Treaty Series

Treaties and international agreements registered or filed and recorded with the Secretariat of the United Nations

VOLUME 3192

Recueil des Traités

Traités et accords internationaux enregistrés ou classés et inscrits au répertoire au Secrétariat de l'Organisation des Nations Unies

United Nations • Nations Unies
New York, 2025

Print ISBN: 978-92-1-003293-3
e-ISBN: 978-92-1-106837-5
ISSN: 0379-8267
e-ISSN: 2412-1495

TABLE OF CONTENTS

I

Treaties and international agreements
registered in June 2017
No. 54545

TABLE DES MATIÈRES

I

Traités et accords internationaux
enregistrés en juin 2017
N° 54545

NOTE BY THE SECRETARIAT

Under Article 102 of the Charter of the United Nations, every treaty and every international agreement entered into by any Member of the United Nations after the coming into force of the Charter shall, as soon as possible, be registered with the Secretariat and published by it. Furthermore, no party to a treaty or international agreement subject to registration which has not been registered may invoke that treaty or agreement before any organ of the United Nations. The General Assembly, by resolution 97 (I), established regulations to give effect to Article 102 of the Charter (see text of the regulations, vol. 859, p. VIII; https://treaties.un.org/Pages/Resource.aspx?path=Publication/Regulation/Page1_en.xml).

The terms "treaty" and "international agreement" have not been defined either in the Charter or in the regulations, and the Secretariat follows the principle that it acts in accordance with the position of the Member State submitting an instrument for registration that, so far as that party is concerned, the instrument is a treaty or an international agreement within the meaning of Article 102. Registration of an instrument submitted by a Member State, therefore, does not imply a judgement by the Secretariat on the nature of the instrument, the status of a party or any similar question. It is the understanding of the Secretariat that its acceptance for registration of an instrument does not confer on the instrument the status of a treaty or an international agreement if it does not already have that status, and does not confer upon a party a status which it would not otherwise have.

*

* *

Disclaimer: All authentic texts in the present Series are published as submitted for registration by a party to the instrument. Unless otherwise indicated, the translations of these texts have been made by the Secretariat of the United Nations, for information.

NOTE DU SECRÉTARIAT

Aux termes de l'Article 102 de la Charte des Nations Unies, tout traité ou accord international conclu par un Membre des Nations Unies après l'entrée en vigueur de la Charte sera, le plus tôt possible, enregistré au Secrétariat et publié par lui. De plus, aucune partie à un traité ou accord international qui aurait dû être enregistré mais ne l'a pas été ne pourra invoquer ledit traité ou accord devant un organe de l'Organisation des Nations Unies. Par sa résolution 97 (I), l'Assemblée générale a adopté un règlement destiné à mettre en application l'Article 102 de la Charte (voir texte du règlement, vol. 859, p. IX; https://treaties.un.org/Pages/Resource.aspx?path=Publication/Regulation/Page1_fr.xml).

Les termes « traité » et « accord international » n'ont été définis ni dans la Charte ni dans le règlement, et le Secrétariat a pris comme principe de s'en tenir à la position adoptée à cet égard par l'État Membre qui a présenté l'instrument à l'enregistrement, à savoir que, en ce qui concerne cette partie, l'instrument constitue un traité ou un accord international au sens de l'Article 102. Il s'ensuit que l'enregistrement d'un instrument présenté par un État Membre n'implique, de la part du Secrétariat, aucun jugement sur la nature de l'instrument, le statut d'une partie ou toute autre question similaire. Le Secrétariat considère donc que son acceptation pour enregistrement d'un instrument ne confère pas audit instrument la qualité de traité ou d'accord international si ce dernier ne l'a pas déjà, et qu'il ne confère pas à une partie un statut que, par ailleurs, elle ne posséderait pas.

*

* *

Déni de responsabilité : Tous les textes authentiques du présent Recueil sont publiés tels qu'ils ont été soumis pour enregistrement par l'une des parties à l'instrument. Sauf indication contraire, les traductions de ces textes ont été établies par le Secrétariat de l'Organisation des Nations Unies, à titre d'information.

I

Treaties and international agreements registered in June 2017 No. 54545

Traités et accords internationaux enregistrés en juin 2017 Nº 54545

No. 54545

Japan
and
Mongolia

Agreement between Japan and Mongolia for an economic partnership (with annexes and implementing agreement). Tokyo, 10 February 2015

Entry into force: *7 June 2016, in accordance with article 17*

Authentic texts: *English, Japanese and Mongol*

Registration with the Secretariat of the United Nations: *Japan, 29 June 2017*

Only the authentic English and Japanese texts of the Agreement and the Implementing Agreement are published in this volume. The authentic texts in the Mongolian language and the corresponding French translations are published in volume 3193. The annexes, which contain highly technical information, are not published herein, in accordance with article 12 (2) of the General Assembly Regulations to give effect to Article 102 of the Charter of the United Nations, as amended, and the publication practice of the UN Secretariat.

Japon
et
Mongolie

Accord de partenariat économique entre le Japon et la Mongolie (avec annexes et accord d'exécution). Tokyo, 10 février 2015

Entrée en vigueur : *7 juin 2016, conformément à l'article 17*

Textes authentiques : *anglais, japonais et mongol*

Enregistrement au Secrétariat de l'Organisation des Nations Unies : *Japon, 29 juin 2017*

Seuls les textes authentiques anglais et japonais de l'Accord et de l'Accord d'exécution sont publiés dans le présent volume, le texte authentique mongol ainsi que la traduction en français figurant dans le volume 3193. Les annexes, qui contiennent des informations hautement techniques, ne sont pas publiées ici, conformément au paragraphe 2 de l'article 12 du règlement de l'Assemblée générale destiné à mettre en application l'Article 102 de la Charte des Nations Unies, tel qu'amendé, et à la pratique du Secrétariat en matière de publication.

[TEXT IN ENGLISH – TEXTE EN ANGLAIS]

AGREEMENT BETWEEN JAPAN AND MONGOLIA FOR AN ECONOMIC PARTNERSHIP

Table of Contents

Annex 8 referred to in Chapter 10	Reservations for Measures referred to in Paragraph 1 of Article 10.8
Annex 9 referred to in Chapter 10	Reservations for Measures referred to in Paragraph 3 of Article 10.8
Annex 10 referred to in Chapter 10	Expropriation

Preamble

Japan and Mongolia,

Conscious of their warm relationship and strong economic and political ties that have developed through growing trade and investment and mutually beneficial cooperation between the Parties;

Realizing that a dynamic and rapidly changing global environment brought about by globalization and closer integration among economies in the world presents many new economic challenges and opportunities to the Parties;

Recognizing that the economies of the Parties are endowed with conditions to complement each other and that this complementarity should contribute to further promoting the sustainable economic development in the Parties, by making use of their respective economic strengths through bilateral trade and investment activities;

Realizing the differences between the Parties in terms of their level of economic development;

Seeking to create a clearly established and secured trade and investment framework through mutually advantageous rules to govern trade and investment between the Parties;

Further seeking to enhance the competitiveness and supply capacity of the economies of the Parties, make their markets more efficient and vibrant, ensure predictable commercial environment for further expansion of trade and investment between them, and contribute to further economic efficiency and growth of the Parties;

Noting the important roles of private sectors for further enhancing commercial and economic relations between the Parties and believing that this Agreement will create new trade and investment opportunities for such private sectors;

Believing that the implementation of this Agreement will contribute to creating new and better employment opportunities through human resource development and thus will improve living standard, including consumer welfares, of the peoples of the Parties;

Reaffirming the view that this Agreement will not only contribute to strengthening the existing political and economic ties between the Parties but also become one of the significant steps in building Japan-Mongolia "Strategic Partnership";

Recalling Article XXIV of the GATT 1994 and Article V of the GATS;

Convinced that this Agreement would open a new era for the relationship between the Parties; and

Determined to establish a legal framework for strengthening the economic partnership between the Parties;

HAVE AGREED as follows:

Chapter 1
General Provisions

Article 1.1
Objective

The objective of this Agreement is to create a new economic dynamism between the Parties by means of the following, taking into account the stage of development and economic needs of the Parties:

(a) liberalizing and facilitating trade in goods and services between the Parties;

(b) facilitating movement of natural persons between the Parties;

(c) increasing investment opportunities and strengthening protection for investments and investment activities in the Parties;

(d) enhancing protection of intellectual property;

(e) promoting cooperation and coordination for the effective enforcement of competition laws in each Party;

(f) establishing a framework for further reinforcing, broadening and deepening bilateral cooperation in all fields relevant to trade and investment and improvement of the business environment; and

(g) creating effective procedures for the implementation and operation of this Agreement and for the prevention and resolution of disputes.

Article 1.2
General Definitions

For the purposes of this Agreement, unless otherwise specified:

(a) the term "Agreement on Customs Valuation" means the Agreement on Implementation of Article VII of the General Agreement on Tariffs and Trade 1994 in Annex 1A to the WTO Agreement;

(b) the term "Area" means:

(i) for Japan, the territory of Japan, and the exclusive economic zone and the continental shelf with respect to which Japan exercises sovereign rights or jurisdiction in accordance with international law; and

(ii) for Mongolia, the territory of Mongolia;

Note: Nothing in this subparagraph shall affect the rights and obligations of the Parties under international law, including those under the UNCLOS.

(c) the term "commercial presence" means any type of business or professional establishment, including through:

(i) the constitution, acquisition or maintenance of a juridical person; or

(ii) the creation or maintenance of a branch or a representative office,

within the Area of a Party for the purposes of supplying a service;

(d) the term "customs authority" means the authority that, according to the legislation of each Party or a non-Party, is responsible for the administration and enforcement of customs laws and regulations:

(i) for Japan, the Ministry of Finance, or its successor; and

(ii) for Mongolia, the Customs General Administration, or its successor;

(e) the term "days" means calendar days, including weekends and holidays;

(f) the term "enterprise" means any juridical person or any other entity duly constituted or organized under the applicable laws and regulations, whether or not for profit, and whether private or government owned or controlled, including any corporation, trust, partnership, sole proprietorship, joint venture, association, organization or company;

(g) the term "enterprise of a Party" means an enterprise constituted or organized under the applicable laws and regulations of that Party;

(h) the term "GATS" means the General Agreement on Trade in Services in Annex 1B to the WTO Agreement;

(i) the term "GATT 1994" means the General Agreement on Tariffs and Trade 1994 in Annex 1A to the WTO Agreement. For the purposes of this Agreement, references to articles in the GATT 1994 include the interpretative notes;

(j) the term "Harmonized System" or "HS" means the Harmonized Commodity Description and Coding System set out in the Annex to the International Convention on the Harmonized Commodity Description and Coding System, and adopted and implemented by the Parties in their respective laws;

(k) the term "investment" means every kind of asset owned or controlled, directly or indirectly, by an investor, including:

(i) an enterprise and a branch of an enterprise;

(ii) shares, stocks or other forms of equity participation in an enterprise, including rights derived therefrom;

(iii) bonds, debentures, loans and other forms of debt, including rights derived therefrom;

(iv) rights under contracts, including turnkey, construction, management, production or revenue-sharing contracts;

(v) claims to money and to any performance under contract having a financial value;

(vi) intellectual property;

Note: Intellectual property means that set out in Article 12.2.

(vii) rights conferred pursuant to laws and regulations or contracts such as concessions, licenses, authorizations and permits, including, but not limited to, those for the supply of financial services, the supply of telecommunications services, the production of nuclear energy and the exploration and exploitation of natural resources; and

(viii) any other tangible and intangible, movable and immovable property, and any related property rights, such as leases, mortgages, liens and pledges;

Note: An investment includes the amount yielded by an investment, in particular, profit, interest, capital gains, dividends, royalties and fees. A change in the form in which assets are invested does not affect their character as an investment.

(l) the term "investor of a Party" means:

(i) a natural person who is a national of a Party under the law of the Party; or

(ii) an enterprise of that Party,

that seeks to make, is making or has made investments in the Area of the other Party;

(m) the term "juridical person" means any legal entity duly constituted or otherwise organized under applicable law, whether for profit or otherwise, and whether private or government owned, including any corporation, trust, partnership, joint venture, sole proprietorship or association;

(n) a juridical person is:

(i) "owned" by persons if more than 50 percent of the equity interest in it is beneficially owned by the persons; and

(ii) "controlled" by persons if the persons have the power to name a majority of its directors or otherwise to legally direct its actions;

(o) the term "originating good" means a good which qualifies as an originating good under the provisions of Chapter 3;

(p) the term "Parties" means Japan and Mongolia and the term "Party" means either Japan or Mongolia;

(q) the term "person" means a natural person or an enterprise/juridical person, as the case may be;

(r) the term "service supplier" means any person that supplies or seeks to supply a service;

Note: Where the service is not supplied or sought to be supplied directly by a juridical person but through other forms of commercial presence such as a branch or a representative office, the service supplier (i.e. the juridical person) shall, nonetheless, through such commercial presence be accorded the treatment provided for service suppliers under Chapter 7. Such treatment shall be extended to the commercial presence through which the service is supplied or sought to be supplied and need not be extended to any other parts of the service supplier located outside the Area of a Party where the service is supplied or sought to be supplied.

(s) the term "SPS Agreement" means the Agreement on the Application of Sanitary and Phytosanitary Measures in Annex 1A to the WTO Agreement;

(t) the term "state enterprise" means a juridical person owned or controlled by a Party;

(u) the term "TRIPS Agreement" means the Agreement on Trade-Related Aspects of Intellectual Property Rights in Annex 1C to the WTO Agreement;

(v) the term "UNCLOS" means the United Nations Convention on the Law of the Sea, done at Montego Bay, December 10, 1982; and

(w) the term "WTO Agreement" means the Marrakesh Agreement Establishing the World Trade Organization, done at Marrakesh, April 15, 1994.

Article 1.3
Transparency

1. Each Party shall promptly publish, or otherwise make publicly available, its laws, regulations and judicial decisions of general application as well as international agreements to which the Party is a party, with respect to any matter covered by this Agreement.

2. Each Party shall make easily available to the public the names and addresses of the competent authorities responsible for the laws and regulations referred to in paragraph 1.

3. Each Party shall, upon request of the other Party, within a reasonable period of time, respond to specific questions from, and provide information to, the other Party with respect to matters referred to in paragraph 1, in the English language to the extent possible.

4. When introducing or changing its laws or regulations that significantly affect the implementation and operation of this Agreement, each Party shall endeavor to provide, except in emergency situations and to the extent covered by its domestic laws, a reasonable interval between the time when such laws or regulations are published or made publicly available and the time when they enter into force.

Article 1.4
Public Comment Procedures

Each Party shall, in accordance with its laws and regulations and to the extent practicable, maintain public comment procedures with respect to any matter covered by this Agreement.

Article 1.5
Administrative Procedures

1. Upon receiving an application submitted by a person who seeks an administrative decision which pertains to or affects the implementation and operation of this Agreement, the competent authorities of a Party shall, in accordance with the laws and regulations of the Party:

(a) inform the applicant of the decision within a reasonable period of time after the submission of the application considered complete in accordance with the laws and regulations of the Party, taking into account the established standard period of time referred to in paragraph 3; and

(b) provide, within a reasonable period of time, information concerning the status of the application, upon request of the applicant.

2. The competent authorities of a Party shall, in accordance with the laws and regulations of the Party, establish criteria for reviewing the application referred to in paragraph 1. The competent authorities shall make such criteria:

(a) as specific as possible; and

(b) publicly available except when it would extraordinarily raise administrative difficulties for the Party.

3. For the purposes of reviewing the applications referred to in paragraph 1, the competent authorities of a Party shall, in accordance with the laws and regulations of the Party:

(a) endeavor to establish standard periods of time between the receipt of the applications and the administrative decisions taken in response to the applications; and

(b) make publicly available such periods of time, if established.

4. The competent authorities of a Party shall endeavor to, in accordance with the laws and regulations of the Party, prior to any final decision which imposes obligations on or restricts legal rights of a person, provide that person with:

(a) a reasonable notice, including a description of the nature of the measure, specific provisions upon which such measure will be based, and the facts which may be a cause of taking such measure; and

(b) a reasonable opportunity to present facts and arguments in support of position of such person,

provided that time, nature of the measure and public interest permit.

Article 1.6
Review and Appeal

1. Each Party shall maintain courts or procedures for the purpose of prompt review and, where warranted, correction of administrative actions regarding matters covered by this Agreement. Such courts or procedures shall be impartial and independent of the authorities entrusted with the administrative enforcement of such actions.

2. Each Party shall ensure that the parties in any such courts or procedures are provided with the right to:

(a) a reasonable opportunity to support or defend their respective positions; and

(b) a decision based on the evidence and submissions of record.

3. Each Party shall ensure, subject to appeal or further review as provided in its laws and regulations, that such decision is implemented by the relevant authorities with respect to the administrative action at issue.

Article 1.7
Measures against Corruption

Each Party shall, in accordance with its laws and regulations, take appropriate measures to prevent and combat corruption of its public officials regarding matters covered by this Agreement.

Article 1.8
Confidential Information

1. Each Party shall, in accordance with its laws and regulations, maintain the confidentiality of information provided in confidence by the other Party in accordance with this Agreement.

2. Unless otherwise provided for in this Agreement, nothing in this Agreement shall require a Party to provide confidential information, the disclosure of which would impede the enforcement of its laws and regulations, or otherwise be contrary to the public interest, or which would prejudice legitimate commercial interests of particular enterprises, public or private.

Article 1.9
Taxation

1. Unless otherwise provided for in this Agreement, the provisions of this Agreement shall not apply to any taxation measures.

2. Nothing in this Agreement shall affect the rights and obligations of either Party under any tax convention. In the event of any inconsistency between this Agreement and any such convention, that convention shall prevail to the extent of the inconsistency.

3. Articles 1.3 and 1.8 shall apply to taxation measures, to the extent that the provisions of this Agreement are applicable to such taxation measures.

Article 1.10
Exceptions

1. For the purposes of this Agreement except Chapters 7, 8 and 12, Articles XX and XXI of the GATT 1994 are incorporated into and form part of this Agreement, *mutatis mutandis*.

2. For the purposes of Chapters 7, 8, 9 and 10, Articles XIV and XIV *bis* of the GATS are incorporated into and form part of this Agreement, *mutatis mutandis*.

3. The Parties may consult with each other on issues related to the situation where:

(a) the export earnings of a Party the economy of which depend on exports of a small number of primary commodities may be seriously reduced by a decline in the sales or the world prices of such commodities; or

(b) promoting the establishment of a particular industry of a Party may be required with a view to raising the general standard of living of its people.

Note: For the purposes of this Article, it is understood that subparagraph (b) of Article XX of the GATT 1994 and subparagraph (b) of Article XIV of the GATS include environmental measures necessary to protect human, animal or plant life or health, and that subparagraph (g) of Article XX of the GATT 1994 applies to measures related to the conservation of living and non-living exhaustible natural resources.

Article 1.11
Relation to Other Agreements

1. The Parties reaffirm their rights and obligations under the WTO Agreement or any other agreements to which both Parties are party.

2. In the event of any inconsistency between this Agreement and the WTO Agreement, the WTO Agreement shall prevail to the extent of the inconsistency.

3. In the event of any inconsistency between this Agreement and any agreement other than the WTO Agreement to which both Parties are party, the Parties shall immediately consult with each other with a view to finding a mutually satisfactory solution, taking into consideration general principles of international law.

Article 1.12
Implementing Agreement

The Governments of the Parties shall conclude a separate agreement setting forth the details and procedures for the implementation of this Agreement, which thereby shall be complementary to this Agreement (hereinafter referred to as "Implementing Agreement").

Article 1.13
Joint Committee

1. The Parties hereby establish a Joint Committee under this Agreement.

2. The functions of the Joint Committee shall be:

(a) reviewing and monitoring the implementation and operation of this Agreement and, when necessary, making appropriate recommendations to the Parties;

(b) considering and recommending to the Parties any amendments to this Agreement;

(c) supervising and coordinating the work of all Sub-Committees established under this Agreement;

(d) adopting:

(i) the Operational Procedures for Trade in Goods and the Operational Procedures for Rules of Origin referred to in Article 2.20 and Article 3.26, respectively; and

(ii) any necessary decisions; and

(e) carrying out other functions as the Parties may agree.

3. The Joint Committee:

(a) shall be composed of representatives of the Governments of the Parties;

(b) may establish other Sub-Committees than those provided for in Article 1.14; and

(c) may delegate its responsibilities to Sub-Committees.

4. The Joint Committee shall establish its rules and procedures.

5. The Joint Committee shall hold the first meeting on the date of entry into force of this Agreement, and thereafter, meet at such times and venues or by means, as may be agreed by the Parties.

Article 1.14
Sub-Committees

1. The following Sub-Committees shall be established on the date of entry into force of this Agreement:

(a) Sub-Committee on Trade in Goods, as provided for in Article 2.19;

(b) Sub-Committee on Rules of Origin, as provided for in Article 3.25;

(c) Sub-Committee on Customs Procedures and Trade Facilitation, as provided for in Article 4.8;

(d) Sub-Committee on Sanitary and Phytosanitary Measures, as provided for in Article 5.6;

(e) Sub-Committee on Technical Regulations, Standards and Conformity Assessment Procedures, as provided for in Article 6.9;

(f) Sub-Committee on Trade in Services, as provided for in Article 7.16;

(g) Sub-Committee on Movement of Natural Persons, as provided for in Article 8.6;

(h) Sub-Committee on Electronic Commerce, as provided for in Article 9.13;

(i) Sub-Committee on Investment, as provided for in Article 10.18;

(j) Sub-Committee on Intellectual Property, as provided for in Article 12.18;

(k) Sub-Committee on Government Procurement, as provided for in Article 13.5;

(l) Sub-Committee on Improvement of the Business Environment, as provided for in Article 14.2; and

(m) Sub-Committee on Cooperation, as provided for in Article 15.4.

2. The Sub-Committees shall carry out the functions specified in the corresponding Articles referred to in paragraph 1.

Article 1.15
Communications

Each Party shall designate a contact point to facilitate communications between the Parties on any matter related to this Agreement.

Chapter 2
Trade in Goods

Section 1
General Rules

Article 2.1
Definitions

For the purposes of this Chapter:

(a) the term "Agreement on Agriculture" means the Agreement on Agriculture in Annex 1A to the WTO Agreement;

(b) the term "Agreement on Anti-Dumping" means the Agreement on Implementation of Article VI of the General Agreement on Tariffs and Trade 1994 in Annex 1A to the WTO Agreement;

(c) the term "Agreement on Safeguards" means the Agreement on Safeguards in Annex 1A to the WTO Agreement;

(d) the term "Agreement on Subsidies and Countervailing Measures" means the Agreement on Subsidies and Countervailing Measures in Annex 1A to the WTO Agreement;

(e) the term "bilateral safeguard measure" means a bilateral safeguard measure provided for in paragraph 2 of Article 2.8;

(f) the term "customs duty" means any customs or import duty imposed in connection with the importation of a good, but does not include any:

    (i) charge equivalent to an internal tax imposed consistently with the provisions of paragraph 2 of Article II and paragraph 2 of Article III of the GATT 1994;

(ii) anti-dumping or countervailing duty applied pursuant to a Party's law and applied consistently with the provisions of Article VI of the GATT 1994, the Agreement on Anti-Dumping and the Agreement on Subsidies and Countervailing Measures; or

(iii) fees or other charges commensurate with the cost of services rendered;

(g) the term "customs value of goods" means the value of goods for the purposes of levying *ad valorem* customs duties on imported goods;

(h) the term "domestic industry" means the producers as a whole of the like or directly competitive goods operating in a Party, or those whose collective output of the like or directly competitive goods constitutes a major proportion of the total domestic production of those goods;

(i) the term "provisional bilateral safeguard measure" means a provisional bilateral safeguard measure provided for in paragraph 1 of Article 2.13;

(j) the term "serious injury" means a significant overall impairment in the position of a domestic industry; and

(k) the term "threat of serious injury" means serious injury that, on the basis of facts and not merely on allegation, conjecture or remote possibility, is clearly imminent.

Article 2.2
Classification of Goods

The classification of goods in trade between the Parties shall be in conformity with the Harmonized System.

Article 2.3
National Treatment

Each Party shall accord national treatment to the goods of the other Party in accordance with Article III of the GATT 1994, and to this end Article III of the GATT 1994 is incorporated into and forms part of this Agreement, *mutatis mutandis*.

Article 2.4
Elimination or Reduction of Customs Duties

1. Unless otherwise provided for in this Agreement, each Party shall eliminate or reduce its customs duties on originating goods of the other Party in accordance with its Schedule in Annex 1.

2. Upon request of either Party, the Parties shall negotiate on issues such as improving market access for originating goods designated for negotiation in the Schedules in Annex 1, in accordance with the terms and conditions set out in such Schedules.

3. In accordance with subparagraph 1(b) of Article II of the GATT 1994, the goods traded between the Parties shall be exempt from other duties or charges of any kind imposed on or in connection with the importation.

4. Nothing in this Article shall prevent a Party from imposing, at any time, a charge equivalent to an internal tax, any anti-dumping or countervailing duty, or fees or other charges referred to in subparagraphs (f)(i) through (iii) of Article 2.1, respectively, on the importation of any good of the other Party.

5. If, as a result of the elimination or reduction of its customs duty on a particular good on a most-favored-nation basis, the most-favored-nation applied rate for the good becomes equal to, or lower than, the rate of customs duty to be applied in accordance with paragraph 1 on the originating good which is classified under the same tariff line as that particular good, each Party shall notify the other Party of such elimination or reduction without delay.

6. In cases where its most-favored-nation applied rate of customs duty on a particular good becomes lower than the rate of customs duty to be applied in accordance with paragraph 1 on the originating good which is classified under the same tariff line as that particular good, each Party shall apply the lower rate with respect to that originating good.

Article 2.5
Customs Valuation

For the purposes of determining the customs value of goods traded between the Parties, the provisions of Part I of the Agreement on Customs Valuation shall apply *mutatis mutandis*.

Article 2.6
Export Subsidies

Neither Party shall introduce or maintain any export subsidies, which are inconsistent with its obligations under the WTO Agreement, on any agricultural good, which is listed in Annex 1 to the Agreement on Agriculture.

Article 2.7
Import and Export Restrictions

1. Neither Party shall introduce or maintain any prohibition or restriction other than customs duties on the importation of any good of the other Party or on the exportation or sale for export of any good destined to the other Party, which is inconsistent with its obligations under the relevant provisions of the WTO Agreement.

2. In the case that a Party introduces a prohibition or restriction other than customs duties taken consistently with the provisions of the WTO Agreement with respect to the importation from, or the exportation to, the other Party of a good upon which the Parties agree, the former Party shall make available, and endeavor to notify, relevant information to the other Party, prior to the introduction of such prohibition or restriction, or as soon as possible thereafter, in a manner consistent with the laws and regulations of the former Party. This paragraph shall apply unless the sharing of such information is considered by the former Party as prejudicial to public interest.

Note: A Party may comply with this paragraph by providing the relevant information to the other Party through the relevant procedures under the WTO Agreement.

Section 2
Safeguard Measures

Article 2.8
Application of Bilateral Safeguard Measures

1. Subject to the provisions of this Section, a Party may apply a bilateral safeguard measure, to the minimum extent necessary to prevent or remedy the serious injury to its domestic industry and to facilitate adjustment thereof, if an originating good of the other Party, as a result of the elimination or reduction of a customs duty in accordance with Article 2.4, is being imported into the former Party in such increased quantities, in absolute terms or relative to domestic production, and under such conditions that the imports of that originating good constitute cause of serious injury, or threat of serious injury, to a domestic industry of the former Party.

2. A Party may, as a bilateral safeguard measure:

(a) suspend the further reduction of any rate of customs duty on the originating good provided for in this Chapter; or

(b) increase the rate of customs duty on the originating good to a level not to exceed the lesser of:

(i) the most-favored-nation applied rate of customs duty in effect on the day when the bilateral safeguard measure is applied; and

(ii) the most-favored-nation applied rate of customs duty in effect on the day immediately preceding the date of entry into force of this Agreement.

Article 2.9
Conditions and Limitations

1. No bilateral safeguard measure shall be maintained except to the extent and for such period of time as may be necessary to prevent or remedy serious injury and to facilitate adjustment, provided that such period of time shall not exceed a period of three years. However, in highly exceptional circumstances, a bilateral safeguard measure may be extended, provided that the total duration of the bilateral safeguard measure, including such extensions, shall not exceed six years. In order to facilitate adjustment in a situation where the expected duration of a bilateral safeguard measure is over one year, the Party maintaining the bilateral safeguard measure shall progressively liberalize the bilateral safeguard measure at regular intervals during the period of application.

2. No bilateral safeguard measure shall be applied again to the import of a particular originating good which has been subject to such a bilateral safeguard measure, for a period of time equal to the duration of the previous bilateral safeguard measure or one year, whichever is longer.

3. Upon the termination of a bilateral safeguard measure, the rate of customs duty for the originating good subject to the measure shall be the rate which would have been in effect if the bilateral safeguard measure had never been applied.

4. A bilateral safeguard measure shall not be applied against an originating good of the exporting Party as long as its share of imports of the good concerned in the importing Party does not exceed three percent.

5. Each Party shall adopt or maintain equitable, timely, transparent and effective procedures relating to bilateral safeguard measures.

Article 2.10
Investigation

1. A Party may apply a bilateral safeguard measure only after an investigation has been carried out by the competent authorities of that Party in accordance with the same procedures as those provided for in Article 3 and paragraph 2 of Article 4 of the Agreement on Safeguards.

2. The investigation referred to in paragraph 1 shall, except in special circumstances, be completed within one year, and in no case more than 18 months, following its date of initiation.

Article 2.11
Notification and Consultations

1. A Party shall immediately make a written notice to the other Party upon:

(a) initiating an investigation referred to in paragraph 1 of Article 2.10 related to serious injury, or threat of serious injury, and the reasons therefor; and

(b) taking a decision to apply or extend a bilateral safeguard measure.

2. The Party making the written notice referred to in paragraph 1 shall provide the other Party with all pertinent information, which shall include:

(a) in the written notice referred to in subparagraph 1(a), the reason for the initiation of the investigation, a precise description of the originating good subject to the investigation and its subheading under the Harmonized System, the period subject to the investigation and the date of initiation of the investigation; and

(b) in the written notice referred to in subparagraph 1(b), evidence of serious injury or threat of serious injury caused by the increased imports of the originating good, a precise description of the originating good subject to the proposed bilateral safeguard measure and its subheading under the Harmonized System, a precise description of the proposed bilateral safeguard measure, and the proposed date of the introduction and expected duration of the bilateral safeguard measure.

3. A Party proposing to apply or extend a bilateral safeguard measure shall provide adequate opportunity for prior consultations with the other Party with a view to reviewing the information arising from the investigation referred to in paragraph 1 of Article 2.10, exchanging views on the bilateral safeguard measure and reaching an agreement on compensation set out in Article 2.12.

Article 2.12
Compensation

1. A Party proposing to apply or extend a bilateral safeguard measure may agree on adequate means of trade compensation in the form of concessions of customs duties whose value is substantially equivalent to that of the additional customs duties expected to result from the bilateral safeguard measure.

2. If the Parties are unable to agree on the compensation within 30 days after the commencement of the consultations in accordance with paragraph 3 of Article 2.11, the Party to whose originating good the bilateral safeguard measure is applied shall be free to suspend the application of concessions of customs duties under this Agreement, which are substantially equivalent to the bilateral safeguard measure. The Party exercising the right of suspension may suspend the application of concessions of customs duties only for the minimum period necessary to achieve the substantially equivalent effects and only while the bilateral safeguard measure is maintained.

Article 2.13
Provisional Bilateral Safeguard Measures

1. In critical circumstances, where delay would cause damage which it would be difficult to repair, a Party may apply a provisional bilateral safeguard measure, which shall take the form of the measure set out in subparagraph 2(a) or 2(b) of Article 2.8, pursuant to a preliminary determination that there is clear evidence that increased imports of an originating good of the other Party have caused or are threatening to cause serious injury to a domestic industry of the former Party.

2. A Party shall make a written notice to the other Party prior to applying a provisional bilateral safeguard measure. Consultations between the Parties on the application of the provisional bilateral safeguard measure shall be initiated immediately after the provisional bilateral safeguard measure is applied.

3. The duration of a provisional bilateral safeguard measure shall not exceed 200 days. During that period, the pertinent requirements of Article 2.10 shall be met. The duration of the provisional bilateral safeguard measure shall be counted as a part of the period referred to in paragraph 1 of Article 2.9.

4. Paragraphs 3 through 5 of Article 2.9 shall apply, *mutatis mutandis*, to a provisional bilateral safeguard measure. The customs duty imposed as a result of the provisional bilateral safeguard measure shall be refunded if the subsequent investigation referred to in paragraph 1 of Article 2.10 does not determine that increased imports of an originating good of the other Party have caused or threatened to cause serious injury to a domestic industry.

Article 2.14
Relation to Safeguard Measures under the WTO Agreement

1. Nothing in this Section shall prevent a Party from applying a safeguard measure to an originating good of the other Party in accordance with:

(a) Article XIX of the GATT 1994 and the Agreement on Safeguards; or

(b) Article 5 of the Agreement on Agriculture.

2. A Party applying a safeguard measure to the importation of an originating good of the other Party in accordance with Article XIX of the GATT 1994 and the Agreement on Safeguards, or Article 5 of the Agreement on Agriculture, shall not apply at the same time a bilateral safeguard measure under this Section to that importation.

3. In the case that a Party has applied a bilateral safeguard measure under this Section to the importation of an originating good of the other Party prior to the application of a safeguard measure in accordance with Article XIX of the GATT 1994 and the Agreement on Safeguards, or Article 5 of the Agreement on Agriculture, the duration of the latter safeguard measure shall be counted as a part of the total duration of the bilateral safeguard measure. The Party may resume the application of the bilateral safeguard measure to that importation upon the termination of the latter safeguard measure up to the remaining period of the bilateral safeguard measure.

Article 2.15
Communications

A written notice referred to in paragraph 1 of Article 2.11 and paragraph 2 of Article 2.13 and any other communication between the Parties in accordance with this Section shall be made in the English language.

Article 2.16
Review

The Parties shall review the provisions of this Section, if necessary, 10 years after the date of entry into force of this Agreement.

Section 3
Other Provisions

Article 2.17
Anti-Dumping and Countervailing Measures

Nothing in this Chapter shall be construed to prevent a Party from taking any measure in accordance with the provisions of Article VI of the GATT 1994, the Agreement on Anti-Dumping and the Agreement on Subsidies and Countervailing Measures.

Article 2.18
Measures to Safeguard the Balance of Payments

1. Nothing in this Chapter shall be construed to prevent a Party from taking any measure for balance-of-payments purposes. A Party taking such measure shall do so in accordance with the conditions established under Article XII of the GATT 1994 and the Understanding on the Balance-of-Payments Provisions of the General Agreement on Tariffs and Trade 1994 in Annex 1A to the WTO Agreement.

2. Nothing in this Chapter shall preclude the use by a Party of exchange controls or exchange restrictions in accordance with the Articles of Agreement of the International Monetary Fund.

Article 2.19
Sub-Committee on Trade in Goods

1. For the purposes of the effective implementation and operation of this Chapter, the Parties hereby establish a Sub-Committee on Trade in Goods (hereinafter referred to in this Article as "the Sub-Committee").

2. The functions of the Sub-Committee shall be:

(a) reviewing and monitoring the implementation and operation of this Chapter;

(b) considering any other matter related to this Chapter as the Parties may agree;

(c) reviewing and making appropriate recommendations, as necessary, to the Joint Committee on the Operational Procedures for Trade in Goods referred to in Article 2.20;

(d) reporting the findings of the Sub-Committee to the Joint Committee; and

(e) carrying out other functions as may be delegated by the Joint Committee.

3. The Sub-Committee shall be composed of representatives of the Governments of the Parties.

4. The Sub-Committee shall hold meetings at such times and venues or by means, as may be agreed by the Parties.

Article 2.20
Operational Procedures for Trade in Goods

Upon the date of entry into force of this Agreement, the Joint Committee shall adopt the Operational Procedures for Trade in Goods that provide detailed regulations pursuant to which the relevant authorities of the Parties shall implement their functions under this Chapter.

Article 2.21
Cooperation with respect to Exports

The Parties shall, in accordance with the provisions of Chapter 15, cooperate with each other in the field of used four-wheeled motor vehicles exported from the exporting Party.

Chapter 3
Rules of Origin

Article 3.1
Definitions

For the purposes of this Chapter:

(a) the term "competent governmental authority" means the authority that, according to the legislation of each Party, is responsible for the issuing of a Certificate of Origin or for the designation of certification entities or bodies;

(b) the term "exporter" means a person located in an exporting Party who exports a good from the exporting Party;

(c) the term "factory ships of the Party" or "vessels of the Party" respectively means factory ships or vessels:

(i) which are registered in the Party;

(ii) which sail under the flag of the Party; and

(iii) which meet one of the following conditions:

(A) they are at least 50 percent owned by nationals of the Parties; or

(B) they are owned by a juridical person which has its head office and its principal place of business in either Party and which does not own any vessel or ship registered in a non-Party;

(d) the term "fungible originating goods of a Party" or "fungible originating materials of a Party" respectively means originating goods or materials of a Party that are interchangeable for commercial purposes, whose properties are essentially identical;

(e) the term "Generally Accepted Accounting Principles" means the recognized consensus or substantial authoritative support within a Party at a particular time as to which economic resources and obligations should be recorded as assets and liabilities, which changes in assets and liabilities should be recorded, how the assets and liabilities and changes in them should be measured, what information should be disclosed and how it should be disclosed, and which financial statements should be prepared. These standards may be broad guidelines of general application as well as detailed practices and procedures;

(f) the term "importer" means a person who imports a good into the importing Party;

(g) the term "indirect materials" means goods used in the production, testing or inspection of another good but not physically incorporated into the good, or goods used in the maintenance of buildings or the operation of equipment associated with the production of another good, including:

(i) fuel and energy;

(ii) tools, dies and molds;

(iii) spare parts and goods used in the maintenance of equipment and buildings;

(iv) lubricants, greases, compounding materials and other goods used in production or used to operate equipment and buildings;

(v) gloves, glasses, footwear, clothing, safety equipment and supplies;

(vi) equipment, devices and supplies used for testing or inspecting the good;

(vii) catalysts and solvents; and

(viii) any other goods that are not incorporated into another good but whose use in the production of the good can reasonably be demonstrated to be a part of that production;

(h) the term "material" means a good that is used in the production of another good;

(i) the term "non-originating material" means a material which does not qualify as originating under this Chapter;

(j) the term "originating material" means a material which qualifies as originating under this Chapter;

(k) the term "packing materials and containers for transportation and shipment" means goods that are used to protect a good during transportation, other than packaging materials and containers for retail sale referred to in Article 3.13;

(l) the term "preferential tariff treatment" means the rate of customs duties applicable to an originating good of the exporting Party in accordance with paragraph 1 of Article 2.4;

(m) the term "producer" means a person who engages in the production of goods or materials; and

(n) the term "production" means a method of obtaining goods including manufacturing, assembling, processing, raising, growing, breeding, mining, extracting, harvesting, fishing, trapping, gathering, collecting, hunting and capturing.

Article 3.2
Originating Goods

Unless otherwise provided for in this Chapter, a good shall qualify as an originating good of a Party where:

(a) the good is wholly obtained or produced entirely in the Party, as defined in Article 3.3;

(b) the good is produced entirely in the Party exclusively from originating materials of the Party; or

(c) the good satisfies the product specific rules (change in tariff classification, qualifying value content or specific manufacturing or processing operation) set out in Annex 2, as well as all other applicable requirements of this Chapter, when the good is produced entirely in the Party using non-originating materials.

Article 3.3
Wholly Obtained Goods

For the purposes of subparagraph (a) of Article 3.2, the following goods shall be considered as being wholly obtained or produced entirely in a Party:

(a) live animals born and raised in the Party;

(b) animals obtained by hunting, trapping, fishing, gathering or capturing in the Party;

(c) goods obtained from live animals in the Party;

(d) plants and plant products harvested, picked or gathered in the Party;

(e) minerals and other naturally occurring substances, not included in subparagraphs (a) through (d), extracted or taken in the Party;

(f) goods of sea-fishing and other goods taken by vessels of the Party from the sea outside the territorial seas of the Parties;

(g) goods produced on board factory ships of the Party outside the territorial seas of the Parties from the goods referred to in subparagraph (f);

(h) goods taken from the seabed or subsoil thereof outside the territorial sea of the Party, provided that the Party has rights to exploit such seabed or subsoil in accordance with the provisions of the UNCLOS;

(i) articles collected in the Party which can no longer perform their original purpose in the Party nor are capable of being restored or repaired and which are fit only for disposal or for the recovery of parts or raw materials;

(j) scrap and waste derived from manufacturing or processing operations or from consumption in the Party and fit only for disposal or for the recovery of raw materials;

(k) parts or raw materials recovered in the Party from articles which can no longer perform their original purpose nor are capable of being restored or repaired; and

(l) goods obtained or produced in the Party exclusively from the goods referred to in subparagraphs (a) through (k).

Article 3.4
Qualifying Value Content

1. For the purposes of subparagraph (c) of Article 3.2, the qualifying value content of a good shall be calculated on the basis of one or the other of the following methods:

(a) Method based on value of non-originating materials ("Build-down method")

$$Q.V.C. = \frac{F.O.B. - V.N.M.}{F.O.B.} \times 100$$

(b) Method based on value of originating materials ("Build-up method")

$$Q.V.C. = \frac{V.O.M. + \text{Direct Labor Cost} + \text{Direct Overhead Cost} + \text{Profit}}{F.O.B.} \times 100$$

Where:

Q.V.C. is the qualifying value content of a good, expressed as a percentage;

F.O.B. is, except as provided for in paragraph 2, the free-on-board value of the good payable by the buyer of the good to the seller of the good, regardless of the mode of shipment, not including any internal excise taxes reduced, exempted or repaid when the good is exported;

V.N.M. is the value of non-originating materials used in the production of the good; and

V.O.M. is the value of originating materials used in the production of the good.

Note: For the purposes of calculating the qualifying value content of a good, the Generally Accepted Accounting Principles in the exporting Party shall apply.

2. F.O.B. referred to in paragraph 1 shall be the value:

(a) adjusted to the first ascertainable price paid for a good from the buyer to the producer of the good, if there is free-on-board value of the good, but it is unknown and cannot be ascertained; or

(b) determined in accordance with Articles 1 through 8 of the Agreement on Customs Valuation, if there is no free-on-board value of a good.

3. For the purposes of calculating the qualifying value content of a good in accordance with paragraph 1, the value of material used in the production of the good in a Party:

(a) shall be determined in accordance with the Agreement on Customs Valuation, and shall include freight, insurance where appropriate, packing and all the other costs incurred in transporting the material to the importation port in the Party where the producer of the good is located; or

(b) if such value is unknown and cannot be ascertained, shall be the first ascertainable price paid for the material in the Party, but may exclude all the costs incurred in the Party in transporting the material from the warehouse of the supplier of the material to the place where the producer is located such as freight, insurance and packing as well as any other known and ascertainable cost incurred in the Party.

4. For the purposes of calculating the qualifying value content of a good to determine whether the good qualifies as an originating good of a Party:

(a) V.N.M. of the good under subparagraph 1(a) shall not include the value of non-originating materials used in the production of originating materials of the Party which are used in the production of the good; and

(b) V.O.M. of the good under subparagraph 1(b) shall include the value of non-originating materials used in the production of originating materials of the Party which are used in the production of the good.

5. For the purposes of subparagraph 2(b) or 3(a), in applying the Agreement on Customs Valuation to determine the value of a good or a material, the Agreement on Customs Valuation shall apply *mutatis mutandis* to domestic transactions or to the cases where there is no transaction of the good or the material.

Article 3.5
Accumulation

For the purposes of determining whether a good qualifies as an originating good of a Party:

(a) an originating good of the other Party which is used as a material in the production of the good in the former Party may be considered as an originating material of the former Party;

(b) the production in the other Party may be considered as that in the former Party; and

(c) the production carried out at different stages by one or more producers within the Party or in the other Party may be taken into account, when the good is produced using non-originating materials,

provided that such good has undergone its last production process in the exporting Party and such production process goes beyond the operations provided for in Article 3.7.

Article 3.6
De Minimis

1. For the application of the product specific rules set out in Annex 2, non-originating materials used in the production of a good that do not satisfy an applicable rule for the good shall be disregarded, provided that the totality of such materials does not exceed specific percentage in value, weight or volume of the good and such percentage is set out in the applicable product specific rule for the good.

2. Paragraph 1 shall not apply to a non-originating material used in the production of a good provided for in Chapters 1 through 24 of the Harmonized System, except where such non-originating material is provided for in a subheading which is different from that of the good for which the origin is being determined under this Article.

Article 3.7
Non-Qualifying Operations

1. A good shall not be considered as an originating good of a Party merely by reason of:

(a) operations to ensure the preservation of products in good condition during transport and storage (such as drying, freezing, keeping in brine) and other similar operations;

(b) changes of packaging and breaking-up and assembly of packages;

(c) disassembly;

(d) placing in bottles, cases, boxes and other simple packaging operations;

(e) collection of parts and components classified as a good in accordance with Rule 2(a) of the General Rules for the Interpretation of the Harmonized System;

(f) mere making-up of sets of articles; or

(g) any combination of operations referred to in subparagraphs (a) through (f).

2. Paragraph 1 shall prevail over the product specific rules set out in Annex 2.

Article 3.8
Consignment Criteria

1. An originating good of the other Party shall be deemed to meet the consignment criteria when it is transported:

(a) directly from the other Party; or

(b) through one or more non-Parties for the purpose of transit or temporary storage in warehouses in such non-Parties, provided that it does not undergo operations other than unloading, reloading and any other operation to preserve it in good condition.

2. If an originating good of the other Party does not meet the consignment criteria referred to in paragraph 1, the good shall not be considered as an originating good of the other Party.

Article 3.9
Unassembled or Disassembled Goods

1. Where a good satisfies the requirements of the relevant provisions of Articles 3.2 through 3.7 and is imported into a Party from the other Party in an unassembled or disassembled form but is classified as an assembled good in accordance with Rule 2(a) of the General Rules for the Interpretation of the Harmonized System, such a good shall be considered as an originating good of the other Party.

2. A good assembled in a Party from unassembled or disassembled materials, which were imported into the Party and classified as an assembled good in accordance with Rule 2(a) of the General Rules for the Interpretation of the Harmonized System, shall be considered as an originating good of the Party, provided that the good would have satisfied the applicable requirements of the relevant provisions of Articles 3.2 through 3.7 if each of the non-originating materials among the unassembled or disassembled materials had been imported into the Party separately and not as an unassembled or disassembled form.

Article 3.10
Fungible Goods and Materials

1. For the purposes of determining whether a good qualifies as an originating good of a Party, where fungible originating materials of the Party and fungible non-originating materials that are commingled in an inventory are used in the production of the good, the origin of the materials may be determined in accordance with an inventory management method under the Generally Accepted Accounting Principles in the Party.

2. Where fungible originating goods of a Party and fungible non-originating goods are commingled in an inventory and, prior to exportation, do not undergo any production process or any operation in the Party where they were commingled other than unloading, reloading and any other operation to preserve them in good condition, the origin of the good may be determined in accordance with an inventory management method under the Generally Accepted Accounting Principles in the Party.

Article 3.11
Indirect Materials

Indirect materials shall be, without regard to where they are produced, considered as originating materials of a Party where the good is produced.

Article 3.12
Accessories, Spare Parts and Tools

1. In determining whether all the non-originating materials used in the production of a good undergo the applicable change in tariff classification or a specific manufacturing or processing operation set out in Annex 2, accessories, spare parts or tools delivered with the good that form part of the good's standard accessories, spare parts or tools, shall be disregarded, provided that:

(a) the accessories, spare parts or tools are not invoiced separately from the good, without regard to whether they are separately described in the invoice; and

(b) the quantities and value of the accessories, spare parts or tools are customary for the good.

2. If a good is subject to a qualifying value content requirement, the value of the accessories, spare parts or tools shall be taken into account as the value of originating materials of a Party where the good is produced or non-originating materials, as the case may be, in calculating the qualifying value content of the good.

Article 3.13
Packaging Materials and Containers for Retail Sale

1. Packaging materials and containers for retail sale, which are classified with the good in accordance with Rule 5 of the General Rules for the Interpretation of the Harmonized System, shall be disregarded in determining the origin of the good, provided that:

(a) the good is wholly obtained or entirely produced as defined in subparagraph (a) of Article 3.2;

(b) the good is produced exclusively from originating materials, as defined in subparagraph (b) of Article 3.2; or

(c) the good has undergone the applicable change in tariff classification or a specific manufacturing or processing operation set out in Annex 2.

2. If a good is subject to a qualifying value content requirement, the value of packaging materials and containers for retail sale shall be taken into account as the value of originating materials of a Party where the good is produced or non-originating materials, as the case may be, in calculating the qualifying value content of the good.

Article 3.14
Packing Materials and Containers for Transportation and Shipment

Packing materials and containers for transportation and shipment of a good shall not be taken into account in determining the origin of the good.

Article 3.15
Claim for Preferential Tariff Treatment

1. The importing Party shall grant preferential tariff treatment in accordance with this Agreement to an originating good of the exporting Party on the basis of a Certificate of Origin.

2. Notwithstanding paragraph 1:

(a) the importing Party shall not require a Certificate of Origin from the importer for an importation of an originating good of the exporting Party whose aggregate customs value does not exceed 1,500 United States dollars or its equivalent amount in the importing Party's currency, or such higher amount as may be established by the importing Party, provided that the importation does not form part of importations that may reasonably be considered to have been made separately for the purpose of avoiding the requirement for a Certificate of Origin; and

(b) the importing Party may waive the requirement for a Certificate of Origin in accordance with its laws and regulations.

3. The importing Party may require, where appropriate, the importer to submit other evidence that the good qualifies as an originating good of the exporting Party.

4. Where an originating good of the exporting Party is imported through one or more non-Parties, the importing Party may require the importer who claims preferential tariff treatment for that good to submit:

(a) a copy of the through bill of lading; or

(b) a certificate or any other information given by the customs authorities of such non-Parties or other relevant entities, which evidences that the good has not undergone operations other than unloading, reloading and any other operation to preserve it in good condition in those non-Parties.

Article 3.16
Certificate of Origin

1. A Certificate of Origin referred to in paragraph 1 of Article 3.15 shall be issued by the competent governmental authority of the exporting Party upon request having been made by the exporter or its authorized agent. Such Certificate of Origin shall include minimum data specified in Annex 3.

2. For the purposes of this Article, the competent governmental authority of the exporting Party may designate other entities or bodies to be responsible for the issuance of Certificate of Origin, under the authorization given in accordance with the applicable laws and regulations of the exporting Party.

3. Where the competent governmental authority of the exporting Party designates other entities or bodies to carry out the issuance of Certificate of Origin, the exporting Party shall notify in writing the other Party of its designees.

4. For the purposes of this Chapter, upon the entry into force of this Agreement, the Parties shall establish each Party's format of Certificate of Origin in the English language in the Operational Procedures for Rules of Origin referred to in Article 3.26.

5. A Certificate of Origin shall be completed in the English language.

6. A Certificate of Origin shall be in a printed format or such other medium agreed upon by the Parties.

7. An issued Certificate of Origin shall be applicable to a single importation of originating goods of the exporting Party into the importing Party and be valid for 12 months from the date of issuance.

8. Where the exporter of a good is not the producer of the good in the exporting Party, the exporter may request a Certificate of Origin on the basis of:

(a) a declaration provided by the exporter to the competent governmental authority or its designees based on the information provided by the producer of the good to that exporter; or

(b) a declaration voluntarily provided by the producer of the good directly to the competent governmental authority or its designees by the request of the exporter.

9. A Certificate of Origin shall be issued only after the exporter who requests the Certificate of Origin, or the producer of a good in the exporting Party referred to in subparagraph 8(b), proves to the competent governmental authority of the exporting Party or its designees that the good to be exported qualifies as an originating good of the exporting Party.

10. The competent governmental authority of the exporting Party shall provide the importing Party with specimen signatures and impressions of stamps used in the offices of the competent governmental authority or its designees.

11. Each Party, in accordance with its laws and regulations, shall ensure that the competent governmental authority or its designees shall keep a record of issued Certificate of Origin for a period of five years after the date on which the Certificate was issued. Such record includes all supporting documents presented to prove the qualification as an originating good of the exporting Party.

12. The competent governmental authority of the exporting Party shall, when it cancels the decision to issue a Certificate of Origin, promptly notify the cancellation to the exporter to whom the Certificate of Origin has been issued, and to the customs authority of the importing Party, except where the Certificate of Origin has been returned to the competent governmental authority.

Article 3.17
Obligations regarding Exportations

Each Party shall, in accordance with its laws and regulations, ensure that an exporter to whom a Certificate of Origin has been issued, or the producer of a good in the exporting Party referred to in subparagraph 8(b) of Article 3.16 shall:

(a) notify in writing the competent governmental authority of the exporting Party or its designees without delay, when such exporter or producer knows that the good for which the Certificate of Origin has been issued does not qualify as an originating good of the exporting Party; and

(b) keep the records related to the origin of the good for five years after the date on which the Certificate of Origin was issued.

Article 3.18
Request for Checking of Certificate of Origin

1. In order to ensure the proper application of this Chapter, the Parties shall assist each other to check the information related to a Certificate of Origin, in accordance with this Agreement and their respective laws and regulations.

2. For the purposes of determining whether a good imported from the exporting Party under preferential tariff treatment qualifies as an originating good of the exporting Party, the customs authority of the importing Party may request information related to the origin of the good from the competent governmental authority of the exporting Party on the basis of a Certificate of Origin.

3. For the purposes of paragraph 2, the competent governmental authority of the exporting Party shall, in accordance with the laws and regulations of the exporting Party, provide the requested information in a period not exceeding four months after the date of receipt of the request. If the customs authority of the importing Party considers necessary, it may require additional information related to the origin of the good. If additional information is requested by the customs authority of the importing Party, the competent governmental authority of the exporting Party shall, in accordance with the laws and regulations of the exporting Party, provide the requested information in a period not exceeding two months after the date of receipt of the request.

4. For the purposes of paragraph 3, the competent governmental authority of the exporting Party may request the exporter to whom the Certificate of Origin has been issued, or the producer of the good in the exporting Party referred to in subparagraph 8(b) of Article 3.16, to provide the former with the requested information.

Article 3.19
Verification Visit

1. If the customs authority of the importing Party is not satisfied with the outcome of the request for checking in accordance with Article 3.18, it may request the exporting Party to:

(a) collect and provide information related to the origin of a good, and check, for that purpose, the facilities used in the production of the good, through a visit by the competent governmental authority of the exporting Party along with the customs authority of the importing Party to the premises of the exporter to whom the Certificate of Origin has been issued, or the producer of the good in the exporting Party referred to in subparagraph 8(b) of Article 3.16; and

(b) provide information related to the origin of the good in the possession of the competent governmental authority of the exporting Party or its designee, during or after the visit referred to in subparagraph (a).

2. When requesting the exporting Party to conduct a visit in accordance with paragraph 1, the customs authority of the importing Party shall deliver a written communication with such request to the exporting Party at least 40 days in advance of the proposed date of the visit, the receipt of which is to be confirmed by the exporting Party. The competent governmental authority of the exporting Party shall request the written consent of the exporter, or the producer of the good in the exporting Party, whose premises are to be visited.

3. The communication referred to in paragraph 2 shall include:

(a) the identity of the customs authority issuing the communication;

(b) the name of the exporter, or the producer of the good in the exporting Party, whose premises are requested to be visited;

(c) the proposed date and place of the visit;

(d) the objective and scope of the proposed visit, including specific reference to the good subject of the verification referred to in the Certificate of Origin; and

(e) the names and titles of the officials of the customs authority of the importing Party to be present during the visit.

4. The exporting Party shall respond in writing to the importing Party, within 30 days after the receipt of the communication referred to in paragraph 2, whether it accepts or refuses to conduct the visit requested in accordance with paragraph 1.

5. The competent governmental authority of the exporting Party shall, in accordance with the laws and regulations of the exporting Party, provide within 45 days or any other mutually agreed period after the last day of the visit, to the customs authority of the importing Party the information obtained in accordance with paragraph 1.

Article 3.20
Determination of Origin and Preferential Tariff Treatment

1. The customs authority of the importing Party may deny preferential tariff treatment to a good for which an importer claims preferential tariff treatment where the good does not qualify as an originating good of the exporting Party or where the importer fails to comply with any of the relevant requirements of this Chapter.

2. The customs authority of the importing Party may determine that a good does not qualify as an originating good of the exporting Party and may deny preferential tariff treatment where it receives the notification from the competent governmental authority of the exporting Party to cancel the decision to issue the Certificate of Origin for the good in accordance with paragraph 12 of Article 3.16.

3. The customs authority of the importing Party may determine that a good does not qualify as an originating good of the exporting Party and may deny preferential tariff treatment, and a written determination thereof shall be sent to the competent governmental authority of the exporting Party where:

(a) the competent governmental authority of the exporting Party fails to provide the information within the period referred to in paragraph 3 of Article 3.18 or paragraph 5 of Article 3.19;

(b) the exporting Party refuses to conduct a visit, or that Party fails to respond to the communication referred to in paragraph 2 of Article 3.19 within the period referred to in paragraph 4 of Article 3.19; or

(c) the information provided to the customs authority of the importing Party in accordance with Article 3.18 or 3.19 is not sufficient to prove that the good qualifies as an originating good of the exporting Party.

4. After carrying out the procedures outlined in Article 3.18 or 3.19 as the case may be, the customs authority of the importing Party shall provide the competent governmental authority of the exporting Party with a written determination of whether or not the good qualifies as an originating good of the exporting Party, including findings of fact and the legal basis for the determination. The competent governmental authority of the exporting Party shall inform such determination by the customs authority of the importing Party to the exporter, or the producer of the good in the exporting Party, whose premises were subject of the visit referred to in Article 3.19.

Article 3.21
Confidentiality

1. Each Party shall maintain, in accordance with its laws and regulations, the confidentiality of information provided to it as confidential in accordance with this Chapter, and shall protect that information from disclosure that could prejudice the competitive position of the persons providing the information.

2. Information obtained by the customs authority of the importing Party in accordance with this Chapter:

(a) may only be used by such authority for the purposes of this Chapter; and

(b) shall not be used by the importing Party in any criminal proceedings carried out by a court or a judge, unless the information is requested to the exporting Party and provided to the importing Party through the diplomatic channels or other channels established in accordance with the applicable laws and regulations of the exporting Party.

Article 3.22
Minor Errors

The customs authority of the importing Party shall disregard minor errors, such as slight discrepancies or omissions, typing errors or protruding from the designated field, provided that these minor errors are not such as to create doubts concerning the accuracy of the information included in the Certificate of Origin.

Article 3.23
Penalties and Measures against False Declaration

1. Each Party shall establish or maintain, in accordance with its laws and regulations, appropriate penalties or other sanctions against its exporters to whom a Certificate of Origin has been issued and the producers of a good in the exporting Party referred to in subparagraph 8(b) of Article 3.16, for providing false declaration or documents to the competent governmental authority of the exporting Party or its designees prior to the issuance of Certificate of Origin.

2. Each Party shall, in accordance with its laws and regulations, take measures which it considers appropriate against its exporters to whom a Certificate of Origin has been issued and the producers of a good in the exporting Party referred to in subparagraph 8(b) of Article 3.16, for failing to notify in writing to the competent governmental authority of the exporting Party or its designees without delay after having known, after the issuance of Certificate of Origin, that the good for which the Certificate of Origin has been issued does not qualify as an originating good of the exporting Party.

Note: For greater certainty, the exporters to whom a Certificate of Origin has been issued and the producers of a good in the exporting Party referred to in subparagraph 8(b) of Article 3.16 are not subject to the measures referred to in this paragraph, in accordance with the laws and regulations of each Party, provided that they notify in writing to the competent governmental authority of the exporting Party or its designees without delay after having known, after the issuance of Certificate of Origin, that the good for which the Certificate of Origin has been issued does not qualify as an originating good of the exporting Party.

Article 3.24
Miscellaneous

Communications between the importing Party and the exporting Party shall be conducted in the English language.

Article 3.25
Sub-Committee on Rules of Origin

1. For the purposes of the effective implementation and operation of this Chapter, the Parties hereby establish a Sub-Committee on Rules of Origin (hereinafter referred to in this Article as "the Sub-Committee").

2. The functions of the Sub-Committee shall be:

(a) reviewing and making appropriate recommendations, as necessary, to the Joint Committee on:

(i) the implementation and operation of this Chapter;

(ii) any amendments to Annex 2 or 3, proposed by either Party; and

(iii) the Operational Procedures for Rules of Origin referred to in Article 3.26;

(b) considering any other matter as the Parties may agree related to this Chapter;

(c) reporting the findings of the Sub-Committee to the Joint Committee; and

(d) carrying out other functions as may be delegated by the Joint Committee.

3. The Sub-Committee shall be composed of representatives of the Governments of the Parties.

4. The Sub-Committee shall hold meetings at such times and venues or by means, as may be agreed by the Parties.

Article 3.26
Operational Procedures for Rules of Origin

Upon the date of entry into force of this Agreement, the Joint Committee shall adopt the Operational Procedures for Rules of Origin that provide detailed regulations pursuant to which the customs authorities, the competent governmental authorities and other relevant authorities of the Parties shall implement their functions under this Chapter.

Chapter 4
Customs Procedures and Trade Facilitation

Article 4.1
Scope and Objectives

1. This Chapter shall apply to customs procedures required for the clearance of goods traded between the Parties.

2. This Chapter shall be implemented by the Parties in accordance with the laws and regulations of each Party and within the available resources of their respective customs authorities.

3. The objectives of this Chapter are to establish a framework to ensure transparency, proper application of customs laws and prompt clearance of goods and to promote cooperation in the field of customs procedures, with a view to facilitating trade in goods between the Parties.

Article 4.2
Definition

For the purposes of this Chapter, the term "customs laws" means such laws and regulations administered and enforced by the customs authority of each Party concerning the importation, exportation and transit of goods, as they relate to customs duties, charges and other taxes, or to prohibitions, restrictions and other similar controls with respect to the movement of controlled items across the boundary of the customs territory of each Party.

Article 4.3
Transparency

1. Each Party shall ensure that all relevant information of general application pertaining to its customs laws is readily available to any interested person.

2. When information that has been made available must be revised due to changes in its customs laws, each Party shall make the revised information readily available, whenever possible in advance of the entry into force of the changes, to enable interested persons to take account of them.

3. Upon request of any interested person of the Parties, each Party shall provide, as quickly and accurately as possible, information related to the specific customs matters raised by the interested person and pertaining to its customs laws. Each Party shall supply not only the information specifically requested but also any other pertinent information which it considers the interested person should be made aware of.

4. Each Party shall designate one or more enquiry points to answer reasonable enquiries from any interested person of the Parties concerning customs matters, and shall make publicly available, including through its website, the names and addresses of such enquiry points.

Article 4.4
Customs Clearance

1. The Parties shall apply their respective customs procedures in a predictable, consistent and transparent manner.

2. For prompt customs clearance of goods traded between the Parties, each Party shall:

(a) make use of information and communications technology;

(b) simplify its customs procedures;

(c) harmonize its customs procedures, to the extent possible, with relevant international standards and recommended practices such as those made under the auspices of the Customs Co-operation Council; and

(d) promote cooperation, where appropriate, between its customs authority and:

(i) other national authorities of the Party;

(ii) the trading communities of the Party; and

(iii) the customs authorities of non-Parties.

3. Each Party shall provide affected parties with easily accessible processes of judicial or administrative review related to the action on the customs matters taken by the Party. Such review shall be independent of the authorities entrusted with the administrative enforcement of such actions and shall be carried out in an impartial and fair manner.

Article 4.5
Temporary Admission and Goods in Transit

1. Each Party shall continue to facilitate the procedures for the temporary admission of goods traded between the Parties in accordance with its laws, regulations and international obligations.

2. Each Party shall continue to facilitate customs clearance of goods in transit from or to the other Party in accordance with paragraph 3 of Article V of the GATT 1994.

3. The Parties shall endeavor to promote, through arrangements such as seminars and courses, the use of A.T.A. carnets in accordance with the international obligations and the facilitation of customs clearance of goods in transit in the Parties or non-Parties.

4. For the purposes of this Article:

(a) the term "A.T.A. carnet" shall have the same meaning as in:

(i) for Japan, the Customs Convention on A.T.A. Carnet for the Temporary Admission of Goods, done at Brussels on December 6, 1961; and

(ii) for Mongolia, the Convention on Temporary Admission, done at Istanbul on June 26, 1990; and

(b) the term "temporary admission" means customs procedures under which certain goods may be brought into a customs territory conditionally, relieved totally or partially from the payment of customs duties. Such goods shall be imported for a specific purpose and shall be intended for re-exportation within a specified period and without having undergone any change except normal depreciation due to the use made of them.

Article 4.6
Advance Rulings

Where a written application is made in accordance with relevant laws, regulations or procedures adopted or maintained by the importing Party and the importing Party has no reasonable grounds to deny the issuance, the importing Party shall endeavor to, prior to the importation of the good, issue a written advance ruling on:

(a) the tariff classification;

(b) the customs valuation; and

(c) the qualification of the good as an originating good of the exporting Party under the provisions of Chapter 3.

Article 4.7
Cooperation and Exchange of Information

1. The Parties shall cooperate and exchange information with each other in the field of customs procedures, including combating the trafficking of prohibited goods and the importation and exportation of goods suspected of infringing intellectual property rights.

2. Such cooperation and exchange of information shall be implemented as provided for in the Implementing Agreement.

3. Paragraph 2 of Article 1.8 shall not apply to the exchange of information under this Article.

Article 4.8
Sub-Committee on Customs Procedures and Trade Facilitation

1. For the purposes of the effective implementation and operation of this Chapter, the Parties hereby establish a Sub-Committee on Customs Procedures and Trade Facilitation (hereinafter referred to in this Article as "the Sub-Committee").

2. The functions of the Sub-Committee shall be:

(a) reviewing and monitoring the implementation and operation of this Chapter;

(b) identifying areas, related to this Chapter, to be improved for facilitating trade between the Parties;

(c) reporting the findings of the Sub-Committee to the Joint Committee; and

(d) carrying out other functions as may be delegated by the Joint Committee.

3. The composition of the Sub-Committee shall be specified in the Implementing Agreement.

4. The Sub-Committee shall hold meetings at such times and venues or by means, as may be agreed by the Parties.

Chapter 5
Sanitary and Phytosanitary Measures

Article 5.1
Scope

This Chapter shall apply to all sanitary and phytosanitary (hereinafter referred to as "SPS") measures of the Parties under the SPS Agreement, that may, directly or indirectly, affect trade in goods between the Parties.

Article 5.2
Reaffirmation of Rights and Obligations

The Parties reaffirm their rights and obligations related to SPS measures under the SPS Agreement.

Article 5.3
Harmonization

The Parties shall endeavor to cooperate on the matters related to the harmonization of SPS measures, on as wide a basis as possible, as prescribed under Article 3 of the SPS Agreement. Such cooperation shall be conducted without requiring either Party to change its appropriate level of protection of human, animal or plant life or health that the Party has determined in accordance with Article 5 of the SPS Agreement.

Article 5.4
Equivalence

1. An importing Party shall accept an exporting Party's SPS measures as equivalent, if the exporting Party objectively demonstrates to the importing Party that its measures achieve the importing Party's appropriate level of SPS protection.

2. Each Party shall, upon request of the other Party, enter into consultations with the aim of achieving bilateral arrangements related to recognition of the equivalence of specified SPS measures.

Article 5.5
Enquiry Point

Each Party shall designate an enquiry point to answer all reasonable enquiries from the other Party regarding SPS measures and, where appropriate, to provide the other Party with relevant information.

Article 5.6
Sub-Committee on Sanitary and Phytosanitary Measures

1. For the purposes of the effective implementation and operation of this Chapter, the Parties hereby establish a Sub-Committee on SPS Measures (hereinafter referred to in this Article as "the Sub-Committee").

2. The functions of the Sub-Committee shall be:

(a) reviewing and monitoring the implementation and operation of this Chapter;

(b) exchanging information on such matters as change or introduction of SPS-related regulations and standards of the Parties and occurrences of SPS incidents in the Areas of the Parties, which may, directly or indirectly, affect trade in goods between the Parties;

(c) undertaking science-based technical consultations to address matters related to harmonization, equivalence, adaptation to regional conditions, and control, inspection and approval procedures as referred to in the SPS Agreement with the objective to achieve mutually acceptable solutions;

(d) discussing technical cooperation between the Parties on SPS measures including capacity building, technical assistance and exchange of experts;

(e) discussing any other issues related to this Chapter;

(f) reporting the findings of the Sub-Committee to the relevant bodies; and

(g) carrying out other functions as may be delegated by the Joint Committee.

3. The Sub-Committee shall be composed of representatives of the Governments of the Parties with appropriate participation of relevant experts.

4. The Sub-Committee shall hold meetings at such times and venues or by means, as may be agreed by the Parties.

Article 5.7
Non-Application of Chapter 16

Chapter 16 shall not apply to this Chapter.

Chapter 6
Technical Regulations, Standards and Conformity Assessment Procedures

Article 6.1
Scope

1. This Chapter shall apply to technical regulations, standards and conformity assessment procedures as defined in the TBT Agreement, that may affect trade in goods between the Parties.

2. This Chapter shall not apply to:

(a) purchasing specifications prepared by governmental bodies for production or consumption requirements of such bodies; or

(b) SPS measures as defined in Annex A of the SPS Agreement.

Article 6.2
Objectives

The objectives of this Chapter are to:

(a) increase and facilitate trade between the Parties, through the improvement of the implementation of the TBT Agreement;

(b) ensure that technical regulations, standards and conformity assessment procedures do not create unnecessary obstacles to trade; and

(c) enhance joint cooperation between the Parties.

Article 6.3
Definitions

For the purposes of this Chapter:

(a) the term "TBT Agreement" means the Agreement on Technical Barriers to Trade in Annex 1A to the WTO Agreement; and

(b) the terms and definitions set out in Annex 1 of the TBT Agreement shall apply.

Article 6.4
Reaffirmation of Rights and Obligations

The Parties reaffirm their rights and obligations related to technical regulations, standards and conformity assessment procedures under the TBT Agreement.

Article 6.5
International Standards

1. Each Party shall use relevant international standards and guides or recommendations to the extent provided in paragraph 4 of Article 2 and paragraph 4 of Article 5 of the TBT Agreement, as a basis for its technical regulations and conformity assessment procedures.

2. Each Party shall encourage its national standardizing bodies to cooperate with the relevant national standardizing bodies of the other Party in international standardizing activities. Such cooperation may take place in regional and international standardizing bodies of which they are both members.

Article 6.6
Technical Regulations

1. Upon request of a Party that has an interest in developing a technical regulation similar to a technical regulation of the other Party, such other Party shall provide, to the extent practicable, relevant information, including studies or documents, except for confidential information, on which it has relied in its development.

2. Each Party shall give positive consideration to accepting as equivalent technical regulations of the other Party, even if these regulations differ from its own, provided it is satisfied that these regulations adequately fulfill the objectives of its own regulations.

3. Where a Party does not accept a technical regulation of the other Party as equivalent to its own, it shall, upon request of the other Party, explain the reasons therefor.

Article 6.7
Acceptance of Results of Conformity Assessment Procedures

1. The Parties recognize that a broad range of mechanisms exists to facilitate the acceptance in a Party of the results of conformity assessment procedures conducted in the other Party. Each Party shall, upon request of the other Party, provide information on the range of such mechanisms used in its Area.

2. Each Party shall ensure, whenever possible, that results of the conformity assessment procedures in the other Party are accepted, even when those procedures differ from its own, provided it is satisfied that the procedures offer an assurance of conformity with applicable technical regulations or standards equivalent to its own procedures.

3. Where a Party does not accept the results of a conformity assessment procedure conducted in the other Party, it shall, upon request of the other Party and subject to the laws and regulations of that Party, explain the reasons therefor so that corrective action may be taken by the other Party where appropriate.

4. Each Party shall, whenever possible, accredit, designate or recognize conformity assessment bodies in the other Party on terms no less favorable than those it accords to conformity assessment bodies in its Area. If a Party accredits, designates or recognizes a body assessing conformity with a particular technical regulation or standard in its Area and it refuses to accredit, designate or recognize a body in the other Party assessing conformity with that technical regulation or standard, it shall, upon request, explain the reasons therefor.

Article 6.8
Enquiry Point

Each Party shall designate an enquiry point to answer all reasonable enquiries from the other Party regarding technical regulations, standards and conformity assessment procedures and, where appropriate, to provide the other Party with other relevant information which it considers the other Party should be made aware of.

Article 6.9
Sub-Committee on Technical Regulations, Standards and Conformity Assessment Procedures

1. For the purposes of the effective implementation and operation of this Chapter, the Parties hereby establish a Sub-Committee on Technical Regulations, Standards and Conformity Assessment Procedures (hereinafter referred to in this Article as "the Sub-Committee").

2. The functions of the Sub-Committee shall be:

(a) reviewing and monitoring the implementation and operation of this Chapter;

(b) enhancing joint cooperation in the development and improvement of technical regulations, standards and conformity assessment procedures;

(c) exchanging information on technical regulations, standards and conformity assessment procedures;

(d) undertaking consultations on issues related to technical regulations, standards and conformity assessment procedures;

(e) exchanging information on the work in regional and multilateral fora engaged in activities related to technical regulations, standards and conformity assessment procedures;

(f) discussing technical cooperation between the Parties on matters related to this Chapter;

(g) discussing any issues including those which may cause disputes between the Parties related to this Chapter with the objective of finding mutually acceptable solutions;

(h) reporting the findings of the Sub-Committee to the relevant bodies; and

(i) carrying out other functions as may be delegated by the Joint Committee.

3. The Sub-Committee shall be composed of representatives of the Governments of the Parties.

4. The Sub-Committee shall hold meetings at such times and venues or by means, as may be agreed by the Parties.

5. For the purposes of this Article, the Sub-Committee shall be coordinated by:

(a) for Japan, the Ministry of Foreign Affairs, or its successor; and

(b) for Mongolia, the Ministry of Industry, or its successor.

Article 6.10
Non-Application of Chapter 16

Chapter 16 shall not apply to this Chapter.

Chapter 7
Trade in Services

Article 7.1
Scope

1. This Chapter shall apply to measures adopted or maintained by a Party affecting trade in services.

2. This Chapter shall not apply to:

(a) cabotage in maritime transport services;

(b) with respect to air transport services, measures affecting traffic rights, however granted, or measures affecting services directly related to the exercise of traffic rights;

(c) government procurement;

(d) subsidies provided by a Party or a state enterprise, including grants, government-supported loans, guarantees and insurance;

(e) measures pursuant to immigration laws and regulations;

(f) measures affecting natural persons of a Party seeking access to the employment market of the other Party, or measures regarding nationality or citizenship, or residence or employment on a permanent basis; and

(g) services supplied in the exercise of governmental authority.

3. Notwithstanding subparagraph 2(b), this Chapter shall apply to measures affecting:

(a) aircraft repair and maintenance services;

(b) the selling and marketing of air transport services; and

(c) computer reservation system services.

4. Annex 4 provides supplementary provisions to this Chapter on financial services, including scope and definitions.

5. Annex 5 provides supplementary provisions to this Chapter on telecommunications services, including scope and definitions.

Article 7.2
Definitions

For the purposes of this Chapter:

(a) the term "aircraft repair and maintenance services" means such activities when undertaken on an aircraft or a part thereof while it is withdrawn from services and does not include so-called line maintenance;

(b) the term "computer reservation system services" means services provided by computerized systems that contain information about air carriers' schedules, availability, fares and fare rules, through which reservations may be made or tickets may be issued;

(c) the term "existing" means in effect on the date of entry into force of this Agreement;

(d) the term "juridical person of the other Party" means a juridical person which is either:

(i) constituted or otherwise organized under the law of the other Party; or

(ii) in the case of the supply of a service through commercial presence, owned or controlled by:

(A) natural persons of the other Party; or

(B) juridical persons of the other Party identified under subparagraph (i);

(e) the term "measure" means any measure, whether in the form of a law, regulation, rule, procedure, decision, administrative action or any other form;

Note: The term "measure" shall include taxation measures to the extent covered by the GATS.

(f) the term "measure adopted or maintained by a Party" means any measure adopted or maintained by:

(i) any level of government or authority of a Party; and

(ii) non-governmental bodies in the exercise of powers delegated by any level of government or authority of a Party;

(g) the term "measures by a Party affecting trade in services" includes measures with respect to:

(i) the purchase, payment or use of a service;

(ii) the access to and use of, in connection with the supply of a service, services which are required by the Party to be offered to the public generally; and

(iii) the presence, including commercial presence, of persons of the other Party for the supply of a service in the Area of the former Party;

(h) the term "monopoly supplier of a service" means any person, public or private, which in the relevant market of the Party, is authorized or established formally or in effect by that Party as the sole supplier of that service;

(i) the term "natural person of a Party" means a national of a Party under the law of the Party;

(j) the term "selling and marketing of air transport services" means opportunities for the air carrier concerned to sell and market freely its air transport services including all aspects of marketing such as market research, advertising and distribution. These activities do not include the pricing of air transport services nor the applicable conditions;

(k) the term "service supplied in the exercise of governmental authority" means any service which is supplied neither on a commercial basis nor in competition with one or more service suppliers;

(l) the term "supply of a service" includes the production, distribution, marketing, sale and delivery of a service;

(m) the term "trade in services" means the supply of a service:

(i) from the Area of a Party into the Area of the other Party ("cross-border supply mode");

(ii) in the Area of a Party to the service consumer of the other Party ("consumption abroad mode");

(iii) by a service supplier of a Party, through commercial presence in the Area of the other Party ("commercial presence mode"); or

(iv) by a service supplier of a Party, through presence of natural persons of that Party in the Area of the other Party ("presence of natural persons mode"); and

(n) the term "traffic rights" means the rights for scheduled and non-scheduled services to operate and/or to carry passengers, cargo and mail for remuneration or hire from, to, within, or over a Party, including points to be served, routes to be operated, types of traffic to be carried, capacity to be provided, tariffs to be charged and their conditions, and criteria for designation of airlines, including such criteria as number, ownership and control.

Article 7.3
National Treatment

1. In the sectors inscribed in its Schedule of Specific Commitments in Annex 6, and subject to any conditions and qualifications set out therein, each Party shall accord to services and service suppliers of the other Party, with respect to all measures affecting the supply of services, treatment no less favorable than that it accords to its own like services and service suppliers.

Note: Specific commitments assumed under this Article shall not be construed to require either Party to compensate for any inherent competitive disadvantages which result from the foreign character of the relevant services or service suppliers.

2. A Party may meet the requirement of paragraph 1 by according to services and service suppliers of the other Party, either formally identical treatment or formally different treatment to that it accords to its own like services and service suppliers.

3. Formally identical or formally different treatment shall be considered to be less favorable if it modifies the conditions of competition in favor of services or service suppliers of a Party compared to like services or service suppliers of the other Party.

Article 7.4
Most-Favored-Nation Treatment

1. Each Party shall accord to services and service suppliers of the other Party treatment no less favorable than that it accords to like services and service suppliers of any non-Party.

2. Each Party may maintain measures inconsistent with paragraph 1 provided that such measures are listed in, and meet the conditions of, the List of Most-Favored-Nation Treatment Exemptions in Annex 6.

Article 7.5
Market Access

1. With respect to market access through the modes of supply identified in subparagraph (m) of Article 7.2, a Party shall accord services and service suppliers of the other Party treatment no less favorable than that provided for under the terms, limitations and conditions agreed and specified in its Schedule of Specific Commitments in Annex 6.

Note: If a Party undertakes a market-access commitment in relation to the supply of a service through the mode of supply referred to in subparagraph (m)(i) of Article 7.2 and if the cross-border movement of capital is an essential part of the service itself, that Party is thereby committed to allow such movement of capital. If a Party undertakes a market-access commitment in relation to the supply of a service through the mode of supply referred to in subparagraph (m)(iii) of Article 7.2, it is thereby committed to allow related transfers of capital into its Area.

2. In sectors where market-access commitments are undertaken, the measures which a Party shall not maintain or adopt either on the basis of a regional subdivision or on the basis of its entire Area, unless otherwise specified in its Schedule of Specific Commitments in Annex 6, are defined as:

(a) limitations on the number of service suppliers whether in the form of numerical quotas, monopolies, exclusive service suppliers or the requirements of an economic needs test;

(b) limitations on the total value of service transactions or assets in the form of numerical quotas or the requirement of an economic needs test;

(c) limitations on the total number of service operations or on the total quantity of service output expressed in terms of designated numerical units in the form of quotas or the requirement of an economic needs test;

Note: This subparagraph does not cover measures of a Party which limit inputs for the supply of services.

(d) limitations on the total number of natural persons that may be employed in a particular service sector or that a service supplier may employ and who are necessary for, and directly related to, the supply of a specific service in the form of numerical quotas or the requirement of an economic needs test;

(e) measures which restrict or require specific types of legal entity or joint venture through which a service supplier may supply a service; and

(f) limitations on the participation of foreign capital in terms of maximum percentage limit on foreign shareholding or the total value of individual or aggregate foreign investment.

Article 7.6
Additional Commitments

The Parties may negotiate commitments with respect to measures affecting trade in services not subject to scheduling under Articles 7.3 and 7.5, including those regarding qualifications, standards or licensing matters. Such commitments shall be inscribed in a Party's Schedule of Specific Commitments in Annex 6.

Article 7.7
Schedule of Specific Commitments

1. Each Party shall set out in a schedule the specific commitments it undertakes under Articles 7.3, 7.5 and 7.6. With respect to sectors or sub-sectors where such commitments are undertaken, each Schedule of Specific Commitments in Annex 6 shall specify:

(a) terms, limitations and conditions on market access;

(b) conditions and qualifications on national treatment;

(c) undertakings related to additional commitments; and

(d) where appropriate, the time-frame for implementation of such commitments.

2. With respect to sectors or sub-sectors where the specific commitments are undertaken and which are indicated with "SS", any terms, limitations, conditions and qualifications, referred to in subparagraphs 1(a) and 1(b), other than those based on measures pursuant to immigration laws and regulations, shall be limited to those based on existing non-conforming measures.

3. Measures inconsistent with both Articles 7.3 and 7.5 shall be inscribed in the column related to Article 7.5. In this case the inscription will be considered to provide a condition or qualification to Article 7.3 as well.

Article 7.8
Domestic Regulation

1. Each Party shall ensure that all measures of general application affecting trade in services are administered in a reasonable, objective and impartial manner.

2. Where authorization is required by a Party for the supply of a service, the competent authorities of that Party shall, within a reasonable period of time after the submission of an application is considered complete under the laws and regulations of that Party, inform the applicant of the decision concerning the application. Upon request of the applicant, the competent authorities of that Party shall provide, without undue delay, information concerning the status of the application.

3. With a view to ensuring that any measure adopted or maintained by a Party in any services sector related to the authorization, qualification requirements and procedures, technical standards and licensing requirements of service suppliers of the other Party does not constitute an unnecessary barrier to trade in services, each Party shall ensure that such measure:

(a) is based on objective and transparent criteria, such as the competence and ability to supply the service;

(b) is not more burdensome than necessary to ensure the quality of the service; and

(c) does not constitute a disguised restriction on the supply of the service.

Article 7.9
Recognition

1. A Party may recognize the education or experience obtained, requirements met, or licenses or certifications granted in the other Party for the purposes of the fulfillment, in whole or in part, of its standards or criteria for the authorization, licensing or certification of service suppliers of the other Party.

2. Recognition referred to in paragraph 1, which may be achieved through harmonization or otherwise, may be based upon an agreement or arrangement between the Parties or may be accorded unilaterally.

3. Where a Party recognizes, by agreement or arrangement between the Party and a non-Party or unilaterally, the education or experience obtained, requirements met, or licenses or certifications granted in the non-Party:

(a) nothing in Article 7.4 shall be construed to require the Party to accord such recognition to the education or experience obtained, requirements met, or licenses or certifications granted in the other Party;

(b) the Party shall accord the other Party an adequate opportunity to negotiate the accession of that other Party to such an agreement or arrangement or to negotiate a comparable one with it between the Parties; and

(c) where the Party accords such recognition unilaterally, the Party shall accord the other Party an adequate opportunity to demonstrate that the education or experience obtained, requirements met, or licenses or certifications granted in the other Party should also be recognized.

Article 7.10
Monopolies and Exclusive Service Suppliers

1. A Party shall ensure that any monopoly supplier of a service in its Area does not, in the supply of the monopoly service in the relevant market, act in a manner inconsistent with that Party's obligations under Articles 7.3, 7.4 and 7.5.

2. Where a Party's monopoly supplier competes, either directly or through an affiliated company, in the supply of a service outside the scope of its monopoly rights, in an area subject to its Specific Commitments, that Party shall ensure that such a supplier does not abuse its monopoly position to act in the Area of that Party in a manner inconsistent with such commitments under Articles 7.3 and 7.5.

3. If a Party has a reason to believe that a monopoly supplier of a service of the other Party is acting in a manner inconsistent with paragraph 1 or 2, the former Party may request the other Party to provide specific information concerning the relevant operations.

4. This Article shall also apply to cases of exclusive service suppliers, where a Party, formally or in effect:

(a) authorizes or establishes a small number of service suppliers; and

(b) substantially prevents competition among those suppliers in its Area.

Article 7.11
Business Practices

1. The Parties recognize that certain business practices of service suppliers, other than those falling under Article 7.10, may restrain competition and thereby restrict trade in services.

2. A Party shall, upon request of the other Party, enter into consultations with a view to eliminating practices referred to in paragraph 1. The Party addressed shall accord full and sympathetic consideration to such a request and shall cooperate through the supply of publicly available non-confidential information of relevance to the matter in question. The Party addressed shall also provide other information available to the requesting Party, subject to its laws and regulations and to the conclusion of a satisfactory agreement concerning the safeguarding of its confidentiality by the requesting Party.

Article 7.12
Payments and Transfers

1. Except under the circumstances envisaged in Article 7.13, a Party shall not apply restrictions on international transfers and payments for current transactions related to trade in services.

2. Nothing in this Chapter shall affect the rights and obligations of the Parties as members of the International Monetary Fund under the Articles of Agreement of the International Monetary Fund, including the use of exchange actions which are in conformity with the Articles of Agreement of the International Monetary Fund. However, a Party shall not impose restrictions on any capital transactions inconsistently with its Specific Commitments regarding such transactions, except under Article 7.13 or upon request of the International Monetary Fund.

Article 7.13
Restrictions to Safeguard the Balance of Payments

1. In the event of serious balance-of-payments and external financial difficulties or threat thereof, a Party may adopt or maintain restrictions on trade in services, including on payments or transfers for transactions.

2. The restrictions referred to in paragraph 1 shall:

(a) be applied on the basis of national treatment and most-favored-nation treatment;

(b) be consistent with the Articles of Agreement of the International Monetary Fund;

(c) avoid unnecessary damage to the commercial, economic and financial interests of the other Party;

(d) not exceed those necessary to deal with the circumstances described in paragraph 1; and

(e) be temporary and be phased out progressively as the situation specified in paragraph 1 improves.

3. In determining the incidence of such restrictions, a Party may give priority to the supply of services which are more essential to its economic or development programs. However, such restrictions shall not be adopted or maintained for the purposes of protecting a particular service sector.

4. Any restrictions adopted or maintained under paragraph 1, or any changes therein, shall be promptly notified to the other Party.

Article 7.14
Transparency

Each Party shall prepare a non-legally binding list providing all relevant measures affecting the obligations under Articles 7.3, 7.4 and 7.5 in all sectors. The list shall be exchanged with the other Party and made publicly available within five years from the date of entry into force of this Agreement and shall also be subject to future review and revision where necessary or as agreed between the Parties. The list shall include the following elements:

(a) sector and sub-sector or matter;

(b) type of inconsistency (i.e. national treatment, most-favored-nation treatment and/or market access);

(c) legal source or authority of the measure; and

(d) brief description of the measure.

Note: The list under this Article is made solely for the purposes of transparency, and shall not be construed to affect the rights and obligations of a Party under this Chapter. Any review or revision under this Article is solely for the purposes of updating such list.

Article 7.15
Denial of Benefits

1. A Party may deny the benefits of this Chapter to a service supplier of the other Party that is a juridical person of the other Party, where the denying Party establishes that the juridical person is owned or controlled by persons of a non-Party, and the denying Party:

(a) does not maintain diplomatic relations with the non-Party; or

(b) adopts or maintains measures regarding the non-Party that:

(i) prohibit transactions with the juridical person; or

(ii) would be violated or circumvented if the benefits of this Chapter were accorded to the juridical person.

2. Subject to prior notification and consultation, a Party may deny the benefits of this Chapter to a service supplier of the other Party that is a juridical person of the other Party, where the denying Party establishes that the juridical person is owned or controlled by persons of a non-Party and has no substantial business activities in the Area of the other Party.

Article 7.16
Sub-Committee on Trade in Services

1. For the purposes of the effective implementation and operation of this Chapter, the Parties hereby establish a Sub-Committee on Trade in Services (hereinafter referred to in this Article as "the Sub-Committee").

2. The functions of the Sub-Committee shall be:

(a) reviewing and monitoring the implementation and operation of this Chapter;

(b) discussing any issues related to this Chapter;

(c) reporting the findings of the Sub-Committee to the Joint Committee; and

(d) carrying out other functions as may be delegated by the Joint Committee.

3. The Sub-Committee shall be composed of representatives of the Governments of the Parties.

4. The Sub-Committee shall hold meetings at such times and venues or by means, as may be agreed by the Parties.

Article 7.17
Review of Commitments

1. With the objective of further liberalizing trade in services between the Parties, including the possibility of renegotiating the format of schedules, the Parties shall consider in due course undertaking a review of this Chapter and the Annexes referred to therein on occasions as may be agreed by the Parties.

2. If, after the entry into force of this Agreement, a Party has undertaken further liberalization autonomously in any of the services sectors, sub-sectors or activities, it shall consider in due course requests from the other Party to incorporate such liberalization into this Agreement.

Chapter 8
Movement of Natural Persons

Article 8.1
General Principles

1. This Chapter reflects the preferential trading relationship between the Parties, the desire of the Parties to facilitate entry and temporary stay of natural persons on a mutually beneficial basis and to establish transparent criteria and procedures for entry and temporary stay, and the need to ensure border security and to protect the domestic labor force and permanent employment in each Party.

2. Each Party shall apply its measures related to the provisions of this Chapter in accordance with the general principles referred to in paragraph 1, and, in particular, shall apply those measures expeditiously so as to avoid unduly impairing or delaying trade in goods or services or investment activities under this Agreement.

Article 8.2
Scope

1. This Chapter shall apply to measures affecting the entry and temporary stay of natural persons of a Party who enter the other Party and fall under one of the categories referred to in paragraph 1 of Article 8.4.

2. This Chapter shall not apply to measures affecting natural persons of a Party seeking access to the employment market of the other Party, nor shall it apply to measures regarding nationality or citizenship, or residence or employment on a permanent basis.

3. This Chapter shall not prevent a Party from applying measures to regulate the entry and temporary stay of natural persons of the other Party, including those measures necessary to protect the integrity of, and to ensure the orderly movement of natural persons across, its borders, provided that such measures are not applied in such a manner as to nullify or impair the benefits accruing to the other Party under the terms of specific commitments set out in Annex 7.

Note: The sole fact of requiring a visa for natural persons of the other Party and not for those of certain non-Parties shall not be regarded as nullifying or impairing benefits under the terms of specific commitments set out in Annex 7.

Article 8.3
Definition

For the purposes of this Chapter, the term "natural person of a Party" means a natural person who resides in a Party or elsewhere and who under the law of the Party is a national of the Party.

Article 8.4
Specific Commitments

1. Each Party shall set out in Annex 7 the specific commitments it undertakes for:

(a) short-term business visitors of the other Party;

(b) intra-corporate transferees of the other Party;

(c) investors of the other Party;

(d) natural persons of the other Party who engage in professional services;

(e) natural persons of the other Party who engage in supplying services, which require technology or knowledge at an advanced level on the basis of a contract with public or private organizations in the former Party; and

(f) spouse and children accompanying those natural persons set out in subparagraphs (b) through (e).

2. Natural persons covered by the categories referred to in paragraph 1 shall be granted entry and temporary stay in accordance with the terms and conditions set out in Annex 7, provided that the natural persons comply with immigration laws and regulations applicable to entry and temporary stay which are not inconsistent with the provisions of this Chapter.

3. Neither Party shall impose or maintain any limitation on the number of natural persons to be granted entry and temporary stay under paragraph 1.

Article 8.5
Requirements and Procedures

1. Each Party shall publish or otherwise make available to the other Party upon the date of entry into force of this Agreement, with respect to natural persons covered by that Party's specific commitments set out in Annex 7, information on requirements and procedures necessary for an effective application by natural persons of the other Party for the grant of:

(a) entry into the former Party;

(b) initial temporary stay in the former Party;

(c) renewal of temporary stay in the former Party;

(d) where applicable, permission to work in the former Party; and

(e) change of status of temporary stay in the former Party.

2. Each Party shall endeavor to provide, upon request by a natural person of the other Party, information on requirements and procedures referred to in paragraph 1.

3. Each Party shall endeavor to promptly inform the other Party of the introduction of any new requirements and procedures, or changes in any existing requirements and procedures referred to in paragraph 1 that affect the effective application by natural persons of the other Party for the grant of entry, temporary stay or permission referred to in subparagraphs 1(a) through (e).

4. Each Party shall ensure that fees charged by its competent authorities on application referred to in paragraph 1 do not in themselves represent an unjustifiable impediment to entry and temporary stay of natural persons of the other Party under this Chapter.

5. Each Party shall endeavor, to the maximum extent possible, to take measures to simplify the requirements and to facilitate and expedite the procedures related to the entry and temporary stay of natural persons of the other Party subject to its laws and regulations.

Article 8.6
Sub-Committee on Movement of Natural Persons

1. For the purposes of the effective implementation and operation of this Chapter, the Parties hereby establish a Sub-Committee on Movement of Natural Persons (hereinafter referred to in this Article as "the Sub-Committee").

2. The functions of the Sub-Committee shall be:

(a) reviewing and monitoring the implementation and operation of this Chapter;

(b) considering the development of measures to further facilitate the entry and temporary stay of natural persons on a reciprocal basis;

(c) exchanging information on measures affecting entry and temporary stay of natural persons referred to in Annex 7;

(d) discussing any issues related to this Chapter as may be agreed upon;

(e) reporting the findings of the Sub-Committee to the Joint Committee; and

(f) carrying out other functions as may be delegated by the Joint Committee.

3. The Sub-Committee shall be composed of representatives of the Governments of the Parties.

4. The Sub-Committee shall hold meetings at such times and venues or by means, as may be agreed by the Parties.

Article 8.7
Dispute Settlement

1. The dispute settlement procedures provided for in Chapter 16 shall not apply to this Chapter unless:

(a) the matter involves a pattern of practice; and

(b) the natural persons of a Party affected by that matter have exhausted the available domestic administrative remedies of the other Party.

2. The remedies referred to in subparagraph 1(b) shall be deemed to be exhausted if a final determination in the matter has not been issued by the competent authority of the other Party within one year after the date of the institution of the administrative remedy, and the failure to issue such a determination is not attributable to the delay caused by the natural persons.

Chapter 9
Electronic Commerce

Article 9.1
General Provisions

1. The Parties recognize the economic growth and opportunities provided by electronic commerce, and the importance of avoiding unnecessary barriers to its use and development.

2. The objective of this Chapter is to contribute to creating an environment of trust and confidence in the use of electronic commerce and to promote electronic commerce between the Parties and the wider use of electronic commerce globally.

3. The Parties recognize the principle of technological neutrality in electronic commerce.

4. In the event of any inconsistency between this Chapter and Chapter 2, 7, 10 or 12, the Chapter other than this Chapter shall prevail to the extent of the inconsistency.

Article 9.2
Definitions

For the purposes of this Chapter:

(a) the term "digital products" means computer programs, text, video, images, sound recordings and other products, that are digitally encoded, regardless of whether they are fixed on a carrier medium or transmitted electronically;

(b) the term "electronic certificate" means an electromagnetic record prepared for certifying that matters used to confirm that the user has performed the electronic signature are pertaining to such user;

(c) the term "electronic signature" means a measure taken with respect to information that can be recorded in an electromagnetic record and which fulfills both of the following requirements:

(i) that the measure indicates that such information has been approved by a person who has taken such measure; and

(ii) that the measure confirms that such information has not been altered; and

(d) the term "trade administration documents" means forms that a Party issues or controls and that must be completed by or for an importer or exporter in connection with the importation or exportation of goods.

Article 9.3
Customs Duties

Each Party shall maintain its practice of not imposing customs duties on electronic transmissions between the Parties.

Article 9.4
Non-Discriminatory Treatment of Digital Products

1. Neither Party shall adopt or maintain:

(a) measures that accord less favorable treatment to digital products of the other Party than it accords to its own like digital products; and

(b) measures that accord less favorable treatment to digital products of the other Party than it accords to like digital products of a non-Party.

2. Paragraph 1 shall not apply to:

(a) government procurement;

(b) subsidies provided by a Party or a state enterprise, including grants, government-supported loans, guarantees and insurance;

(c) measures maintained by a Party in accordance with paragraph 2 of Article 7.4;

(d) measures adopted or maintained by a Party within the scope of Article 7.3 or 7.5 which are:

(i) related to the sectors not committed in its Schedule of Specific Commitments in Annex 6; or

(ii) not inconsistent with the terms, limitations, conditions and qualifications agreed and specified in its Schedule of Specific Commitments in Annex 6; and

(e) non-conforming measures adopted or maintained by a Party in accordance with Article 10.8.

3. In implementing its obligations under paragraph 1, each Party shall, where necessary, determine in good faith whether a digital product is a digital product of a Party, of the other Party or of a non-Party. Such determination shall be made in a transparent, objective, reasonable and fair manner.

4. Each Party shall, upon request of the other Party, explain how it determines the origin of a digital product where it determines such origin in implementing its obligations under paragraph 1.

5. The Parties shall cooperate in international organizations and fora to foster the development of criteria for the determination of the origin of a digital product, with a view to considering the incorporation of such criteria into this Agreement.

Article 9.5
Electronic Signature

1. Neither Party shall adopt or maintain measures regulating electronic signature that would:

(a) prohibit parties to an electronic transaction from mutually determining the appropriate electronic signature methods for their transaction; or

(b) prevent parties to an electronic transaction from having the opportunity to prove in court that their electronic transactions comply with any legal requirements.

2. Notwithstanding paragraph 1, each Party may require that, for a particular category of electronic transactions, the electronic signatures meet certain performance standards or are based on a specific electronic certificate issued by a supplier of certification services accredited or recognized in accordance with the laws and regulations of the Party, provided that the requirement:

(a) serves a legitimate policy objective; and

(b) is substantially related to achieving that objective.

Article 9.6
Consumer Protection

1. The Parties recognize the importance of adopting and maintaining transparent and effective consumer protection measures for electronic commerce as well as measures conducive to the development of consumer confidence.

2. The Parties recognize the importance of cooperation between their respective competent authorities in charge of consumer protection on activities related to electronic commerce in order to enhance consumer protection.

3. The Parties shall adopt or maintain measures, in accordance with their respective laws and regulations, to protect the personal data of electronic commerce users.

Article 9.7
Unsolicited Commercial E-mail

Each Party shall endeavor to take appropriate and necessary measures to regulate unsolicited commercial e-mail for advertising purposes.

Article 9.8
Paperless Trade Administration

1. Each Party shall endeavor to make all trade administration documents available to the public in electronic form.

2. Each Party shall endeavor to accept trade administration documents submitted electronically as the legal equivalent of the paper version of such documents.

3. The Parties shall cooperate bilaterally and in international fora to enhance the acceptance of electronic versions of trade administration documents.

Article 9.9
Domestic Regulation

Each Party shall ensure that all its measures affecting electronic commerce are administered in a transparent, objective, reasonable and impartial manner, and are not more burdensome than necessary to meet legitimate policy objectives.

Article 9.10
Prohibition on Requirement concerning the Location of Computing Facilities

1. Neither Party shall require:

(a) a service supplier of the other Party;

(b) an investor of the other Party; or

(c) an investment of an investor of the other Party in the Area of the former Party,

as a condition for conducting its business in the Area of the former Party, to use or locate computing facilities in that Area.

2. Notwithstanding paragraph 1, nothing in this Article shall be construed to prevent a Party from adopting or maintaining measures affecting the use or location of computing facilities necessary to achieve a legitimate public policy objective, provided that such measures are not applied in a manner which would constitute a means of arbitrary or unjustifiable discrimination or a disguised restriction on trade.

Article 9.11
Source Code

1. Neither Party shall require the transfer of, or access to, source code of software owned by a person of the other Party, as a condition of the import, distribution, sale or use of such software, or of products containing such software, in its Area.

2. For the purposes of this Article, software subject to paragraph 1 is limited to mass-market software or products containing such software, and does not include software used for critical infrastructure.

Article 9.12
Cooperation

1. The Parties shall, where appropriate, cooperate bilaterally and participate actively in regional and multilateral fora to promote the development of electronic commerce.

2. The Parties shall, where appropriate, share information and experiences, including on related laws, regulations and best practices with respect to electronic commerce, related to, *inter alia*, consumer confidence, cyber-security, combatting unsolicited commercial e-mail, intellectual property, electronic government and personal data protection.

3. The Parties shall cooperate to overcome obstacles encountered by small and medium enterprises in the use of electronic commerce.

4. Each Party shall encourage, through existing means available to it, the activities of non-profit organizations in that Party aimed at promoting electronic commerce, including the exchange of information and views.

5. The Parties recognize the importance of working to maintain cross-border flows of information as an essential element for a vibrant electronic commerce environment.

6. The Parties recognize the importance of further enhancement of trade in digital products.

Article 9.13
Sub-Committee on Electronic Commerce

1. For the purposes of the effective implementation and operation of this Chapter, the Parties hereby establish a Sub-Committee on Electronic Commerce (hereinafter referred to in this Article as "the Sub-Committee").

2. The functions of the Sub-Committee shall be:

(a) reviewing and monitoring the implementation and operation of this Chapter;

(b) discussing any issues related to this Chapter including, where appropriate, the possible review of Article 9.4;

(c) seeking new opportunities to further enhance trade in digital products;

(d) reporting the findings of the Sub-Committee to the Joint Committee; and

(e) carrying out other functions as may be delegated by the Joint Committee.

3. The Sub-Committee shall be composed of representatives of the Governments of the Parties.

4. The Sub-Committee shall hold meetings at such times and venues or by means, as may be agreed by the Parties.

Chapter 10
Investment

Article 10.1
Scope

1. This Chapter shall apply to measures adopted or maintained by a Party related to:

(a) investors of the other Party;

(b) investments of investors of the other Party in the Area of the former Party; and

(c) with respect to Articles 10.7 and 10.17, all investments in the Area of the former Party.

Note 1: For greater certainty, this Chapter shall also apply to measures adopted or maintained by a Party related to investments made by investors of the other Party in the Area of the former Party prior to the entry into force of this Agreement.

Note 2: For greater certainty, this Chapter shall not apply to claims arising out of events which occurred prior to the entry into force of this Agreement.

2. In the event of any inconsistency between this Chapter and Chapter 7:

(a) with respect to matters covered by Articles 10.3, 10.4 and 10.7, Chapter 7 shall prevail to the extent of the inconsistency; and

(b) with respect to matters not falling under subparagraph (a), this Chapter shall prevail to the extent of the inconsistency.

3. Nothing in this Chapter shall impose any obligation on either Party regarding measures pursuant to immigration laws and regulations.

Article 10.2
Definitions

For the purposes of this Chapter:

(a) the term "Bilateral Investment Agreement" means the Agreement between Japan and Mongolia concerning the Promotion and Protection of Investment signed at Tokyo on February 15, 2001;

(b) an enterprise is:

(i) "owned" by an investor if more than 50 percent of the equity interest in it is owned by the investor; and

(ii) "controlled" by an investor if the investor has the power to name a majority of its directors or otherwise to legally direct its actions;

(c) the term "existing" means in effect on the date of entry into force of this Agreement;

(d) the term "freely usable currency" means freely usable currency as defined under the Articles of Agreement of the International Monetary Fund;

(e) the term "investment activities" means establishment, acquisition, expansion, operation, management, maintenance, use, enjoyment and sale or other disposal of an investment; and

(f) the term "measure" means any measure, whether in the form of a law, regulation, rule, procedure, decision, administrative action or any other form.

Article 10.3
National Treatment

1. Each Party shall in its Area accord to investors of the other Party and to their investments treatment no less favorable than the treatment it accords in like circumstances to its own investors and to their investments with respect to investment activities.

2. Paragraph 1 shall not be construed to prevent a Party from adopting or maintaining a measure that prescribes special formalities in connection with investment activities of investors of the other Party in its Area, provided that such special formalities do not impair the substance of the rights of such investors under this Chapter.

Article 10.4
Most-Favored-Nation Treatment

Each Party shall in its Area accord to investors of the other Party and to their investments treatment no less favorable than the treatment it accords in like circumstances to investors of a non-Party and to their investments with respect to investment activities.

Article 10.5
General Treatment

1. Each Party shall in its Area accord to investments of investors of the other Party treatment in accordance with international law, including fair and equitable treatment and full protection and security.

Note 1: This paragraph prescribes the customary international law minimum standard of treatment of aliens as the minimum standard of treatment to be afforded to investments of investors of the other Party. The concepts of "fair and equitable treatment" and "full protection and security" do not require treatment in addition to or beyond that which is required by the customary international law minimum standard of treatment of aliens. A determination that there has been a breach of another provision of this Agreement, or of a separate international agreement, does not establish that there has been a breach of this paragraph.

Note 2: "Fair and equitable treatment" includes the obligation of the Party not to deny justice in criminal, civil or administrative adjudicatory proceedings in accordance with the principle of due process of law.

2. Each Party shall observe any written obligation it may have entered into with respect to a specific investment by an investor of the other Party, which the investor could have relied on at the time of establishment, acquisition or expansion of such investment.

3. This Article shall apply to taxation measures.

Article 10.6
Access to the Courts

1. Each Party shall in its Area accord to investors of the other Party treatment no less favorable than the treatment it accords in like circumstances to its own investors or to investors of a non-Party with respect to access to the courts and administrative agencies in all degrees of jurisdiction, both in pursuit and in defense of such investors' rights.

2. This Article shall apply to taxation measures.

Article 10.7
Prohibition of Performance Requirements

1. Neither Party shall impose or enforce any of the following requirements, or enforce any commitment or undertaking, in connection with investment activities of an investor of a Party or of a non-Party in its Area to:

(a) export a given level or percentage of goods or services;

(b) achieve a given level or percentage of domestic content;

(c) purchase, use or accord a preference to goods produced or services provided in its Area, or to purchase goods or services from persons in its Area;

(d) relate in any way the volume or value of imports to the volume or value of exports or to the amount of foreign exchange inflows associated with an investment of the investor;

(e) restrict sales of goods or services in its Area that an investment of the investor produces or provides by relating such sales in any way to the volume or value of its exports or foreign exchange earnings;

(f) restrict the exportation or sale for export;

(g) appoint, as executives, managers or members of boards of directors, individuals of any particular nationality;

(h) locate the headquarters of that investor for a specific region or the world market in its Area;

(i) hire a given number or percentage of its nationals;

(j) supply one or more of the goods that the investor produces or the services that the investor provides to a specific region or the world market, exclusively from the Area of the former Party; or

(k) adopt:

(i) given rate or amount of royalty under a license contract; or

(ii) a given duration of the term of a license contract,

with respect to any license contract freely entered into between the investor and a person in its Area, whether it has been entered into or not, provided that the requirement is imposed or the commitment or undertaking is enforced by an exercise of governmental authority of the Party.

Note: A "license contract" referred to in this subparagraph means any license contract concerning transfer of technology, a production process, or other proprietary knowledge.

2. Neither Party shall condition the receipt or continued receipt of an advantage, in connection with investment activities of an investor of a Party or of a non-Party in its Area, on compliance with any of the following requirements to:

(a) achieve a given level or percentage of domestic content;

(b) purchase, use or accord a preference to goods produced or services provided in its Area, or to purchase goods or services from persons in its Area;

(c) relate in any way the volume or value of imports to the volume or value of exports or to the amount of foreign exchange inflows associated with an investment of the investor;

(d) restrict sales of goods or services in its Area that an investment of the investor produces or provides by relating such sales in any way to the volume or value of its exports or foreign exchange earnings; or

(e) restrict the exportation or sale for export.

3. (a) Nothing in paragraph 2 shall be construed to prevent a Party from conditioning the receipt or continued receipt of an advantage, in connection with investment activities of an investor of a Party or of a non-Party in its Area, on compliance with a requirement to locate production, supply a service, train or employ workers, construct or expand particular facilities, or carry out research and development, in its Area.

(b) Subparagraph 1(k) shall not apply when the requirement is imposed or the commitment or undertaking is enforced by a court or competition authority to remedy an alleged violation of laws controlling the anti-competitive activities.

(c) Subparagraphs 1(a), 1(b), 1(c), 2(a) and 2(b) shall not apply to qualification requirements for goods or services with respect to foreign aid programs.

(d) Subparagraphs 2(a) and 2(b) shall not apply to requirements imposed by an importing Party related to the content of goods necessary to qualify for preferential tariffs or preferential quotas.

4. Paragraphs 1 and 2 shall not apply to any requirement other than the requirements set out in those paragraphs.

Article 10.8
Non-Conforming Measures

1. Articles 10.3, 10.4 and 10.7 shall not apply to:

(a) any existing non-conforming measure that is maintained by the central government of a Party, as set out in its Schedule in Annex 8;

(b) any existing non-conforming measure that is maintained by a local government of a Party;

(c) the continuation or prompt renewal of any non-conforming measure referred to in subparagraphs (a) and (b); or

(d) an amendment or modification to any non-conforming measure referred to in subparagraphs (a) and (b), to the extent that the amendment or modification does not decrease the conformity of the measure, as it existed immediately before the amendment or modification, with Articles 10.3, 10.4 and 10.7.

2. If a Party considers that the non-conforming measure referred to in subparagraph 1(b) and adopted or maintained by a prefecture or the city of Ulaanbaatar or a province of the other Party creates an impediment to investment activities of an investor of the former Party, that former Party may request consultations with respect to the application of that measure with a view to achieving mutually satisfactory solution.

3. Articles 10.3, 10.4 and 10.7 shall not apply to any measure that a Party adopts or maintains with respect to sectors, sub-sectors or activities, as set out in its Schedule in Annex 9.

4. Neither Party shall, under any measure adopted after the date of entry into force of this Agreement and covered by its Schedule in Annex 9, require an investor of the other Party, by reason of its nationality, to sell or otherwise dispose of an investment that exists at the time when the measure becomes effective.

5. In cases where a Party makes an amendment or a modification to any existing non-conforming measure set out in its Schedule in Annex 8 or where a Party adopts any new or more restrictive measure with respect to sectors, sub-sectors or activities set out in its Schedule in Annex 9 after the date of entry into force of this Agreement, the Party shall, prior to the implementation of the amendment or modification or the new or more restrictive measure, or in exceptional circumstances, as soon as possible thereafter:

(a) notify the other Party of detailed information on such amendment, modification or measure; and

(b) hold, upon request of the other Party, consultations in good-faith with the other Party with a view to achieving mutual satisfaction.

6. Each Party shall endeavor, where appropriate, to reduce or eliminate the non-conforming measures specified in its Schedules in Annexes 8 and 9 respectively.

7. Articles 10.3 and 10.4 shall not apply to any measure covered by the exceptions to, or derogations from, obligations under Articles 3 and 4 of the TRIPS Agreement, as specifically provided in Articles 3 through 5 of the TRIPS Agreement.

8. Articles 10.3, 10.4 and 10.7 shall not apply to any measure that a Party adopts or maintains with respect to government procurement.

Article 10.9
Expropriation and Compensation

1. Neither Party shall expropriate or nationalize an investment in its Area of investors of the other Party or take any measure equivalent to expropriation or nationalization (hereinafter referred to as "expropriation") except:

(a) for a public purpose;

(b) in a non-discriminatory manner;

(c) upon payment of prompt, adequate and effective compensation in accordance with paragraphs 2 through 4; and

(d) in accordance with due process of law and Article 10.5.

2. The compensation shall be equivalent to the fair market value of the expropriated investment at the time when the expropriation was publicly announced or when the expropriation took place, whichever is earlier. The fair market value shall not reflect any change in value occurring because the intended expropriation had become publicly known earlier.

3. The compensation shall be paid without delay and shall include interest at a commercially reasonable rate, taking into account the length of time until the time of payment. It shall be effectively realizable and freely transferable, and shall be freely convertible into the currency of the Party of the investors concerned and into freely usable currencies at the market exchange rate prevailing on the date of expropriation.

4. Without prejudice to the provisions of Article 10.13, the investors affected by expropriation shall have a right of access to the courts or administrative agencies of the Party making the expropriation to seek a prompt review of the investors' case and the amount of compensation in accordance with the principles set out in this Article.

5. This Article shall apply to taxation measures, to the extent that such taxation measures constitute expropriation.

6. This Article shall be interpreted in accordance with Annex 10.

Article 10.10
Protection from Strife

1. Each Party shall accord to investors of the other Party that have suffered loss or damage related to their investments in the Area of the former Party due to armed conflict or a state of emergency such as revolution, insurrection, civil disturbance or any other similar event in the Area of that former Party, treatment, as regards restitution, indemnification, compensation or any other settlement, that is no less favorable than the treatment it accords to its own investors or to investors of a non-Party, whichever is more favorable to the investors of the other Party.

2. Any payment as a means of settlement referred to in paragraph 1 shall be effectively realizable, freely transferable and freely convertible at the market exchange rate into the currency of the Party of the investors concerned and freely usable currencies.

3. Notwithstanding the provisions of Article 1.10, neither Party shall be relieved of its obligation under paragraph 1 by reason of its measures taken in accordance with that Article.

Article 10.11
Transfers

1. Each Party shall ensure that all transfers related to investments in its Area of an investor of the other Party may be freely made into and out of its Area without delay. Such transfers shall include, in particular, though not exclusively:

(a) the initial capital and additional amounts to maintain or increase investments;

(b) profits, interest, capital gains, dividends, royalties, fees and other current incomes accruing from investments;

(c) payments made under a contract including loan payments in connection with investments;

(d) proceeds of the total or partial sale or liquidation of investments;

(e) earnings and remuneration of personnel from the other Party engaged in activities in connection with investments in the Area of the former Party;

(f) payments made in accordance with Articles 10.9 and 10.10; and

(g) payments arising out of the settlement of a dispute under Article 10.13.

2. Each Party shall further ensure that such transfers may be made without delay in freely usable currencies at the market exchange rate prevailing on the date of the transfer.

3. Notwithstanding paragraphs 1 and 2, a Party may delay or prevent a transfer through the equitable, non-discriminatory and good-faith application of its laws and regulations related to:

(a) bankruptcy, insolvency or the protection of the rights of creditors;

(b) issuing, trading or dealing in securities;

(c) criminal or penal offenses; or

(d) ensuring compliance with orders or judgments in adjudicatory proceedings.

Article 10.12
Subrogation

If a Party or its designated agency makes a payment to any investor of that Party under an indemnity, guarantee or insurance contract, pertaining to an investment of such investor in the Area of the other Party, the latter Party shall recognize the assignment to the former Party or its designated agency of any right or claim of such investor on account of which such payment is made and shall recognize the right of the former Party or its designated agency to exercise by virtue of subrogation any such right or claim to the same extent as the original right or claim of the investor. As regards payment to be made to that former Party or its designated agency by virtue of such assignment of right or claim and the transfer of such payment, the provisions of Articles 10.9, 10.10 and 10.11 shall apply *mutatis mutandis*.

Article 10.13
Settlement of Investment Disputes between a Party and an Investor of the Other Party

1. For the purposes of this Article:

(a) the term "disputing investor" means an investor who is a party to an investment dispute;

(b) the term "disputing Party" means a Party that is a party to an investment dispute;

(c) the term "disputing parties" means the disputing investor and the disputing Party;

(d) the term "ICSID Convention" means the Convention on the Settlement of Investment Disputes between States and Nationals of Other States, done at Washington, March 18, 1965;

(e) the term "ICSID Additional Facility Rules" means the Rules Governing the Additional Facility for the Administration of Proceedings by the Secretariat of the International Centre for Settlement of Investment Disputes;

(f) the term "investment dispute" means a dispute between a Party and an investor of the other Party that has incurred loss or damage by reason of, or arising out of, an alleged breach of any obligation of the former Party under this Chapter with respect to the investor of that other Party or its investment in the Area of the former Party; and

(g) the term "New York Convention" means the Convention on the Recognition and Enforcement of Foreign Arbitral Awards, done at New York, June 10, 1958.

2. Subject to subparagraph 6(a)(i), nothing in this Article shall be construed to prevent a disputing investor from seeking administrative or judicial settlement within the Area of the disputing Party.

3. An investment dispute shall, as far as possible, be settled amicably through consultations between the disputing parties.

4. If the investment dispute cannot be settled through such consultations within 120 days from the date on which the disputing investor requested in writing the disputing Party for the consultations, the disputing investor may, subject to paragraph 6, submit the investment dispute to one of the following international arbitrations:

(a) arbitration in accordance with the ICSID Convention, so long as the ICSID Convention is in force between the Parties;

(b) arbitration under the ICSID Additional Facility Rules, provided that either Party, but not both, is a party to the ICSID Convention;

(c) arbitration under the Arbitration Rules of the United Nations Commission on International Trade Law; and

(d) if agreed with the disputing Party, any arbitration in accordance with other arbitration rules.

5. The applicable arbitration rules shall govern the arbitration set forth in paragraph 4 except to the extent modified in this Article.

6. (a) Notwithstanding paragraphs 4 and 8, no claim may be submitted to the arbitration set forth in paragraph 4 unless:

(i) the disputing investor gives the disputing Party written waiver of any right to initiate before any court under the law of either Party or other dispute settlement procedures including the investment dispute settlement procedures under the Bilateral Investment Agreement, any proceedings with respect to any measure of the disputing Party alleged to constitute a breach referred to in subparagraph 1(f); and

(ii) the disputing investor has not initiated before the investment dispute settlement procedures under the Bilateral Investment Agreement, any proceedings with respect to any measure of the disputing Party alleged to constitute a breach referred to in subparagraph 1(f).

(b) Notwithstanding subparagraph (a), the disputing investor may initiate or continue an action that seeks interim injunctive relief that does not involve the payment of monetary damages before any competent court of the disputing Party.

7. The disputing investor who intends to submit the investment dispute to arbitration in accordance with paragraph 4 shall give to the disputing Party written notice of intent to do so at least 90 days before the investment dispute is submitted. The notice of intent shall specify:

(a) the name and address of the disputing investor;

(b) the specific measures of the disputing Party at issue and a brief summary of the factual and legal basis of the investment dispute sufficient to present the problem clearly, including the obligations under this Chapter alleged to have been breached;

(c) arbitration set forth in paragraph 4 which the disputing investor chooses to invoke; and

(d) the relief sought and the approximate amount of damages claimed.

8. (a) Each Party hereby consents to the submission of investment disputes by a disputing investor to arbitration set forth in paragraph 4 chosen by the disputing investor.

(b) The consent given under subparagraph (a) and the submission by a disputing investor of an investment dispute to arbitration shall satisfy the requirements of:

(i) Chapter II of the ICSID Convention or the ICSID Additional Facility Rules, for written consent of the parties to a dispute; and

(ii) Article II of the New York Convention for an agreement in writing.

9. Notwithstanding paragraph 8, no investment disputes may be submitted to arbitration set forth in paragraph 4, if more than three years have elapsed since the date on which the disputing investor acquired or should have first acquired, whichever is the earlier, the knowledge that the disputing investor had incurred loss or damage referred to in subparagraph 1(f).

10. Unless the disputing parties otherwise agree, an arbitral tribunal established under paragraph 4 shall comprise three arbitrators, one arbitrator appointed by each of the disputing parties and the third, who shall be the presiding arbitrator, appointed by agreement of the disputing parties. If the disputing investor or the disputing Party fails to appoint an arbitrator or arbitrators within 60 days from the date on which the investment dispute was submitted to arbitration, the Secretary-General of the International Centre for Settlement of Investment Disputes in the case of arbitration referred to in subparagraph 4(a) or 4(b), or the Secretary-General of the Permanent Court of Arbitration, at The Hague in the case of arbitration referred to in subparagraph 4(c) or 4(d), may be requested by either of the disputing parties, to appoint the arbitrator or arbitrators not yet appointed, subject to the requirements of paragraph 11.

11. Unless the disputing parties otherwise agree, the third arbitrator shall not be a national of either Party, nor have his or her usual place of residence in either Party, nor be employed by either of the disputing parties, nor have dealt with the investment dispute in any capacity.

12. Unless the disputing parties otherwise agree, the arbitration shall be held in a country that is a party to the New York Convention.

13. An arbitral tribunal established under paragraph 4 shall decide the issues in dispute in accordance with this Chapter and other provisions of this Agreement as applicable and applicable rules of international law.

14. The disputing Party shall deliver to the other Party:

(a) written notice of the investment dispute submitted to the arbitration no later than 30 days after the date on which the investment dispute was submitted; and

(b) copies of all pleadings filed in the arbitration.

15. The Party which is not the disputing Party may, upon written notice to the disputing parties, make submissions to the arbitral tribunal on a question of interpretation of this Chapter and other provisions of this Agreement as applicable.

16. The arbitral tribunal may order an interim measure of protection to preserve the rights of the disputing investor, or to facilitate the conduct of arbitral proceedings, including an order to preserve evidence in the possession or control of either of the disputing parties. The arbitral tribunal shall not order attachment or enjoin the application of the measure alleged to constitute a breach referred to in subparagraph 1(f).

17. Before ruling on the merits, the arbitral tribunal shall address and, if warranted, decide as a preliminary question any objection by the disputing Party to the jurisdiction of the arbitral tribunal and to the admissibility of the claim of the disputing investor. When the arbitral tribunal decides such an objection as a preliminary question, it may, if warranted, award to the prevailing disputing party reasonable costs and attorney's fees incurred in submitting or opposing the objection. In determining whether such an award is warranted, the arbitral tribunal shall consider whether either the disputing investor's claim or the disputing Party's objection was frivolous. In doing so, the arbitral tribunal shall provide the disputing parties a reasonable opportunity to comment.

18. The arbitral tribunal may award only:

(a) a judgment whether or not there has been a breach by the disputing Party of any obligation under this Chapter with respect to the disputing investor and its investment; and

(b) one or both of the following remedies, only if there has been such a breach:

(i) monetary damages and applicable interest; and

(ii) restitution of property, in which case the award shall provide that the disputing Party may pay monetary damages and any applicable interest, in lieu of restitution.

The arbitral tribunal may also award costs and attorneys' fees in accordance with this Article and the applicable arbitration rules.

19. The disputing Party may make available to the public in a timely manner all documents, including an award, submitted to, or issued by, an arbitral tribunal established under paragraph 4, subject to redaction of:

(a) confidential business information;

(b) information which is privileged or otherwise protected from disclosure under the applicable laws and regulations of either Party; and

(c) information which shall be withheld in accordance with the relevant arbitration rules.

20. The award rendered by the arbitral tribunal shall be final and binding upon the disputing parties. This award shall be executed in accordance with the applicable laws and regulations, as well as relevant international law including the ICSID Convention and the New York Convention, concerning the execution of award in force in the country where such execution is sought.

21. Neither Party shall give diplomatic protection, or bring an international claim, with respect to an investment dispute which the other Party and an investor of the former Party have consented to submit or submitted to arbitration set forth in paragraph 4, unless the other Party has failed to abide by and comply with the award rendered in such investment dispute. Diplomatic protection, for the purposes of this paragraph, shall not include informal diplomatic exchanges for the sole purpose of facilitating a settlement of the investment dispute.

22. This Article shall apply to disputes regarding taxation measures to the extent covered by Article 10.5, 10.6 or 10.9.

Article 10.14
Temporary Safeguard Measures

1. A Party may adopt or maintain restrictive measures with respect to cross-border capital transactions as well as payment and transfers related to investments:

(a) in the event of serious balance-of-payments and external financial difficulties or threat thereof; or

(b) in exceptional cases where movements of capital cause or threaten to cause serious difficulties for macroeconomic management, in particular monetary and exchange rate policies.

2. Restrictive measures referred to in paragraph 1:

(a) shall be applied on the basis of national treatment and most-favored-nation treatment;

(b) shall be consistent with the Articles of Agreement of the International Monetary Fund;

(c) shall avoid unnecessary damage to the commercial, economic and financial interests of the other Party;

(d) shall not exceed those necessary to deal with the circumstances described in paragraph 1; and

(e) shall be temporary and be phased out progressively as the situation specified in paragraph 1 improves.

3. Any restrictions adopted or maintained in accordance with paragraph 1, or any changes therein, shall be promptly notified to the other Party.

4. Nothing in this Article shall be construed to alter the rights enjoyed and obligations undertaken by a Party as a party to the Articles of Agreement of the International Monetary Fund.

Article 10.15
Prudential Measures

1. Notwithstanding any other provisions of this Chapter, a Party shall not be prevented from adopting or maintaining measures related to financial services for prudential reasons, including measures for the protection of investors, depositors, policy holders or persons to whom a fiduciary duty is owed by an enterprise supplying financial services, or to ensure the integrity and stability of its financial system.

2. Where the measures adopted or maintained by a Party in accordance with paragraph 1 do not conform with this Chapter, they shall not be used as a means of avoiding the obligations of the Party under this Chapter.

Article 10.16
Denial of Benefits

1. A Party may deny the benefits of this Chapter to an investor of the other Party that is an enterprise of the other Party and to its investment if the enterprise is owned or controlled by an investor of a non-Party and the denying Party:

(a) does not maintain diplomatic relations with the non-Party; or

(b) adopts or maintains measures with respect to the non-Party that prohibit transactions with the enterprise or that would be violated or circumvented if the benefits of this Chapter were accorded to the enterprise or to its investment.

2. A Party may deny the benefits of this Chapter to an investor of the other Party that is an enterprise of the other Party and to its investment if the enterprise is owned or controlled by an investor of a non-Party and the enterprise has no substantial business activities in the Area of the other Party.

Article 10.17
Health, Safety and Environmental Measures
and Labor Standards

The Parties shall refrain from encouraging investment by investors of each Party or of a non-Party by relaxing their respective health, safety or environmental measures or by lowering its labor standards. To this effect each Party should not waive or otherwise derogate from such measures or standards as an encouragement for the establishment, acquisition or expansion in its Area of investments by investors of each Party or of a non-Party.

Article 10.18
Sub-Committee on Investment

1. For the purposes of the effective implementation and operation of this Chapter, the Parties hereby establish a Sub-Committee on Investment (hereinafter referred to in this Article as "the Sub-Committee").

2. The functions of the Sub-Committee shall be:

(a) reviewing and monitoring the implementation and operation of this Chapter;

(b) exchanging information on any matters related to this Chapter;

(c) discussing any issues related to this Chapter;

(d) reporting the findings and the outcome of discussions of the Sub-Committee to the Joint Committee; and

(e) carrying out other functions as may be delegated by the Joint Committee.

3. The Sub-Committee shall be composed of representatives of the Governments of the Parties.

4. The Sub-Committee may invite representatives of relevant entities other than the Governments of the Parties with the necessary expertise relevant to the issues to be discussed.

5. The Sub-Committee shall hold meetings at such times and venues or by means, as may be agreed by the Parties.

6. This Article shall apply to matters regarding taxation measures to the extent covered by Article 10.5, 10.6 or 10.9.

Article 10.19
Relation to the Bilateral Investment Agreement

1. Notwithstanding paragraph 2 of Article 17 of the Bilateral Investment Agreement, the Bilateral Investment Agreement shall be terminated upon the date of entry into force of this Agreement.

2. The Parties confirm that with respect to investments and returns acquired prior to the date of termination of the Bilateral Investment Agreement, the provisions of Articles 1 through 16 of the Bilateral Investment Agreement shall continue to be effective for a further period of 15 years from that date in accordance with paragraph 3 of Article 17 of the Bilateral Investment Agreement.

3. For the purposes of paragraph 2, nothing in this Agreement shall affect the rights and obligations of a Party under the relevant provisions of the Bilateral Investment Agreement.

Article 10.20
Duration and Termination

With respect to investments acquired prior to the date of termination of this Agreement, the provisions of this Chapter, as well as provisions of this Agreement which are directly related to this Chapter, shall continue to be effective for a period of 10 years from the date of termination of this Agreement.

Chapter 11
Competition

Article 11.1
Anticompetitive Activities

1. Each Party shall, in accordance with its laws and regulations, take measures which it considers appropriate against anticompetitive activities, in order to facilitate trade and investment flows between the Parties through the efficient functioning of its markets.

2. For the purposes of this Chapter, the term "anticompetitive activities" means any conduct or transaction that may be subject to penalties or relief under the competition laws and regulations of the respective Parties.

Article 11.2
Cooperation on Controlling Anticompetitive Activities

1. The Parties shall, in accordance with their respective laws and regulations, cooperate and assist each other for controlling anticompetitive activities within their respective available resources.

2. The details and procedures concerning the implementation of cooperation under this Article shall be specified in the Implementing Agreement.

Article 11.3
Non-Discrimination

Each Party shall apply its competition laws and regulations in a manner which does not discriminate between persons in like circumstances on the basis of their nationality.

Article 11.4
Procedural Fairness

Each Party shall implement administrative and judicial procedures in a fair manner to control anticompetitive activities, in accordance with its relevant laws and regulations.

Article 11.5
Transparency

Each Party shall promote transparency of the implementation of its competition laws and regulations and its competition policy.

Article 11.6
Non-Application of Paragraph 2 of Article 1.8
and Chapter 16

Paragraph 2 of Article 1.8 and Chapter 16 shall not apply to this Chapter.

Chapter 12
Intellectual Property

Article 12.1
General Provisions

1. The Parties shall grant and ensure adequate, effective and non-discriminatory protection of intellectual property and provide for measures for the enforcement of intellectual property rights against infringement thereof, in accordance with the provisions of this Chapter and the international agreements related to intellectual property to which both Parties are party.

2. The Parties shall also promote efficiency and transparency in the administration of intellectual property system.

3. Nothing in this Chapter shall derogate from existing rights and obligations that the Parties have under the TRIPS Agreement or other international agreements related to intellectual property to which both Parties are party.

Article 12.2
Definition

The term "intellectual property" referred to in this Chapter shall mean all categories of intellectual property that are under the TRIPS Agreement.

Article 12.3
National Treatment

Each Party shall accord to nationals of the other Party treatment no less favorable than the treatment it accords to its own nationals with regard to the protection of intellectual property in accordance with Articles 3 and 5 of the TRIPS Agreement.

Note: For the purposes of this Article:

(a) the term "nationals" shall have the same meaning as in the TRIPS Agreement;

(b) the term "protection" shall include matters affecting the availability, acquisition, scope, maintenance and enforcement of intellectual property rights as well as those matters affecting the use of intellectual property rights specifically addressed in this Chapter; and

(c) for greater certainty, the term "protection of intellectual property" shall include the repression of unfair competition as provided for in Article 12.12.

Article 12.4
Procedural Matters

1. For the purposes of providing efficient administration of intellectual property system, each Party shall take appropriate measures to improve its administrative procedures concerning intellectual property rights.

2. Neither Party shall require the authentication of signatures or other means of self-identification on documents to be submitted to the competent authority of the Party, including applications, translations into a language accepted by such authority of any earlier application whose priority is claimed, powers of attorney and certifications of assignment, in the course of application procedure or other administrative procedures on patents, utility models, industrial designs or trademarks.

3. Notwithstanding paragraph 2, a Party may require:

(a) the authentication of signatures or other means of self-identification, if the law of the Party so provides, where the signatures or other means of self-identification concern the surrender of a patent or a registration of utility models, industrial designs or trademarks; and

(b) the submission of evidence if there is reasonable doubt as to the authenticity of signatures or other means of self-identification on documents submitted to the competent authority of the Party. Where the competent authority notifies the person that the submission of evidence is required, the notification shall state the reason for requiring the submission.

4. Neither Party shall require that the submission of a power of attorney be completed together with the filing of the application as a condition for according a filing date to the application.

5. Each Party shall endeavor to improve patent attorney or registered intellectual property rights authorized representative system.

6. Where the acquisition of an intellectual property right is subject to the right being granted or registered, each Party shall ensure that, irrespective of whether an application for the granting or registration of an intellectual property right is filed as a national or as an international application in accordance with the applicable international agreement, the procedures for granting or registration of the right, subject to compliance with the substantive conditions for acquisition of the right, provide the granting or registration within a reasonable period of time so as to avoid undue curtailment of the period of protection.

7. Each Party shall provide a system for the registration of trademarks, industrial designs and patents which shall include:

(a) a requirement to provide to the applicant a communication in writing, which may be electronic, of the decision with reasons for a refusal of the application;

(b) an opportunity for the applicant to appeal against administrative refusal;

(c) an opportunity for the applicant to ask for judicial review of the final administrative refusal; and

(d) an opportunity for interested parties, if so provided in its laws and regulations:

(i) to petition to oppose an application or a registration; and

(ii) to seek cancellation or invalidation of the registration.

Article 12.5
Transparency

For the purposes of further promoting transparency in the administration of its intellectual property system, each Party shall take appropriate measures available to the extent possible in accordance with its laws and regulations to:

(a) publish information on, at least:

(i) intention to grant patents, or applications for and grant of patents;

(ii) registrations of utility models;

(iii) intention to grant rights of industrial designs, or registrations of industrial designs; and

(iv) registrations of trademarks and/or applications therefor,

and provide the relevant information contained in the files thereof at least to interested persons upon request; and

(b) make available to the public information on its efforts to ensure effective enforcement of intellectual property rights and other information with respect to its intellectual property system.

Article 12.6
Promotion of Public Awareness concerning Protection of Intellectual Property

The Parties shall take necessary measures to enhance public awareness of protection of intellectual property including educational and dissemination projects on the use of intellectual property as well as on the enforcement of intellectual property rights.

Article 12.7
Patents

1. Each Party shall ensure that any patent application is not rejected solely on the ground that the subject matter claimed in the application is related to a computer program. Nevertheless, the provision of this Article shall not prejudice the autonomy of each Party to exclude from patentability computer programs as such in accordance with the laws and regulations of each Party.

2. Each Party shall ensure that an applicant may, on its own initiative, divide a patent application containing more than one invention into a certain number of divisional patent applications within the time limit provided for in the laws and regulations of the Party.

Article 12.8
Industrial Designs

Each Party shall provide adequate and effective protection of industrial designs of an article as a whole, and, where appropriate, of a part thereof.

Article 12.9
Trademarks

1. Each Party shall refuse or cancel the registration of a trademark, which is identical or similar to a trademark well-known in either Party as indicating the goods or services of the owner of the well-known trademark, if use of that trademark is for unfair intentions, *inter alia*, intention to gain an unfair profit or intention to cause damage to the owner of the well-known trademark, and/or if such use would result in a likelihood of confusion.

Note: Each Party may determine in accordance with its laws and regulations whether a trademark is a well-known trademark.

2. Each Party shall ensure that an applicant may file a request to the competent authority that examination of its application for registration of a trademark be accelerated, subject to reasonable grounds and procedural requirements. Where such a request has been filed, the competent authority shall, where appropriate, accelerate the examination of the application.

Article 12.10
Copyright and Related Rights

1. Each Party shall provide to authors, performers and producers of phonograms the right to authorize the making available to the public of their works, performances fixed in phonograms and phonograms respectively, by wire or wireless means, in such a way that members of the public may access them from a place and at a time individually chosen by them.

2. Each Party shall provide to broadcasting organizations the right to prohibit the following acts when undertaken without their consent:

(a) the rebroadcasting of their broadcasts;

(b) the fixation of their broadcasts; or

(c) the reproduction of fixations of their broadcasts.

3. Each Party shall, in accordance with its laws and regulations, take appropriate measures to facilitate the activities to be conducted by the collective management organizations for copyright and related rights in that Party.

Article 12.11
Geographical Indications

Each Party shall ensure adequate and effective protection of geographical indications in accordance with its laws and regulations and with the TRIPS Agreement.

Article 12.12
Unfair Competition

1. Each Party shall provide for effective protection against acts of unfair competition in accordance with Article 10 *bis* of the Paris Convention.

2. Each Party shall ensure that provisions of Article 10 *bis* of the Paris Convention shall apply *mutatis mutandis* with respect to services.

3. For the purposes of this Article, the term "Paris Convention" means the Paris Convention for the Protection of Industrial Property of March 20, 1883, as revised at Brussels on December 14, 1900, at Washington on June 2, 1911, at The Hague on November 6, 1925, at London on June 2, 1934, at Lisbon on October 31, 1958, and at Stockholm on July 14, 1967 and as amended on September 28, 1979.

Article 12.13
Protection of Undisclosed Information

Each Party shall ensure, in its laws and regulations, adequate and effective protection of undisclosed information in accordance with paragraph 2 of Article 39 of the TRIPS Agreement including not taking measures that limit the duration of protection of the undisclosed information stipulated in private contracts, or measures that force the disclosure of undisclosed information without legitimate reasons.

Article 12.14
Enforcement - Border Measures

1. Each Party shall adopt or maintain procedures with respect to import shipments under which:

(a) its customs authorities may act upon their own initiative to suspend the release of goods suspected of infringing rights to trademarks and/or copyrights and related rights (hereinafter referred to in this Article as "suspected goods"); and

(b) a right holder may request that Party's competent authorities to suspend the release of suspected goods.

2. Each Party shall adopt or maintain procedures by which its competent authorities may determine, within a reasonable period after the initiation of the procedures described in paragraph 1, whether the suspected goods infringe rights to trademarks and/or copyrights and related rights.

3. In the case of the suspension with respect to import shipments in accordance with paragraph 1, the importer and the right holder shall be promptly notified of the suspension and shall be provided with all the information available about suspected goods.

Article 12.15
Enforcement - Civil Remedies

Each Party shall ensure that a right holder of intellectual property has the right to claim against the infringer damages adequate to compensate for the injury the right holder has suffered because of an infringement of that person's intellectual property right by an infringer who knowingly, or with reasonable grounds to know, engaged in infringing activity.

Article 12.16
Enforcement - Criminal Remedies

1. Each Party shall provide for criminal procedures and penalties to be applied at least in cases of willful trademark counterfeiting or copyright piracy on a commercial scale in accordance with Article 61 of the TRIPS Agreement.

2. With respect to the offences specified in paragraph 1, each Party shall provide that its competent authorities have the authority in accordance with its laws and regulations to order the forfeiture or destruction of all infringing goods.

Article 12.17
Enforcement - In the Digital Environment

Each Party's enforcement procedures shall apply to infringement of copyright or related rights over digital networks, which may include the unlawful use of means of widespread distribution for infringing purposes. These procedures shall be implemented in a manner that avoids the creation of barriers to legitimate activity, including electronic commerce, and, consistent with the laws and regulations of that Party, preserves fundamental principles such as freedom of expression, fair process and privacy.

Article 12.18
Sub-Committee on Intellectual Property

1. For the purposes of the effective implementation and operation of this Chapter, the Parties hereby establish a Sub-Committee on Intellectual Property (hereinafter referred to in this Article as "the Sub-Committee").

2. The functions of the Sub-Committee shall be:

(a) reviewing and monitoring the implementation and operation of this Chapter;

(b) discussing any issues related to intellectual property with a view to enhancing protection of intellectual property and enforcement of intellectual property rights in accordance with the provisions of this Chapter and to promoting efficient and transparent administration of intellectual property system;

(c) reporting the findings and the outcome of discussions of the Sub-Committee to the Joint Committee; and

(d) carrying out other functions as may be delegated by the Joint Committee.

3. The Sub-Committee shall be composed of representatives of the Governments of the Parties.

4. The Sub-Committee shall hold meetings at such times and venues or by means, as may be agreed by the Parties.

Article 12.19
Security Exceptions

For the purposes of this Chapter, Article 73 of the TRIPS Agreement is incorporated into and forms part of this Agreement, *mutatis mutandis*.

Chapter 13
Government Procurement

Article 13.1
Procurement Principle

Recognizing the importance of government procurement in furthering the expansion of production and trade so as to promote growth and employment, each Party shall ensure transparency of the measures regarding government procurement in accordance with its laws and regulations. The Parties also recognize the need to take into account the development, financial and trade needs of the Parties. Each Party shall ensure a fair and effective implementation of the measures regarding government procurement.

Article 13.2
Exchange of Information

The Parties shall at the central government level, subject to their respective laws and regulations, exchange information, to the extent possible in the English language and in a timely manner, on their respective laws and regulations, policies and practices on government procurement, as well as on any reforms to their existing government procurement regimes.

Article 13.3
Further Negotiations

The Parties shall enter into negotiations to review this Chapter with a view to achieving a comprehensive Chapter on Government Procurement, when Mongolia expresses its intention to become a party to the Agreement on Government Procurement in Annex 4 to the WTO Agreement (hereinafter referred to in this Article as "the GPA").

Note: If the GPA is amended or is superseded by another agreement, "the GPA", for the purposes of this Article, shall refer to the GPA as amended or such other agreement.

Article 13.4
Negotiation on Non-Discrimination

In the event that, after the entry into force of this Agreement, a Party offers a non-Party any advantages of access to its government procurement market or any advantageous treatment concerning the measures regarding government procurement, the former Party shall, upon request of the other Party, afford adequate opportunity to enter into negotiations with the other Party with a view to extending these advantages or advantageous treatment to the other Party on a reciprocal basis.

Article 13.5
Sub-Committee on Government Procurement

1. For the purposes of the effective implementation and operation of this Chapter, the Parties hereby establish a Sub-Committee on Government Procurement (hereinafter referred to in this Article as "the Sub-Committee").

2. The functions of the Sub-Committee shall be:

(a) reviewing and monitoring the implementation and operation of this Chapter;

(b) analyzing available information on each Party's government procurement market;

(c) cooperating on e-procurement and human resource development;

(d) reporting the findings of the Sub-Committee to the Joint Committee; and

(e) carrying out other functions as may be delegated by the Joint Committee.

3. The Sub-Committee shall be composed of representatives of the Governments of the Parties.

4. The Sub-Committee shall hold meetings at such times and venues or by means, as may be agreed by the Parties.

Chapter 14
Improvement of the Business Environment

Article 14.1
Basic Principles

1. Each Party shall, in accordance with its laws and regulations, take appropriate measures to further improve the business environment for the persons of the other Party conducting their business activities in the former Party.

2. The Parties shall, in accordance with their respective laws and regulations, promote cooperation to further improve the business environment in the respective Parties.

Article 14.2
Sub-Committee on Improvement of the Business Environment

1. For the purposes of the effective implementation and operation of this Chapter, the Parties hereby establish a Sub-Committee on Improvement of the Business Environment (hereinafter referred to in this Chapter as "the Sub-Committee").

2. The functions of the Sub-Committee shall be:

(a) reviewing findings reported by a Liaison Office on Improvement of the Business Environment (hereinafter referred to in this Chapter as "the Liaison Office") to be designated by each Party in accordance with Article 14.3;

(b) addressing, and seeking ways to promptly resolve, issues related to the business environment on its own initiative or based on the findings reported by the Liaison Office;

(c) reporting its findings and making recommendations, including those on measures that should be taken by the Parties, to the Parties;

(d) reviewing, where appropriate, the measures taken by the Parties related to such recommendations referred to in subparagraph (c);

(e) making available to the public, in an appropriate manner, the recommendations referred to in subparagraph (c) and the results of the review referred to in subparagraph (d);

(f) cooperating, in an appropriate manner, with other Sub-Committees established under this Agreement, with a view to avoiding unnecessary duplication of works. The forms of such cooperation may include:

(i) informing the results of its consideration to such other Sub-Committees;

(ii) seeking opinions from such other Sub-Committees;

(iii) inviting to the Sub-Committee the members of such other Sub-Committees; and

(iv) where appropriate, transferring the relevant issues to such other Sub-Committees;

(g) reporting promptly the findings and recommendations referred to in subparagraph (c) to the Joint Committee; and

(h) carrying out other functions as may be delegated by the Joint Committee.

3. The Sub-Committee shall be composed of representatives of the Governments of the Parties including officials of relevant Ministries or Agencies in charge of the issues to be addressed. The Sub-Committee may invite representatives of relevant entities other than the Governments of the Parties with the necessary expertise relevant to the issues to be addressed.

4. The Sub-Committee shall hold meetings at such times and venues or by means, as may be agreed by the Parties.

Article 14.3
Liaison Office

1. Each Party shall designate and maintain a Liaison Office for the purposes of this Chapter.

2. The functions and other details of the Liaison Office shall be set forth in the Implementing Agreement.

Article 14.4
Non-Application of Chapter 16

Chapter 16 shall not apply to this Chapter.

Chapter 15
Cooperation

Article 15.1
Basic Principles

The Parties shall, in accordance with their respective laws and regulations, promote cooperation under this Agreement for their mutual benefit, in order to further liberalize and facilitate trade in goods and services as well as investment between the Parties and to promote the well-being of the people and sustainable development of the Parties. For this purpose, the Parties shall enhance further cooperation between their Governments, and encourage and facilitate mutual cooperation between relevant entities of the Parties, one or both of whom are entities other than the Governments of the Parties, in the following fields:

(a) agriculture, forestry and fisheries, including matters related to SPS measures referred to in Chapter 5;

(b) manufacturing industry, including matters related to technical regulations, standards and conformity assessment procedures referred to in Chapter 6;

(c) small and medium enterprises;

(d) trade and investment;

(e) infrastructure, construction and urban development;

(f) science and technology and intellectual property;

(g) financial services;

(h) education and human resource development;

(i) tourism;

(j) environment;

(k) mining and energy;

(l) healthcare;

(m) competition;

(n) information and communications technology; and

(o) other fields to be mutually agreed upon by the Governments of the Parties.

Article 15.2
Areas and Forms of Cooperation

The areas and forms of cooperation under this Chapter shall be set forth in the Implementing Agreement.

Article 15.3
Costs of Cooperation

1. The Parties shall initiate discussion, after the entry into force of this Agreement, to explore potential cooperation activities in the fields referred to in Article 15.1 and to ensure timely, efficient and effective implementation of cooperation activities under this Chapter.

2. The Parties shall endeavor to make available the necessary funds and other resources for the implementation of cooperation under this Chapter in accordance with their respective laws and regulations.

3. Costs for cooperation under this Chapter shall be borne in such a manner to be mutually agreed upon by the Parties through efficient and effective utilization of funds and resources.

Article 15.4
Sub-Committee on Cooperation

1. For the purposes of the effective implementation and operation of this Chapter, the Parties hereby establish a Sub-Committee on Cooperation (hereinafter referred to in this Article as "the Sub-Committee").

2. The functions of the Sub-Committee shall be:

(a) reviewing and monitoring the effective implementation and operation of this Chapter;

(b) exchanging information on cooperation in each of the fields referred to in Article 15.1;

(c) identifying ways for further cooperation between the Parties;

(d) discussing any issues related to this Chapter;

(e) discussing proposals on cooperation presented by other Sub-Committees established under this Agreement;

(f) making recommendations to the Joint Committee, where appropriate, on cooperation activities under this Chapter;

(g) reporting to the Joint Committee the findings and outcome of discussions of the Sub-Committee regarding the implementation of this Chapter, including the measures to be taken by the Parties; and

(h) carrying out other functions as may be delegated by the Joint Committee.

3. The Sub-Committee shall, where appropriate, recognize and share information with the Parties' existing consultation mechanisms for Official Development Assistance and other cooperation schemes to ensure timely, effective and efficient implementation of cooperation activities under this Agreement.

4. The Sub-Committee shall be composed of representatives of the Governments of the Parties. The Sub-Committee may invite representatives of relevant entities other than the Governments of the Parties with the necessary expertise relevant to the issues to be discussed.

5. The Sub-Committee shall hold meetings at such times and venues or by means, as may be agreed by the Parties. The Sub-Committee shall endeavor to hold the first meeting within one year after the entry into force of this Agreement.

Article 15.5
Non-Application of Chapter 16

Chapter 16 shall not apply to this Chapter.

Chapter 16
Dispute Settlement

Article 16.1
Scope

Unless otherwise provided for in this Agreement, the dispute settlement procedure of this Chapter shall apply with respect to the avoidance and the settlement of disputes between the Parties arising out of the interpretation and/or application of this Agreement.

Article 16.2
General Principle

The Parties shall at all times endeavor to agree on the interpretation and application of this Agreement. They shall make every attempt through cooperation, consultations or other means to arrive at a prompt and mutually satisfactory resolution of any matter concerning the interpretation and/or application of this Agreement.

Article 16.3
Choice of Forum

1. Nothing in this Chapter shall prejudice any rights of the Parties to have recourse to dispute settlement procedures available under any other international agreement to which both Parties are party, including the WTO Agreement. The complaining Party may select the forum in which to settle the dispute.

2. Notwithstanding paragraph 1, once the complaining Party has requested the establishment of an arbitral tribunal under this Chapter or any other international agreement to which both Parties are party, including a panel under the Understanding on Rules and Procedures Governing the Settlement of Disputes in Annex 2 to the WTO Agreement with respect to a particular dispute, the arbitral tribunal or panel selected shall be used to the exclusion of any other procedure for that particular dispute.

Article 16.4
Consultations

1. Either Party may request in writing consultations to the other Party with respect to any matter on the interpretation and/or application of this Agreement.

2. In the request for consultations referred to in paragraph 1, the complaining Party shall set out the reasons for the request, including identification of the measure at issue and an indication of the legal and factual basis of the complaint.

3. The Party complained against shall promptly respond in writing to such request and enter into consultations with the complaining Party in good faith within 40 days after the date of receipt of the request. In cases of urgency, including those which concern perishable goods, the Party complained against shall enter into consultations within 20 days after the date of receipt of the request.

4. The Parties shall make every effort to arrive at a mutually satisfactory resolution of the matter through consultations under this Article. During the consultations the Parties shall provide to each other sufficient information to enable a full examination of the matter.

5. During the consultations under this Article, the Parties shall endeavor to make available personnel of their relevant agencies and organizations with expertise in the matter subject to the consultations.

6. The consultations under this Article shall be confidential and without prejudice to the rights of either Party in any further proceedings.

7. The consultations under this Article may be held in person or by any technological means available to the Parties upon agreement by the Parties. If the Parties agree to hold consultations in person, the consultations shall be held in a venue agreed upon by the Parties, or if there is no agreement on the venue, in the capital of the Party complained against.

Article 16.5
Good Offices, Conciliation or Mediation

1. Good offices, conciliation or mediation may be requested at any time by either Party. They may begin at any time by agreement of the Parties, and be terminated at any time upon request of either Party.

2. If the Parties agree, good offices, conciliation or mediation may continue while procedures of the arbitral tribunal provided for in this Chapter are in progress.

3. Proceedings involving good offices, conciliation or mediation and positions taken by the Parties during these proceedings shall be confidential and without prejudice to the rights of either Party in any further proceedings.

Article 16.6
Establishment of Arbitral Tribunals

1. The complaining Party may request in writing the establishment of an arbitral tribunal to the Party complained against if:

(a) the Party complained against does not enter into consultations under Article 16.4 within 40 days, or within 20 days in cases of urgency, including those which concern perishable goods, after the date of receipt of the request for such consultations; or

(b) the Parties fail to resolve the dispute through consultations under Article 16.4 within 60 days, or within 30 days in cases of urgency, including those which concern perishable goods, after the date of receipt of the request for such consultations,

provided that the complaining Party considers that any benefit accruing to it directly or indirectly under this Agreement is being nullified or impaired as a result of the failure of the Party complained against to carry out its obligations under this Agreement, or as a result of the application by the Party complained against of measures which are in conflict with its obligations under this Agreement.

2. Any request to establish an arbitral tribunal in accordance with this Article shall identify the reasons for the request including:

(a) the legal basis of the complaint including the provisions of this Agreement alleged to have been breached and any other relevant provisions of the applicable international law; and

(b) the factual basis of the complaint.

Article 16.7
Composition of Arbitral Tribunals

1. An arbitral tribunal shall comprise three arbitrators, who should have relevant technical or legal expertise.

2. Each Party shall, within 30 days after the date of receipt of the request for the establishment of an arbitral tribunal, appoint one arbitrator who may be its national and propose up to three candidates to serve as the third arbitrator who shall be the chair of the arbitral tribunal. The third arbitrator shall not be a national of either Party, nor have his or her usual place of residence in either Party, nor be employed by either Party, nor have dealt with the dispute in any capacity.

3. The Parties shall endeavor to agree on and appoint the third arbitrator within 45 days after the date of receipt of the request for the establishment of an arbitral tribunal, taking into account the candidates proposed in accordance with paragraph 2.

4. If a Party has not appointed the one arbitrator in accordance with paragraph 2, or if the Parties fail to agree on the third arbitrator in accordance with paragraph 3, the arbitrator or arbitrators not yet appointed shall be chosen within 10 days by lot from the candidates proposed in accordance with paragraph 2.

5. The date of the establishment of an arbitral tribunal shall be the date on which the chair is appointed.

6. If an arbitrator appointed under this Article resigns, dies or otherwise becomes unable to act, a replacement arbitrator shall be appointed in the same manner as prescribed for the appointment of the original arbitrator. The replacement arbitrator shall have all the powers and duties of the original arbitrator. The work of the arbitral tribunal shall be suspended until the replacement arbitrator is appointed.

Article 16.8
Functions of Arbitral Tribunals

1. The functions of the arbitral tribunal established in accordance with Articles 16.6 and 16.7 shall be to:

(a) make an objective assessment of the matter before it, including an objective assessment of the facts of the case and the applicability of and conformity with this Agreement;

(b) consult regularly with the Parties offering them equal opportunities for such consultations and provide adequate opportunities for the development of a mutually satisfactory resolution;

(c) make its award in accordance with this Agreement and applicable rules of international law;

(d) include in its award, its findings of law and fact, together with the reasons for the findings; and

(e) attach to its award suggested implementation options including suggested period of time for implementing the award, for the Parties to consider in conjunction with Article 16.11, if requested by either Party.

2. The arbitral tribunal may seek, from the Parties, such relevant information as it considers necessary and appropriate. The Parties shall respond promptly and fully to any request by the arbitral tribunal for such information as the arbitral tribunal considers necessary and appropriate.

3. The arbitral tribunal may seek information from any relevant source and may consult experts to obtain their opinion on certain aspects of the matter. With respect to factual issues concerning a scientific or other technical matter raised by a Party, the arbitral tribunal may request advisory reports in writing from experts.

4. Any information obtained by the arbitral tribunal in accordance with paragraph 3 shall be made available to the Parties.

Article 16.9
Proceedings of Arbitral Tribunals

1. The arbitral tribunal shall meet in closed session. The Parties shall be present at the meetings only when invited by the arbitral tribunal to appear before it.

2. The venue for the proceedings of the arbitral tribunal shall be decided by mutual consent of the Parties, failing which it shall alternate between the Parties with the first meeting of the arbitral tribunal proceedings to be held in the capital of the Party complained against.

3. The deliberations of the arbitral tribunal and the documents submitted to it shall be kept confidential.

4. Notwithstanding paragraph 3, either Party may make public statements as to its views regarding the dispute, but shall treat as confidential, information and written submissions submitted by the other Party to the arbitral tribunal which that other Party has designated as confidential. Where a Party has provided information or written submissions designated as confidential, the other Party may request a non-confidential summary of the information or written submission which may be disclosed publicly. The Party to which such a request is made may agree to the request and submit such a summary, or refuse the request without needing to ascribe any reasons or justification.

5. The Parties shall be given the opportunity to attend any of the presentations, statements or rebuttals in the proceedings. Any information or written submissions submitted by a Party to the arbitral tribunal, including any comments on the descriptive part of the draft award and responses to questions put by the arbitral tribunal, shall be made available to the other Party.

6. The award of the arbitral tribunal shall be drafted without the presence of the Parties.

7. The arbitral tribunal shall, within 120 days, or within 60 days in cases of urgency including those which concern perishable goods, after the date of its establishment, submit to the Parties its draft award, including both the descriptive part and its findings and conclusions, for the purposes of enabling the Parties to review it. When the arbitral tribunal considers that it cannot submit its draft award within the aforementioned 120 days or 60 days period, it may extend that period with the consent of the Parties. However, in no case should the period from the establishment of the arbitral tribunal to the submission of the draft award to the Parties exceed 150 days. Either Party may submit comments in writing to the arbitral tribunal on the draft award within 30 days after the date of submission of the draft award.

8. The arbitral tribunal shall present its award to the Parties within 45 days after the date of submission of the draft award.

9. The arbitral tribunal shall attempt to make its decisions, including its award, by consensus, but may also make its decisions, including its award, by majority vote.

10. The award of the arbitral tribunal shall be final and binding on the Parties.

Article 16.10
Termination of the Proceedings

The Parties may agree to terminate the proceedings of the arbitral tribunal by jointly so notifying the chair of the arbitral tribunal at any time before the issuance of the award to the Parties, in which case the chair shall terminate the proceedings of the arbitral tribunal without delay.

Article 16.11
Implementation of Award

1. Unless the Parties otherwise agree, the Party complained against shall promptly comply with the award of the arbitral tribunal issued in accordance with Articles 16.8 and 16.9. If this is not practicable, the Party complained against shall comply with the award within a reasonable period of time.

2. The reasonable period of time referred to in paragraph 1 shall be mutually determined by the Parties, taking into account, where appropriate, the suggested period of time attached to the award by the arbitral tribunal. Where the Parties fail to agree on the reasonable period of time within 45 days after the date of issuance of the award of the arbitral tribunal, either Party may refer the matter to an arbitral tribunal, which shall determine the reasonable period of time.

3. (a) If the Party complained against considers it impracticable to comply with the award within the reasonable period of time, the Party complained against shall, no later than the expiry of that period, enter into consultations with the complaining Party, with a view to developing mutually satisfactory compensation or any alternative arrangement.

(b) If no satisfactory compensation or any alternative arrangement has been agreed within 30 days after the date of expiry of the reasonable period of time, the complaining Party may suspend the application to the Party complained against of concessions or other obligations under this Agreement, after giving notification of such suspension 30 days in advance.

4. If the complaining Party considers that the Party complained against has failed to comply with the award within the reasonable period of time and if the Party complained against has not entered into consultations in accordance with subparagraph 3(a), the complaining Party may suspend the application to the Party complained against of concessions or other obligations under this Agreement, after giving notification of such suspension 30 days in advance.

5. The suspension of the application of concessions or other obligations under paragraph 3 or 4 shall:

(a) not be effected if, with respect to the dispute to which the suspension relates, consultations or proceedings before the arbitral tribunal are in progress;

(b) be temporary, and be discontinued when the Parties reach a mutually satisfactory resolution or where compliance with the award is effected;

(c) be restricted to the same level of nullification or impairment that is attributable to the failure to comply with the award; and

(d) be restricted to the same sector or sectors to which the nullification or impairment relates, unless it is not practicable or effective to suspend the application of concessions or other obligations in such sector or sectors.

6. If the Party complained against considers that the requirements for the suspension of the application of concessions or other obligations under this Agreement by the complaining Party set out in paragraph 3, 4 or 5 have not been met, it may request consultations with the complaining Party. The complaining Party shall enter into consultations within 10 days after the date of receipt of the request. If the Parties fail to resolve the matter within 30 days after the date of receipt of the request for consultations in accordance with this paragraph, the Party complained against may refer the matter to an arbitral tribunal, which then shall determine whether the said requirements have been met.

7. The arbitral tribunal that is established for the purposes of this Article shall, whenever possible, have as its arbitrators, the arbitrators of the original arbitral tribunal. If this is not possible, then the arbitrators to the arbitral tribunal that is established for the purposes of this Article shall be appointed in accordance with paragraphs 2, 3 and 4 of Article 16.7. Unless the Parties agree on a different period, the arbitral tribunal established under this Article shall make its determinations within 60 days after the date when the matter is referred to it. Such determinations shall be final and binding on the Parties.

Article 16.12
Modification of Time Periods

Any time period provided for in this Chapter may be modified for a particular dispute by mutual consent of the Parties.

Article 16.13
Expenses

Each Party shall bear the costs of the arbitrator appointed by it and its representation in the proceedings of the arbitral tribunal. The other costs of the arbitral tribunal shall be borne by the Parties in equal shares, unless the Parties otherwise agree.

Article 16.14
Language

All proceedings of the arbitral tribunal and all documents and information submitted to the arbitral tribunal shall be in the English language.

Chapter 17
Final Provisions

Article 17.1
Table of Contents and Headings

The table of contents and headings of the Chapters, Sections and Articles of this Agreement are inserted for convenience of reference only and shall not affect the interpretation of this Agreement.

Article 17.2
Annexes and Notes

The Annexes and Notes to this Agreement shall form an integral part of this Agreement.

Article 17.3
Amendment

1. This Agreement may be amended by written agreement between the Parties.

2. Such amendment shall be approved by the Parties in accordance with their respective legal procedures, and shall enter into force on the date to be agreed upon by the Parties and by means of diplomatic notes exchanged between the Governments of the Parties informing each other that their respective legal procedures necessary for its entry into force have been completed.

3. Notwithstanding paragraph 2, amendments related only to the following may be made by diplomatic notes exchanged between the Governments of the Parties:

(a) Annex 1, provided that the amendments are made in accordance with the amendment of the Harmonized System, and include no change on the rates of customs duty to be applied by a Party to the originating goods of the other Party in accordance with Annex 1;

(b) Annex 2; and

(c) Annex 3.

Article 17.4
Entry into Force

This Agreement shall enter into force on the thirtieth day after the date on which the Governments of the Parties exchange diplomatic notes informing each other that their respective legal procedures necessary for entry into force of this Agreement have been completed. It shall remain in force unless terminated as provided for in Article 17.5.

Article 17.5
Termination

Either Party may terminate this Agreement by giving one year's advance notice in writing through the diplomatic channel to the other Party.

Article 17.6
Authentic Texts

1. The texts of this Agreement in the Japanese, Mongolian and English languages shall be equally authentic.

2. Notwithstanding paragraph 1:

(a) (i) Part 2 of Annex 1 is in the Japanese and English languages, such texts being equally authentic; and

(ii) Part 3 of Annex 1 is in the Mongolian and English languages, such texts being equally authentic;

(b) (i) Part 1A and Part 2 of Annex 6 are in the Japanese and English languages, such texts being equally authentic; and

(ii) Part 1B of Annex 6 is in the Mongolian and English languages, such texts being equally authentic;

(c) (i) Part 1 of Annex 7 is in the Japanese and English languages, such texts being equally authentic; and

(ii) Part 2 of Annex 7 is in the Mongolian and English languages, such texts being equally authentic; and

(d) (i) Part 1 of Annex 8 and Part 1 of Annex 9 are in the Japanese and English languages, such texts being equally authentic; and

(ii) Part 2 of Annex 8 and Part 2 of Annex 9 are in the Mongolian and English languages, such texts being equally authentic.

3. In the event of any divergence among the texts, the English text shall prevail.

IN WITNESS WHEREOF, the undersigned, being duly authorized by their respective Governments, have signed this Agreement.

DONE at Tokyo on this tenth day of February in the year 2015 in duplicate in the Japanese, Mongolian and English languages.

For Japan:	For Mongolia:
安倍晋三	Chimed Saikhanbileg

IMPLEMENTING AGREEMENT BETWEEN THE GOVERNMENT OF JAPAN AND THE GOVERNMENT OF MONGOLIA PURSUANT TO ARTICLE 1.12 OF THE AGREEMENT BETWEEN JAPAN AND MONGOLIA FOR AN ECONOMIC PARTNERSHIP

Table of Contents

Preamble

The Government of Japan and the Government of Mongolia,

In accordance with Article 1.12 of the Agreement between Japan and Mongolia for an Economic Partnership (hereinafter referred to as "the Basic Agreement"),

HAVE AGREED as follows:

Chapter 1
General Provisions

Article 1.1
Definitions

For the purposes of this Agreement:

(a) the term "Countries" means Japan and Mongolia and the term "Country" means either Japan or Mongolia; and

(b) the term "Parties" means the Government of Japan and the Government of Mongolia and the term "Party" means either the Government of Japan or the Government of Mongolia.

Chapter 2
Customs Procedures and Trade Facilitation

Article 2.1
Cooperation

1. The Parties shall endeavor to assist each other through their customs authorities to ensure proper application of customs laws, and to prevent, investigate and repress any violation or attempted violation of customs laws.

2. The Parties shall endeavor to cooperate through their customs authorities, where necessary and appropriate, in the areas of research, development and testing of new customs procedures and new enforcement aids and techniques, training activities of customs officers, and exchange of personnel between them.

Article 2.2
Information and Communications Technology

The customs authorities of the Parties shall make cooperative efforts to promote the use of information and communications technology in their customs procedures, including sharing best practices, for the purpose of improving their customs procedures.

Article 2.3
Risk Management

1. In order to facilitate customs clearance of goods traded between the Countries, the customs authorities of the Parties shall maintain risk management systems that enable them to concentrate inspection activities on high risk goods and that simplify the clearance and movement of low risk goods.

2. The Parties shall endeavor to promote, through arrangements such as seminars and courses, the use of risk management and the improvement of risk management techniques in the Parties.

3. The customs authorities of the Parties shall share best practices on risk management techniques and other enforcement techniques.

Article 2.4
Combating Illicit Trafficking

1. The customs authorities of the Parties shall cooperate in the field of combating illicit trafficking of goods.

2. The Parties shall endeavor to promote regional cooperation under the Customs Co-operation Council in the field of combating illicit trafficking of goods.

Article 2.5
Intellectual Property Rights

The customs authorities of the Parties shall endeavor to cooperate in the field of combating the importation and exportation of goods suspected of infringing intellectual property rights.

Article 2.6
Exchange of Information

1. Each Party shall maintain the confidentiality of any information communicated to it in confidence by the other Party in accordance with Article 4.7 of the Basic Agreement and this Chapter, unless the latter Party consents to the disclosure of such information.

2. Each Party may limit the information it communicates to the other Party when the latter Party is unable to give the assurance requested by the former Party with respect to the limitations of purposes for which the information will be used.

3. If a Party that requests information would be unable to comply with a similar request in case such a request were made by the other Party, it shall draw attention to that fact in its request. Execution of such a request shall be at the discretion of the latter Party.

4. Information provided from the customs authority of a Party to the customs authority of the other Party in accordance with Article 4.7 of the Basic Agreement and this Chapter shall be used only for the discharge of functions of the latter customs authority under its Country's customs laws.

5. Information provided in accordance with Article 4.7 of the Basic Agreement and this Chapter shall not be used by the receiving Party in criminal proceedings carried out by a court or a judge.

6. In the event that information communicated by a Party to the other Party in accordance with Article 4.7 of the Basic Agreement and this Chapter is needed for presentation to a court or a judge in criminal proceedings, the latter Party shall submit a request for such information to the former Party through the diplomatic channel or other channels established in accordance with the laws and regulations of the Country of the former Party. The former Party will make its best efforts to respond promptly and favorably to meet any reasonable deadlines indicated by the other Party.

7. Notwithstanding any other provision of this Chapter, a Party shall not be required to communicate information to the other Party if such communication is prohibited by the laws and regulations of the Country of the former Party or if the former Party considers such communication incompatible with its important interests.

Article 2.7
Sub-Committee on Customs Procedures and Trade Facilitation

1. The Sub-Committee on Customs Procedures and Trade Facilitation established in accordance with Article 4.8 of the Basic Agreement (hereinafter referred to in this Article as "the Sub-Committee") shall comprise:

(a) an official from the Ministry of Finance of Japan, or its successor, and an official from the Customs General Administration of Mongolia, or its successor, as co-chairs;

(b) for Japan, officials from the Ministry of Finance and the Ministry of Foreign Affairs, or their successors, and other government officials with the necessary expertise relevant to the issues to be discussed who may be included on an *ad hoc* basis; and

(c) for Mongolia, officials from the Customs General Administration, or its successor, and other government officials with the necessary expertise relevant to the issues to be discussed who may be included on an *ad hoc* basis.

2. The Sub-Committee may, by mutual consent of the Parties, invite representatives of relevant entities other than the Parties with the necessary expertise relevant to the issues to be discussed.

Chapter 3
Competition

Article 3.1
Objective

The objective of this Chapter is to provide for the details and procedures concerning the implementation of the cooperation set forth in Article 11.2 of the Basic Agreement.

Article 3.2
Definitions

For the purposes of this Chapter:

(a) the term "competition authority" means:

(i) for Japan, the Fair Trade Commission, or its successor; and

(ii) for Mongolia, the Authority for Fair Competition and Consumer Protection, or its successor;

(b) the term "competition law" means:

(i) for Japan, the Law Concerning Prohibition of Private Monopoly and Maintenance of Fair Trade (Law No. 54 of 1947) (hereinafter referred to in this Chapter as "the Antimonopoly Law") and its implementing regulations as well as any amendment thereto; and

(ii) for Mongolia, the Law of Mongolia on Competition of June 10, 2010 and its implementing regulations as well as any amendment thereto; and

(c) the term "enforcement activities" means any investigation or proceeding conducted by a Party in relation to the application of the competition law of its Country, but shall not include:

(i) the review of business conduct or routine filings; and

(ii) research, studies or surveys with the objective of examining the general economic situation or general conditions in specific sectors.

Article 3.3
Notification

1. The competition authority of each Party shall notify, to the extent consistent with the laws and regulations of its Country, the competition authority of the other Party of the enforcement activities of the notifying Party that the notifying competition authority considers may affect the important interests of the other Party.

2. Enforcement activities of a Party that may affect the important interests of the other Party include those that:

(a) are relevant to enforcement activities of the other Party;

(b) are against a national of the Country of the other Party, or against an enterprise incorporated or organized under the applicable laws and regulations of the Country of the other Party;

(c) involve mergers or acquisitions in which:

(i) one or more of the parties to the transaction; or

(ii) an enterprise controlling one or more of the parties to the transaction,

is an enterprise incorporated or organized under the applicable laws and regulations of the Country of the other Party;

(d) involve anticompetitive activities, other than mergers or acquisitions, substantially carried out in the Country of the other Party;

(e) involve conduct considered by the notifying competition authority to have been required, encouraged or approved by the other Party; or

(f) involve relief that requires or prohibits conduct in the Country of the other Party.

3. Provided that it is not contrary to the laws and regulations of the Country of the notifying competition authority and does not affect any investigation being carried out by the notifying competition authority, notification in accordance with paragraph 1 shall be given as promptly as possible when the competition authority of a Party becomes aware that the enforcement activities of its Party may affect the important interests of the other Party.

4. Notifications provided in accordance with this Article shall be sufficiently detailed to enable the notified competition authority to make an initial evaluation of the effect on the important interests of its Party.

Article 3.4
Cooperation in Enforcement Activities

The competition authority of each Party shall render assistance to the competition authority of the other Party in its enforcement activities to the extent consistent with the laws and regulations of the Country of the assisting competition authority and the important interests of the Party of the assisting competition authority, and within its reasonably available resources.

Article 3.5
Exchange of Information

For the purpose of cooperation provided for in Article 3.4, the competition authority of each Party shall, to the extent consistent with the laws and regulations of the Country of the competition authority and important interests of the Party of the competition authority:

(a) inform the competition authority of the other Party with respect to its enforcement activities involving anticompetitive activities that it considers may also have an adverse effect on competition in the Country of the other Party;

(b) provide the competition authority of the other Party with any significant information, within its possession and that comes to its attention, about anticompetitive activities that it considers may be relevant to, or may warrant, enforcement activities by the competition authority of the other Party; and

(c) provide the competition authority of the other Party, upon request and in accordance with the provisions of this Chapter, with information within its possession that is relevant to the enforcement activities of the competition authority of the other Party.

Article 3.6
Coordination of Enforcement Activities

1. Where the competition authorities are pursuing enforcement activities with respect to matters that are related to each other:

(a) the competition authorities shall consider coordination of their enforcement activities; and

(b) the competition authority of each Party shall consider, upon request of the competition authority of the other Party and where consistent with the important interests of the former Party, inquiring whether persons who have provided confidential information in connection with the enforcement activities will consent to the sharing of such information with the competition authority of the other Party.

2. In considering whether particular enforcement activities should be coordinated, the competition authorities should take into account, among others, the following factors:

(a) the effect of such coordination on their ability to achieve the objectives of their enforcement activities;

(b) the relative abilities of the competition authorities to obtain information necessary to conduct the enforcement activities;

(c) the extent to which the competition authority of either Party can secure effective relief against the anticompetitive activities involved;

(d) the possible reduction of cost to the Parties and to the persons subject to the enforcement activities; and

(e) the potential advantages of coordinated relief to the Parties and to the persons subject to the enforcement activities.

3. The competition authority of each Party may, subject to appropriate notification to the competition authority of the other Party, at any time, limit or terminate the coordination of enforcement activities and pursue its enforcement activities independently.

Article 3.7
Cooperation regarding Anticompetitive Activities in the Country of a Party that Adversely Affect the Interests of the Other Party

1. If the competition authority of a Party believes that anticompetitive activities carried out in the Country of the other Party adversely affect the important interests of the former Party, the competition authority of the former Party, taking into account the importance of avoiding conflicts resulting from its enforcement activities with respect to such anticompetitive activities and taking into account that the competition authority of the other Party may be in a position to conduct more effective enforcement activities with respect to such anticompetitive activities, may request that the competition authority of the other Party initiate appropriate enforcement activities.

2. The request made in accordance with paragraph 1 shall be as specific as possible about the nature of the anticompetitive activities and their effect on the important interests of the Party of the requesting competition authority, and shall include an offer of such further information and other cooperation as the requesting competition authority is able to provide.

3. The requested competition authority shall carefully consider whether to initiate enforcement activities, or whether to expand ongoing enforcement activities, with respect to the anticompetitive activities identified in the request made in accordance with paragraph 1. The requested competition authority shall inform the requesting competition authority of its decision as soon as practically possible. If enforcement activities are initiated, the requested competition authority shall inform the requesting competition authority of their outcome and, to the extent possible, of significant interim developments.

4. Nothing in this Article limits the discretion of the requested competition authority under the competition law and enforcement policies of its Country as to whether or not to undertake enforcement activities with respect to the anticompetitive activities identified in the request, or precludes the requesting competition authority from withdrawing its request.

Article 3.8
Avoidance of Conflicts over Enforcement Activities

1. Each Party shall give careful consideration to the important interests of the other Party throughout all phases of its enforcement activities, including decisions regarding the initiation of enforcement activities, the scope of enforcement activities and the nature of penalties or relief sought in each case.

2. When a Party informs the other Party that specific enforcement activities of the latter Party may affect the important interests of the former Party, the latter Party shall endeavor, to the extent consistent with the laws and regulations of its Country, to provide timely notice of significant developments of such enforcement activities.

3. Where a Party considers that its enforcement activities may adversely affect the important interests of the other Party, the Parties should consider the following factors, in addition to any other factor that may be relevant, in seeking an appropriate accommodation of the competing interests:

(a) the relative significance to the anticompetitive activities of conduct or transactions occurring in the Country of the Party conducting the enforcement activities as compared to conduct or transactions occurring in the other Country;

(b) the relative impact of the anticompetitive activities on the important interests of the respective Parties;

(c) the presence or absence of evidence of an intention on the part of those engaged in the anticompetitive activities to affect consumers, suppliers or competitors in the Country of the Party conducting the enforcement activities;

(d) the extent to which the anticompetitive activities substantially lessen competition in the market of each Country;

(e) the degree of conflict or consistency between the enforcement activities of the Party and the laws and regulations of the Country of the other Party, or the policies or important interests of that other Party;

(f) whether private persons, either natural or legal, will be placed under conflicting requirements by the Parties;

(g) the location of relevant assets and parties to the transaction;

(h) the degree to which effective sanctions or other relief can be secured by the enforcement activities of the Party against the anticompetitive activities; and

(i) the extent to which enforcement activities of the other Party with respect to the same private persons, either natural or legal, would be affected.

Article 3.9
Technical Cooperation

1. The Parties agree that it is in their common interest that their competition authorities work together in technical cooperation activities aimed at strengthening competition policy and implementing the competition law of each Country.

2. The forms of technical cooperation activities referred to in paragraph 1 shall be:

(a) exchange of personnel of the competition authorities for training purposes;

(b) participation of personnel of the competition authorities as lecturers or consultants at training courses on strengthening of competition policy and implementation of the competition law organized or sponsored by either or both competition authorities; and

(c) other forms to be agreed upon by the competition authorities.

Article 3.10
Transparency

The competition authority of each Party shall:

(a) promptly inform the competition authority of the other Party of any modification of the competition law and any adoption of new laws and regulations by its Country that control anticompetitive activities;

(b) provide, where appropriate, the competition authority of the other Party with copies of its publicly-released guidelines or policy statements issued in relation to the competition law of its Country; and

(c) provide, where appropriate, the competition authority of the other Party with copies of its annual reports and/or any other publication that are made generally available to the public.

Article 3.11
Consultations

The competition authorities shall consult with each other, upon request of either competition authority, on any matter which may arise in connection with this Chapter.

Article 3.12
Confidentiality of Information

1. (a) Information, other than publicly available information, provided by a Party to the other Party in accordance with this Chapter shall only be used by the other Party for the purpose of effective enforcement of the competition law of its Country and shall not be communicated to a third party, unless the Party providing the information has approved otherwise.

(b) Information, other than publicly available information, provided by the competition authority of a Party to the competition authority of the other Party in accordance with this Chapter shall only be used by the competition authority receiving the information for the purpose of effective enforcement of the competition law of its Country and shall not be communicated to a third party or other authorities, unless the competition authority providing the information has approved otherwise.

2. Notwithstanding subparagraph 1(b), the competition authority of a Party which receives information, other than publicly available information, in accordance with this Chapter may, unless otherwise notified by the competition authority of the other Party, communicate such information, for the purpose of enforcement of competition law, to relevant law enforcement authorities of the former Party, which may use the information under the conditions referred to in Article 3.13.

3. Each Party shall, in accordance with the laws and regulations of its Country, maintain the confidentiality of any information provided to it in confidence by the other Party in accordance with this Chapter, unless the latter Party consents to the disclosure of such information.

4. Each Party may limit the information it provides to the other Party when the other Party is unable to give the assurance requested by the former Party with respect to confidentiality or the limitations of purposes for which the information will be used.

5. Notwithstanding any other provisions of this Chapter, neither Party shall be required to provide information to the other Party if it is prohibited from providing the information by the laws and regulations of its Country or it finds providing the information incompatible with its important interests. In particular:

(a) the Government of Japan shall not be required to provide "trade secrets of entrepreneurs" covered by the provisions of Article 39 of the Antimonopoly Law to the Government of Mongolia, except for those provided in accordance with subparagraph 1(b) of Article 3.6 and with the consent of the entrepreneurs concerned; and

(b) the Government of Mongolia shall not be required to provide "secrets of organizations" covered by the provisions of Article 3 of the Law on Organization's Secret of May 16, 1995 to the Government of Japan.

6. This Article shall not preclude the use or disclosure of information to the extent that there is an obligation to do so under the laws and regulations of the Country of the Party receiving the information. Such Party shall, whenever possible, give advance notice of any such use or disclosure to the Party which provided the information.

Article 3.13
Use of Information for Criminal Proceedings

1. Information provided by a Party to the other Party in accordance with this Chapter, except publicly available information, shall not be used in criminal proceedings carried out by a court or a judge of the Country of that other Party.

2. In the event that information provided by a Party to the other Party in accordance with this Chapter, except publicly available information, is needed for presentation in criminal proceedings carried out by a court or a judge of the Country of that other Party, that other Party shall submit a request for such information to the former Party through the diplomatic channel or other channels established in accordance with the laws and regulations of the Country of the former Party.

Article 3.14
Communications

Unless otherwise provided for in this Chapter, communications under this Chapter may be directly carried out between the competition authorities. Notifications in accordance with Article 3.3 and requests in accordance with paragraph 1 of Article 3.7, however, shall be confirmed in writing through the diplomatic channel. Such confirmation shall be made as promptly as practically possible after the communication concerned between the competition authorities.

Article 3.15
Miscellaneous

1. Detailed arrangements to implement this Chapter may be made between the competition authorities.

2. Nothing in this Chapter shall prevent the Parties from seeking or providing assistance to each other in accordance with other bilateral or multilateral agreements or arrangements.

3. Nothing in this Chapter shall be construed to prejudice the policy or legal position of either Party regarding any issues related to jurisdiction.

4. Nothing in this Chapter shall be construed to affect the rights and obligations of either Party under other international agreements or arrangements or under the laws of its Country.

Chapter 4
Improvement of the Business Environment

Article 4.1
Sub-Committee on Improvement of the Business Environment

The issues to be addressed by the Sub-Committee on Improvement of the Business Environment (hereinafter referred to in this Chapter as "the Sub-Committee") referred to in subparagraph 2(b) of Article 14.2 of the Basic Agreement may include:

(a) improvement of transparency in business related rules, regulations, administrative and judicial procedures, and administrative and judicial decisions;

(b) measures to simplify and expedite administrative procedures;

(c) ways to facilitate business activities in both Countries; and

(d) other issues related to business environment.

Article 4.2
Liaison Office

1. The functions of the Liaison Office designated in each Country in accordance with paragraph 1 of Article 14.3 of the Basic Agreement shall be:

(a) receiving complaints and inquiries from the enterprises of the other Country with respect to the laws, regulations and other measures of the former Country which may adversely affect the business activities of the enterprises of the other Country;

(b) transmitting the complaints and inquiries referred to in subparagraph (a) to the relevant authorities of the former Country;

(c) seeking responses from the relevant authorities of the former Country referred to in subparagraph (b) within a reasonable period of time, where appropriate, in writing with sufficient explanations, reasons and legal basis, if any;

(d) transmitting the responses referred to in subparagraph (c) to the enterprises referred to in subparagraph (a);

(e) providing the enterprises referred to in subparagraph (a) with necessary information and advice in collaboration with the relevant authorities of the former Country; and

(f) reporting the findings to the Sub-Committee.

2. Each Party may designate an entity located in the other Country that will facilitate the communications between the Liaison Office of the other Country and the enterprises of the former Country.

3. Paragraphs 1 and 2 shall not be construed to prevent or restrict any contacts made by the enterprises of a Country directly to the relevant authorities of the other Country.

Chapter 5
Cooperation

Article 5.1
Agriculture, Forestry and Fisheries,
including Matters related to SPS Measures referred to in Chapter 5 of the Basic Agreement

Pursuant to Article 15.2 of the Basic Agreement, in the field referred to in subparagraph (a) of Article 15.1 of the Basic Agreement:

(a) the areas of cooperation may include:

(i) genetic resources for foods and agriculture;

(ii) irrigation and seed production;

(iii) establishing demonstration and model farms and facilities;

(iv) production of dairy products, beef, organic foods, grains and vegetables;

(v) horticulture;

(vi) beekeeping;

(vii) fodder production and pet food processing;

(viii) animal breeding biotechnology;

(ix) animal health and veterinary services;

(x) any matters on sanitary and phytosanitary (hereinafter referred to as "SPS") measures, including the following matters:

(A) establishment of pest or disease free zones; and

(B) control, inspection and approval procedures on SPS measures;

(xi) food processing, including heat processing meat production;

(xii) food marketing;

(xiii) agricultural cooperatives;

(xiv) wood processing;

(xv) aquaculture;

(xvi) human resource development; and

(xvii) other areas as may be agreed by the Parties; and

(b) the forms of cooperation may include:

(i) conducting feasibility studies of food value chain;

(ii) development study;

(iii) joint research work;

(iv) exchanging views, information and experts;

(v) providing vocational and practical trainings;

(vi) providing and encouraging the participation in trade fairs, seminars, workshops, business matching events and exhibitions;

(vii) encouraging public private partnership;

(viii) technical consulting service;

(ix) dissemination of technology;

(x) technical assistance on harmonization and recognition of equivalence of SPS measures; and

(xi) other forms as may be agreed by the Parties.

Article 5.2
Manufacturing Industry, including Matters related to Technical Regulations, Standards and Conformity Assessment Procedures referred to in Chapter 6 of the Basic Agreement

Pursuant to Article 15.2 of the Basic Agreement, in the field referred to in subparagraph (b) of Article 15.1 of the Basic Agreement:

(a) the areas of cooperation may include:

(i) enhancing diversification of manufacturing industry;

(ii) industrial and technological parks;

(iii) strengthening management, competitiveness and technological capabilities of manufacturing industry;

(iv) promoting environmental protection through environmentally sound technologies;

(v) technical assistance for the following matters:

(A) encouraging the enforcement of Chapter 6 of the Basic Agreement and the Agreement on Technical Barriers to Trade in Annex 1A to the Marrakesh Agreement Establishing the World Trade Organization, done at Marrakesh, April 15, 1994;

(B) strengthening the corresponding bodies of standardization, technical regulation and conformity assessment, including the formation and training of human resources; and

(C) increasing the collaboration in international organizations in the areas of standardization and conformity assessment;

(vi) human resource development; and

(vii) other areas as may be agreed by the Parties; and

(b) the forms of cooperation may include:

(i) conducting feasibility study and development study;

(ii) exchanging information on policies and best practices;

(iii) encouraging exchanges of experts;

(iv) providing training programs;

(v) organizing seminars and workshops;

(vi) technical assistance;

(vii) dissemination of technology by introducing international and advanced standards; and

(viii) other forms as may be agreed by the Parties.

Article 5.3
Small and Medium Enterprises

Pursuant to Article 15.2 of the Basic Agreement, in the field referred to in subparagraph (c) of Article 15.1 of the Basic Agreement:

(a) the areas of cooperation may include:

(i) promotion of innovative activities of small and medium enterprises (hereinafter referred to in this Article as "SMEs"), including support for the creation, protection and exploitation of intellectual properties;

(ii) strengthening management, competitiveness and technological capabilities of SMEs;

(iii) human resource development; and

(iv) other areas as may be agreed by the Parties; and

(b) the forms of cooperation may include:

(i) exchanging information on policies and best practices;

(ii) encouraging exchanges of experts;

(iii) providing training programs;

(iv) organizing seminars and workshops; and

(v) other forms as may be agreed by the Parties.

Note: For the purposes of this Article, the term "small and medium enterprises" or "SMEs" includes micro-enterprises.

Article 5.4
Trade and Investment

Pursuant to Article 15.2 of the Basic Agreement, in the field referred to in subparagraph (d) of Article 15.1 of the Basic Agreement:

(a) the areas of cooperation may include:

(i) promoting trade and investment;

(ii) promoting service sector development;

(iii) encouraging bilateral cooperation between Japan External Trade Organization, or its successor, and Invest Mongolia Agency, or its successor;

(iv) human resource development; and

(v) other areas as may be agreed by the Parties; and

(b) the forms of cooperation may include:

(i) exchanging views and information on trade and investment, including investment environment and laws and regulations related to business, to further promote trade and investment between the Countries and relevant business operations;

(ii) encouraging exchanges of experts, trainees and researchers to promote and improve knowledge on trade and investment;

(iii) organizing and encouraging the participation in trade missions, trade fairs, seminars, business matching events and exhibitions;

(iv) capacity building for government officials; and

(v) other forms as may be agreed by the Parties.

Article 5.5
Infrastructure, Construction and Urban Development

Pursuant to Article 15.2 of the Basic Agreement, in the field referred to in subparagraph (e) of Article 15.1 of the Basic Agreement:

(a) the areas of cooperation may include:

(i) introducing maritime transportation;

(ii) improving quality of airports;

(iii) introducing and developing intelligent transportation system;

(iv) developing safety standards related to vehicles;

(v) enhancing ability of monitoring and supervising of roads and transportation;

(vi) strengthening capacity of research and development in the areas of roads and transportation;

(vii) introducing technologies for:

(A) energy efficiency;

(B) earthquake resistance;

(C) re-use and re-cycle of construction solid waste; and

(D) membrane for treatment and purification of drinking water;

(viii) improving regulations, controls and enforcement mechanisms for construction safety;

(ix) human resource development; and

(x) other areas as may be agreed by the Parties; and

(b) the forms of cooperation may include:

(i) joint study on the development of the cities around airports;

(ii) exchanging views and information;

(iii) encouraging and facilitating visits and exchanges of experts;

(iv) providing training programs;

(v) promoting seminars and workshops;

(vi) capacity building for engineers and technicians; and

(vii) other forms as may be agreed by the Parties.

Article 5.6
Science and Technology and Intellectual Property

Pursuant to Article 15.2 of the Basic Agreement, in the field referred to in subparagraph (f) of Article 15.1 of the Basic Agreement:

(a) the areas of cooperation may include:

(i) encouraging innovation;

(ii) advanced science and technology;

(iii) utilization of intellectual property rights for innovation and economic growth;

(iv) capacity building in the field of enforcement of intellectual property rights at the border;

(v) capacity building for organizations for collective management of copyrights and related rights;

(vi) development of human resources with advanced knowledge and skills; and

(vii) other areas as may be agreed by the Parties; and

(b) the forms of cooperation may include:

(i) encouraging joint research and development;

(ii) exchanging information on policies, laws and regulations;

(iii) encouraging exchanges of scientists, technical personnel or other experts;

(iv) promoting the holding of joint seminars, dialogues, workshops and trainings with a view to enhancing awareness and knowledge of scientists;

(v) encouraging cooperation among institutes on advanced science and technology; and

(vi) other forms as may be agreed by the Parties.

Article 5.7
Financial Services

Pursuant to Article 15.2 of the Basic Agreement, in the field referred to in subparagraph (g) of Article 15.1 of the Basic Agreement:

(a) the areas of cooperation may include:

(i) facilitating development of financial and capital markets in the Asian region;

(ii) improving financial market infrastructure, including enhancement of capabilities in monitoring financial and other relevant transactions;

(iii) promoting regulatory cooperation in the field of financial services;

(iv) strengthening functions of non-banking and insurance;

(v) human resource development; and

(vi) other areas as may be agreed by the Parties; and

(b) the forms of cooperation may include:

(i) exchanging information, experiences and skills;

(ii) promoting trainings; and

(iii) other forms as may be agreed by the Parties.

Article 5.8
Education and Human Resource Development

Pursuant to Article 15.2 of the Basic Agreement, in the field referred to in subparagraph (h) of Article 15.1 of the Basic Agreement:

(a) the areas of cooperation may include:

(i) development of human resources with advanced knowledge and skills; and

(ii) other areas as may be agreed by the Parties; and

(b) the forms of cooperation may include:

(i) exchanging information, including good practices;

(ii) encouraging visits and exchanges of experts, scholars, teachers, trainers and government officials;

(iii) providing technical and vocational trainings for engineers and technical staffs;

(iv) encouraging recognition of the education or experience obtained in universities;

(v) promoting joint seminars, workshops and meetings;

(vi) encouraging cooperation among educational institutions; and

(vii) other forms as may be agreed by the Parties.

Article 5.9
Tourism

Pursuant to Article 15.2 of the Basic Agreement, in the field referred to in subparagraph (i) of Article 15.1 of the Basic Agreement:

(a) the areas of cooperation may include:

(i) encouraging tourism industry;

(ii) sustainable development of tourism;

(iii) strengthening management and competence in tourism;

(iv) human resource development; and

(v) other areas as may be agreed by the Parties; and

(b) the forms of cooperation may include:

(i) providing appropriate assistance for tourism promotion and development programs;

(ii) exchanging information and sharing experiences;

(iii) encouraging exchanges of experts;

(iv) promoting trainings for persons engaged in the tourism industry;

(v) encouraging and facilitating cooperation between private entities; and

(vi) other forms as may be agreed by the Parties.

Article 5.10
Environment

Pursuant to Article 15.2 of the Basic Agreement, in the field referred to in subparagraph (j) of Article 15.1 of the Basic Agreement:

(a) the areas of cooperation may include:

(i) conservation and improvement of the environment;

(ii) enhancing the mechanism of environmental inspection;

(iii) establishing and promoting strategies and technology for sustainable green development, including tackling of climate change and low-carbon development;

(iv) introducing water purifying technology;

(v) improving waste management and technology;

(vi) reducing vehicle emission;

(vii) human resource development; and

(viii) other areas as may be agreed by the Parties; and

(b) the forms of cooperation may include:

(i) exchanging information, including policies, laws and regulations;

(ii) encouraging and facilitating visits and exchanges of experts;

(iii) enhancing training opportunities;

(iv) promoting capacity building; and

(v) other forms as may be agreed by the Parties.

Article 5.11
Mining and Energy

Pursuant to Article 15.2 of the Basic Agreement, in the field referred to in subparagraph (k) of Article 15.1 of the Basic Agreement:

(a) the areas of cooperation may include:

(i) development and promotion of technologies related to mining and energy;

(ii) human resource development; and

(iii) other areas as may be agreed by the Parties; and

(b) the forms of cooperation may include:

(i) conducting feasibility study and development study;

(ii) exchanging views and information on policies, laws and regulations;

(iii) encouraging exchanges of experts and technical personnel to promote and improve knowledge on the development of mining and energy;

(iv) promoting the holding of joint seminars, dialogues and workshops;

(v) encouraging public private partnership; and

(vi) other forms as may be agreed by the Parties.

Article 5.12
Healthcare

Pursuant to Article 15.2 of the Basic Agreement, in the field referred to in subparagraph (l) of Article 15.1 of the Basic Agreement:

(a) the areas of cooperation may include:

(i) development and promotion of advanced health and science technology;

(ii) human resource development; and

(iii) other areas as may be agreed by the Parties; and

(b) the forms of cooperation may include:

(i) encouraging joint research and development;

(ii) exchanging information;

(iii) providing trainings for medical professionals and encouraging field visits and exchanges of experts;

(iv) promoting activities by public and private health organizations; and

(v) other forms as may be agreed by the Parties.

Article 5.13
Competition

Pursuant to Article 15.2 of the Basic Agreement, in the field referred to in subparagraph (m) of Article 15.1 of the Basic Agreement:

(a) the areas of cooperation may include:

(i) human resource development; and

(ii) other areas as may be agreed by the Parties; and

(b) the forms of cooperation may include:

(i) exchanging views and information;

(ii) encouraging and facilitating visits and exchanges of experts;

(iii) promoting seminars and workshops; and

(iv) other forms as may be agreed by the Parties.

Article 5.14
Information and Communications Technology

Pursuant to Article 15.2 of the Basic Agreement, in the field referred to in subparagraph (n) of Article 15.1 of the Basic Agreement:

(a) the areas of cooperation may include:

(i) strengthening management, competitiveness and technological capabilities in information and communications technology;

(ii) development of human resources with advanced knowledge and skills; and

(iii) other areas as may be agreed by the Parties; and

(b) the forms of cooperation may include:

(i) encouraging joint research and development;

(ii) exchanging information on policies, laws and regulations;

(iii) encouraging exchanges of scientists, technical personnel or other experts;

(iv) promoting the holding of joint seminars, dialogues, workshops and trainings;

(v) encouraging cooperation among institutes of advanced information and communications technology;

(vi) promoting business matching; and

(vii) other forms as may be agreed by the Parties.

Chapter 6
Final Provisions

Article 6.1
Implementation

This Agreement shall be implemented by the Parties in accordance with the Basic Agreement and the laws and regulations in force in their respective Countries, and within the available resources of each Party.

Article 6.2
Table of Contents and Headings

The table of contents and headings of the Chapters and Articles of this Agreement are inserted for convenience of reference only and shall not affect the interpretation of this Agreement.

Article 6.3
Amendment

This Agreement may be amended by agreement between the Parties. Any such amendment shall enter into force in accordance with the procedures specified in the instrument of amendment.

Article 6.4
Entry into Force

This Agreement shall enter into force at the same time as the Basic Agreement and shall remain in force as long as the Basic Agreement remains in force.

Article 6.5
Dispute Settlement

Chapter 16 of the Basic Agreement shall apply *mutatis mutandis* with respect to the settlement of disputes between the Parties concerning the interpretation and/or application of Chapter 1, Chapter 2 and this Chapter.

IN WITNESS WHEREOF, the undersigned, being duly authorized by their respective Governments, have signed this Agreement.

DONE at Tokyo on this tenth day of February in the year 2015 in duplicate in the Japanese, Mongolian and English languages, all texts being equally authentic. In the event of any divergence among the texts, the English text shall prevail.

For the Government of Japan:

安倍晋三

For the Government of Mongolia:

Chimed Saikhanbileg

日本国政府のために

安倍晋三

モンゴル国政府のために

チメド・サイハンビレグ

第六・四条　効力発生

この取極は、基本協定の効力発生の時に効力を生じ、基本協定が有効である限り効力を有する。

第六・五条　紛争解決

基本協定第十六章の規定は、必要な変更を加えた上で、この取極の第一章、第二章及びこの章の規定の解釈又は適用に関する両締約国政府間の紛争の解決について適用する。

以上の証拠として、下名は、各自の政府から正当に委任を受けてこの取極に署名した。

二千十五年二月十日に東京で、ひとしく正文である日本語、モンゴル語及び英語により本書二通を作成した。正文の間に相違がある場合には、英語の本文による。

(v) 高度な情報通信技術に係る団体間の協力の奨励

(vi) 事業取引のあっせんの促進

(vii) 両締約国政府が合意するその他の形態

第六章　最終規定

第六・一条　実施

この取極は、両締約国政府により、基本協定及び両締約国それぞれにおいて効力を有する法令に従って、かつ、各締約国政府の利用可能な資源の範囲内で実施される。

第六・二条　目次及び見出し

この取極の目次並びにこの取極中の章及び条の見出しは、引用上の便宜のためにのみ付されたものであって、この取極の解釈に影響を及ぼすものではない。

第六・三条　改正

この取極は、両締約国政府間の合意により改正することができる。改正は、改正に係る文書において特定する手続に従って効力を生ずる。

(iv) 両締約国政府が合意するその他の形態

第五・十四条　情報通信技術

基本協定第十五・二条の規定に基づき、基本協定第十五・一条(n)に規定する分野における協力については、次のとおりとする。

(a) 当該協力の範囲には、次の事項を含めることができる。

(i) 情報通信技術における経営、競争力及び技術的能力の強化

(ii) 高度な知識及び技術を有する人材の養成

(iii) 両締約国政府が合意するその他の範囲

(b) 当該協力の形態には、次の事項を含めることができる。

(i) 共同研究開発の奨励

(ii) 政策及び法令に関する情報の交換

(iii) 科学者、技術者その他の専門家の交流の奨励

(iv) 共同セミナー、対話、研究集会及び研修の開催の促進

(iii) 医療専門家のための研修の提供並びに専門家の現場視察及び交流の奨励

(iv) 官民の保健機関の活動の促進

(v) 両締約国政府が合意するその他の形態

第五・十三条　競争

基本協定第十五・二条の規定に基づき、基本協定第十五・一条(m)に規定する分野における協力については、次のとおりとする。

(a) 当該協力の範囲には、次の事項を含めることができる。

(i) 人材養成

(ii) 両締約国政府が合意するその他の範囲

(b) 当該協力の形態には、次の事項を含めることができる。

(i) 意見及び情報の交換

(ii) 専門家の訪問及び交流の奨励及び円滑化

(iii) セミナー及び研究集会の促進

(iv) 共同セミナー、対話及び研究集会の開催の促進

(v) 官民間の連携の奨励

(vi) 両締約国政府が合意するその他の形態

第五・十二条 保健

基本協定第十五・二条の規定に基づき、基本協定第十五・一条(1)に規定する分野における協力については、次のとおりとする。

(a) 当該協力の範囲には、次の事項を含めることができる。

(i) 高度な保健技術及び科学技術の開発及び促進

(ii) 人材養成

(iii) 両締約国政府が合意するその他の範囲

(b) 当該協力の形態には、次の事項を含めることができる。

(i) 共同研究開発の奨励

(ii) 情報の交換

(iv) 能力開発の促進

(v) 両締約国政府が合意するその他の形態

第五・十一条　鉱業及びエネルギー

基本協定第十五・二条の規定に基づき、基本協定第十五・一条(k)に規定する分野における協力については、次のとおりとする。

(a) 当該協力の範囲には、次の事項を含めることができる。

(i) 鉱業及びエネルギーに関連する技術の開発及び促進

(ii) 人材養成

(iii) 両締約国政府が合意するその他の範囲

(b) 当該協力の形態には、次の事項を含めることができる。

(i) 実行可能性調査及び開発調査の実施

(ii) 政策及び法令に関する意見及び情報の交換

(iii) 鉱業及びエネルギーの開発に関する知識の普及及び改善のための専門家及び技術者の交流の奨励

(i) 環境の保全及び改善

(ii) 環境検査の制度の強化

(iii) 持続可能なかつ自然に配慮した開発（気候変動への対処及び炭素の排出が少ない開発を含む。）のための戦略及び技術の確立及び促進

(iv) 浄水技術の導入

(v) 廃棄物の管理及び廃棄物に係る技術の改善

(vi) 車両からの排出ガスの削減

(vii) 人材養成

(viii) 両締約国政府が合意するその他の範囲

(b) 当該協力の形態には、次の事項を含めることができる。

(i) 情報（政策及び法令に関するものを含む。）の交換

(ii) 専門家の訪問及び交流の奨励及び円滑化

(iii) 研修の機会の増大

(iv) 人材養成

(v) 両締約国政府が合意するその他の範囲

(b) 当該協力の形態には、次の事項を含めることができる。

(i) 観光の促進及び開発計画に対する適当な支援の提供

(ii) 情報の交換及び経験の共有

(iii) 専門家の交流の奨励

(iv) 観光産業に従事する者に対する研修の促進

(v) 民間団体間の協力の奨励及び円滑化

(vi) 両締約国政府が合意するその他の形態

第五・十条　環境

基本協定第十五・二条の規定に基づき、基本協定第十五・一条(j)に規定する分野における協力については、次のとおりとする。

(a) 当該協力の範囲には、次の事項を含めることができる。

(ii) 専門家、学者、教員、研修指導者及び政府職員の訪問及び交流の奨励
(iii) 技師及び技術職員の技術訓練及び職業訓練の提供
(iv) 大学において得る教育又は経験の認定の奨励
(v) 共同セミナー、研究集会及び会合の促進
(vi) 教育機関間の協力の奨励
(vii) 両締約国政府が合意するその他の形態

第五・九条　観光

基本協定第十五・二条の規定に基づき、基本協定第十五・一条(i)に規定する分野における協力については、次のとおりとする。

(a) 当該協力の範囲には、次の事項を含めることができる。
(i) 観光産業の奨励
(ii) 観光の持続可能な発展
(iii) 観光における経営及び能力の強化

(vi) 両締約国政府が合意するその他の範囲

(b) 当該協力の形態には、次の事項を含めることができる。

(i) 情報の交換並びに経験及び技能の交流

(ii) 研修の促進

(iii) 両締約国政府が合意するその他の形態

第五・八条　教育及び人材養成

基本協定第十五・二条の規定に基づき、基本協定第十五・一条(h)に規定する分野における協力については、次のとおりとする。

(a) 当該協力の範囲には、次の事項を含めることができる。

(i) 高度な知識及び技術を有する人材の養成

(ii) 両締約国政府が合意するその他の範囲

(b) 当該協力の形態には、次の事項を含めることができる。

(i) 情報（良き慣行に関するものを含む。）の交換

(iv) 科学者の意識及び知識を向上させることを目的とする共同セミナー、対話、研究集会及び研修の開催の促進

(v) 先端科学技術に係る団体間の協力の奨励

(vi) 両締約国政府が合意するその他の形態

第五・七条　金融サービス

基本協定第十五・二条の規定に基づき、基本協定第十五・一条(g)に規定する分野における協力については、次のとおりとする。

(a) 当該協力の範囲には、次の事項を含めることができる。

(i) アジア地域における金融市場及び資本市場の発展の円滑化

(ii) 金融市場の基盤の整備（金融その他の関連する取引の監視における能力の向上を含む。）

(iii) 金融サービスの分野における規制に関する協力の促進

(iv) 銀行以外の金融及び保険の機能の強化

(v) 人材養成

は、次のとおりとする。

(a) 当該協力の範囲には、次の事項を含めることができる。

(i) イノベーションの奨励

(ii) 先端科学技術

(iii) イノベーション及び経済成長のための知的財産権の利用

(iv) 国境における知的財産権の行使の分野での能力の開発

(v) 著作権及び関連する権利を集中管理する団体の能力の開発

(vi) 高度な知識及び技能を有する人材の養成

(vii) 両締約国政府が合意するその他の範囲

(b) 当該協力の形態には、次の事項を含めることができる。

(i) 共同研究開発の奨励

(ii) 政策及び法令に関する情報の交換

(iii) 科学者、技術者その他の専門家の交流の奨励

(viii) 建築の安全に関する規則、規制及び執行の制度の改善

(ix) 人材養成

(x) 両締約国政府が合意するその他の範囲

(b) 当該協力の形態には、次の事項を含めることができる。

(i) 空港周辺の都市の開発に関する共同研究

(ii) 意見及び情報の交換

(iii) 専門家の訪問及び交流の奨励及び円滑化

(iv) 研修プログラムの提供

(v) セミナー及び研究集会の促進

(vi) 技師及び技術者の能力の開発

(vii) 両締約国政府が合意するその他の形態

第五・六条　科学技術及び知的財産

基本協定第十五・二条の規定に基づき、基本協定第十五・一条(f)に規定する分野における協力について

は、次のとおりとする。

(a) 当該協力の範囲には、次の事項を含めることができる。

(i) 海運の導入

(ii) 空港の質の改善

(iii) 高度道路交通システムの導入及び開発

(iv) 車両に関する安全基準の向上

(v) 道路及び輸送についての監視能力及び監督能力の向上

(vi) 道路及び輸送の分野における研究及び開発の能力の強化

(vii) 次の事項のための技術の導入

(A) エネルギー効率

(B) 耐震

(C) 建設廃棄物の再使用及び再生利用

(D) 飲料水の処理用及び浄化用の薄膜

の奨励

(iv) 人材養成

(v) 両締約国政府が合意するその他の範囲

(b) 当該協力の形態には、次の事項を含めることができる。

(i) 両締約国間の貿易及び投資並びに関連する業務の更なる促進のための貿易及び投資（投資環境及び企業に関係する法令を含む。）に関する意見及び情報の交換

(ii) 貿易及び投資に関する知識の普及及び改善のための専門家、研修生及び研究者の交流の奨励

(iii) 貿易ミッション、貿易見本市、セミナー、事業取引のあっせんの催し及び展示会の開催並びにこれらへの参加の奨励

(iv) 政府職員の能力の開発

(v) 両締約国政府が合意するその他の形態

第五・五条　公共基盤、建設及び都市開発

基本協定第十五・二条の規定に基づき、基本協定第十五・一条(e)に規定する分野における協力について

(i) 政策及び最良の慣行に関する情報の交換
(ii) 専門家の交流の奨励
(iii) 研修プログラムの提供
(iv) セミナー及び研究集会の開催
(v) 両締約国政府が合意するその他の形態

注釈 この条の規定の適用上、「中小企業」には、零細企業を含む。

第五・四条 貿易及び投資

基本協定第十五・二条の規定に基づき、基本協定第十五・一条(d)に規定する分野における協力については、次のとおりとする。

(a) 当該協力の範囲には、次の事項を含めることができる。
(i) 貿易及び投資の促進
(ii) サービス分野の発展の促進
(iii) 独立行政法人日本貿易振興機構又はその後継機関とモンゴル投資庁又はその後継機関との間の協力

(v) セミナー及び研究集会の開催

(vi) 技術援助

(vii) 国際的かつ高度な任意規格の導入による技術の普及

(viii) 両締約国政府が合意するその他の形態

第五・三条　中小企業

基本協定第十五・二条の規定に基づき、基本協定第十五・一条(c)に規定する分野における協力については、次のとおりとする。

(a) 当該協力の範囲には、次の事項を含めることができる。

(i) 中小企業の革新的な活動の促進（知的財産の創造、保護及び利用のための支援を含む。）

(ii) 中小企業の経営、競争力及び技術的能力の強化

(iii) 人材養成

(iv) 両締約国政府が合意するその他の範囲

(b) 当該協力の形態には、次の事項を含めることができる。

(iv) 環境上適正な技術による環境保護の促進

(v) 次の事項のための技術援助

(A) 基本協定第六章及び千九百九十四年四月十五日にマラケシュで作成された世界貿易機関を設立するマラケシュ協定附属書一A貿易の技術的障害に関する協定の執行の奨励

(B) 標準化、強制規格及び適合性評価に関連する機関の強化（人的資源の形成及び訓練を含む。）

(C) 標準化及び適合性評価の分野における国際機関における協力の増進

(vi) 人材養成

(vii) 両締約国政府が合意するその他の範囲

(b) 当該協力の形態には、次の事項を含めることができる。

(i) 実行可能性調査及び開発調査の実施

(ii) 政策及び最良の慣行に関する情報の交換

(iii) 専門家の交流の奨励

(iv) 研修プログラムの提供

(vii) 官民間の連携の奨励

(viii) 技術に関する相談サービス

(ix) 技術の普及

(x) 衛生植物検疫措置の調和及び同等の認定に関する技術援助

(xi) 両締約国政府が合意するその他の形態

第五・二条　製造業（基本協定第六章に規定する強制規格、任意規格及び適合性評価手続に関連する事項を含む。）

基本協定第十五・二条の規定に基づき、基本協定第十五・一条(b)に規定する分野における協力については、次のとおりとする。

(a)　当該協力の範囲には、次の事項を含めることができる。

(i)　製造業の多角化の強化

(ii)　工業団地及び技術団地

(iii)　製造業の経営、競争力及び技術的能力の強化

(xiii) 農業協同組合

(xiv) 木材の加工

(xv) 養殖

(xvi) 人材養成

(xvii) 両締約国政府が合意するその他の範囲

(b) 当該協力の形態には、次の事項を含めることができる。

(i) フード・バリューチェーンに関する実行可能性調査の実施

(ii) 開発調査

(iii) 共同研究活動

(iv) 意見及び情報の交換並びに専門家の交流

(v) 職業訓練及び実地研修の実施

(vi) 貿易見本市、セミナー、研究集会、事業取引のあっせんの催し及び展示会の機会の提供並びにこれらへの参加の奨励

(ii) 灌漑及び種子の生産

(iii) 演示のための及び模範となる農場及び施設の設置

(iv) 乳製品、牛肉、有機食品、穀物及び野菜の生産

(v) 園芸

(vi) 養蜂

(vii) 飼料の生産及びペットフードの加工

(viii) 動物の繁殖に関するバイオテクノロジー

(ix) 動物の保健及び獣医のサービス

(x) 次の事項を含む衛生植物検疫措置に関する全ての事項

(A) 有害動植物又は病気の無発生区域の設置

(B) 衛生植物検疫措置に関する管理、検査及び承認の手続

(xi) 食品の加工（加熱加工をした食肉の生産を含む。）

(xii) 食品のマーケティング

(e) 自国の関係当局と協力して、(a)に規定する企業に対し、必要な情報及び助言を提供すること。

(f) 小委員会に対して所見を報告すること。

2 一方の締約国政府は、他方の締約国に所在する団体であって当該他方の締約国の連絡事務所と自国の企業との間の連絡を円滑にするものを指定することができる。

3 1及び2の規定は、一方の締約国の企業が他方の締約国の関係当局に直接接触することを妨げ、又は制限するものと解してはならない。

第五章　協力

第五・一条　農業、林業及び漁業（基本協定第五章に規定する衛生植物検疫措置に関連する事項を含む。）

基本協定第十五・二条の規定に基づき、基本協定第十五・一条(a)に規定する分野における協力については、次のとおりとする。

(a) 当該協力の範囲には、次の事項を含めることができる。

(i) 食料及び農業のための遺伝資源

向上

(b) 行政上の手続を簡素化し、及び迅速にするための措置

(c) 両締約国における事業活動を円滑化するための方法

(d) ビジネス環境に関連するその他の問題

第四・二条　連絡事務所

1　基本協定第十四・三条1の規定に従って各締約国において指定される連絡事務所は、次のことを任務とする。

(a) 自国の法令その他の措置であって、他方の締約国の企業の事業活動に悪影響を及ぼすおそれがあるものに関する当該他方の締約国の企業からの苦情及び照会を受領すること。

(b) 自国の関係当局に対し、(a)に規定する苦情及び照会を送付すること。

(c) (b)に規定する自国の関係当局から、合理的な期間内に、適当な場合には書面にて、十分な説明、理由及び法的根拠（該当する場合に限る。）を付した回答を求めること。

(d) (a)に規定する企業に対し、(c)に規定する回答を送付すること。

第三・十五条　雑則

1　この章の規定を実施するための詳細な取決めは、両競争当局間で行うことができる。

2　この章のいかなる規定も、他の二国間又は多数国間の協定又は取決めに従って両締約国政府が相互に支援を求め、又は提供することを妨げるものではない。

3　この章のいかなる規定も、管轄権に関連するあらゆる問題に関するいずれの締約国政府の政策又は法的立場をも害するものと解してはならない。

4　この章のいかなる規定も、他の国際協定若しくは国際的な取決め又は自国の法律に基づくいずれの締約国政府の権利及び義務にも影響を及ぼすものと解してはならない。

第四章　ビジネス環境の整備

第四・一条　ビジネス環境の整備に関する小委員会

基本協定第十四・二条2(b)に規定する問題であってビジネス環境の整備に関する小委員会（以下この章において「小委員会」という。）が取り組むものには、次の事項を含めることができる。

(a)　ビジネスに関連する規則、行政上及び司法上の手続並びに行政上及び司法上の決定における透明性の

第三・十三条　刑事手続のための情報の使用

1　この章の規定に従って一方の締約国政府から他方の締約国政府に提供される情報（公に利用可能な情報を除く。）については、当該他方の締約国の裁判所又は裁判官が行う刑事手続において使用してはならない。

2　この章の規定に従って一方の締約国政府から他方の締約国政府に提供される情報（公に利用可能な情報を除く。）を当該他方の締約国の裁判所又は裁判官が行う刑事手続において提示することが必要とされる場合には、当該他方の締約国政府は、当該情報に対する要請を外交上の経路又は当該一方の締約国の法令に従って設けられたその他の経路を通じて当該一方の締約国政府に提出する。

第三・十四条　連絡

この章に別段の定めがある場合を除くほか、この章の規定に基づく連絡については、両競争当局間で直接行うことができる。ただし、第三・三条の規定に基づく通報及び第三・七条1の規定に基づく要請については、外交上の経路を通じ、書面により確認する。その確認については、関係する連絡が両競争当局間において行われた後、実行可能な限り速やかに行う。

4　一方の締約国政府は、秘密性又は情報の使用目的の制限に関し、自己が要請する保証を他方の締約国政府から得ることができない場合には、当該他方の締約国政府に提供する情報を限定することができる。

5　この章の他の規定にかかわらず、いずれの一方の締約国政府も、自国の法令によって禁止されている場合又は自己の重要な利益と両立しないと認める場合には、他方の締約国政府に情報を提供することを要しない。特に、

(a)　日本国政府は、独占禁止法第三十九条の規定の適用を受ける「事業者の秘密」（第三・六条1(b)の規定に従って行われる照会の結果として関係事業者の同意を得て提供されるものを除く。）をモンゴル国政府に提供することを要しない。

(b)　モンゴル国政府は、千九百九十五年五月十六日の組織の秘密に関する法律第三条の規定の適用を受ける「組織の秘密」を日本国政府に提供することを要しない。

6　この条の規定は、情報を受領した締約国政府が、自国の法令に従って義務付けられている限度において、当該情報の使用又は開示を行うことを妨げない。当該情報を受領した締約国政府は、可能な限り、当該情報を提供した締約国政府に対し当該使用又は開示について事前に通報する。

約国政府は、自国の競争法の効果的な執行のためにのみ使用するものとし、かつ、第三者に伝達してはならない。

(b) この章の規定に従って一方の締約国政府の競争当局から他方の締約国政府の競争当局に提供される情報（公に利用可能な情報を除く。）については、当該一方の締約国政府の競争当局が別段の承認を与えた場合を除くほか、当該他方の締約国政府の競争当局は、自国の競争法の効果的な執行のためにのみ使用するものとし、かつ、第三者又は他の当局に伝達してはならない。

2 1(b)の規定にかかわらず、この章の規定に従って情報（公に利用可能な情報を除く。）を受領する一方の締約国政府の競争当局は、他方の締約国政府の競争当局が別段の通報を行う場合を除くほか、当該情報を競争法の執行のために当該一方の締約国政府の関連する法執行当局に伝達することができる。当該法執行当局は、次条に規定する条件に従って当該情報を使用することができる。

3 一方の締約国政府は、自国の法令に従い、他方の締約国政府がこの章の規定に従って秘密のものとして提供するあらゆる情報の秘密性を保持する。ただし、当該他方の締約国政府が当該情報の開示に同意する場合は、この限りでない。

一方の締約国政府の競争当局は、次のことを行う。

(a) 自国の競争法の改正及び反競争的行為を規制する自国の新たな法令の制定について他方の締約国政府の競争当局に速やかに通報すること。

(b) 適当な場合には、自国の競争法に関連して発出し、及び公表した指針又は政策声明の写しを他方の締約国政府の競争当局に提供すること。

(c) 適当な場合には、当該一方の締約国政府の競争当局の年次報告その他の公表資料であって、公衆が一般に利用可能であるものの写しを他方の締約国政府の競争当局に提供すること。

第三・十一条　協議

両競争当局は、いずれかの競争当局の要請があった場合には、この章の規定に関連して生ずることがあるいかなる事項についても、相互に協議する。

第三・十二条　情報の秘密性

1(a) この章の規定に従って一方の締約国政府から他方の締約国政府に提供される情報（公に利用可能な情報を除く。）については、当該一方の締約国政府が別段の承認を与えた場合を除くほか、当該他方の締

(h) 締約国政府の執行活動が、反競争的行為に対する効果的な制裁その他の排除に係る措置を確保することができる程度

(i) 同一の私人（自然人であるか法人であるかを問わない。）に関する他方の締約国政府の執行活動が影響を受ける程度

第三・九条　技術協力

1　両締約国政府は、両競争当局が競争政策を強化し、及び自国の競争法を実施するための技術協力活動において協力することが共通の利益であることに合意する。

2　1に規定する技術協力活動の形態は、次のとおりとする。

(a) 研修のため両競争当局の職員を交流させること。

(b) 競争政策の強化及び競争法の実施に関する研修課程であって、一方又は双方の競争当局が組織し、又は後援するものにおいて、両競争当局の職員が講師又はコンサルタントとして参加すること。

(c) 両競争当局が合意するその他の形態

第三・十条　透明性

方の締約国政府が認める場合には、両締約国政府は、利害の競合を適切に調整しようとするに当たり、次の要素その他関連し得る要素を考慮すべきである。

(a) 執行活動を行う側の締約国における行動又は取引が、他方の締約国における行動又は取引に比して有している反競争的行為についての相対的な重要性

(b) 反競争的行為がそれぞれの締約国政府の重要な利益に及ぼす相対的な影響

(c) 反競争的行為に関与している者が、執行活動を行う側の締約国における消費者、供給者又は競争者に影響を及ぼす意図を有することに関する証拠の存否

(d) 反競争的行為が各締約国の市場における競争を実質的に減殺する程度

(e) 一方の締約国政府の執行活動と他方の締約国の法令又は当該他方の締約国政府の政策若しくは重要な利益との間の抵触又は一貫性の程度

(f) 私人（自然人であるか法人であるかを問わない。）が両締約国政府による相反する要求の下に置かれることとなるか否か。

(g) 関連する資産及び取引の当事者の所在地

行活動を開始する場合には、当該要請を受けた競争当局は、当該要請を行った競争当局に対し、当該執行活動の最終的な結果を通報し、かつ、暫定的な進展のうち重要なものを可能な範囲で通報する。

4　この条のいかなる規定も、1の規定に基づく要請において特定された反競争的行為について執行活動を行うか否かに関し、当該要請を受けた競争当局が自国の競争法及び執行政策の下で有する裁量を制限するものではなく、また、当該要請を行った競争当局が当該要請を取り下げることを妨げるものでもない。

第三・八条　執行活動に関する紛争の回避

1　一方の締約国政府は、自己の執行活動のあらゆる局面（執行活動の開始及び範囲に関する決定並びに各事案における罰則又は排除に係る措置の性質に関する決定を含む。）において、他方の締約国政府の重要な利益に慎重な考慮を払う。

2　いずれか一方の締約国政府が、他方の締約国政府による特定の執行活動が自己の重要な利益に影響を及ぼす可能性があることを当該他方の締約国政府に通報した場合には、当該他方の締約国政府は、自国の法令に適合する限りにおいて、当該執行活動の重要な進展について適時に通報するよう努める。

3　一方の締約国政府の執行活動が他方の締約国政府の重要な利益に悪影響を及ぼす可能性があると当該一

第三・七条　一方の締約国における反競争的行為であって他方の締約国政府の利益に悪影響を及ぼすものに関する協力

1　一方の締約国政府の競争当局は、他方の締約国において行われた反競争的行為が自国政府の重要な利益に悪影響を及ぼすと信ずる場合には、当該反競争的行為に関する自己の執行活動から生ずる紛争を回避することの重要性及び当該他方の締約国政府の競争当局が当該反競争的行為に関してより効果的な執行活動を行うことができる可能性があることに留意して、当該他方の締約国政府の競争当局に対し、適切な執行活動を開始するよう要請することができる。

2　1の規定に基づく要請には、反競争的行為の性質及び当該要請を行う競争当局が属する締約国政府の重要な利益に当該反競争的行為が及ぼす影響について、できる限り具体的な説明を付するものとし、また、当該要請を行う競争当局が提供することができる追加的な情報その他協力についての申出を含める。

3　1の規定に基づく要請を受けた競争当局は、当該要請において特定される反競争的行為に関し、執行活動を開始するか否か、又は現に行われている執行活動を拡大するか否かを慎重に検討する。当該要請を受けた競争当局は、当該要請を行った競争当局に対し、実行可能な限り速やかに自己の決定を通報する。執

(b) 一方の締約国政府の競争当局は、他方の締約国政府の競争当局の要請があった場合において、自国政府の重要な利益に適合するときは、自己の執行活動に関連して秘密の情報を提供した者に対し、当該情報を当該他方の締約国政府の競争当局と共有することに同意するか否かを照会することを検討する。

2 両競争当局は、特定の執行活動の調整を行うべきか否かを検討するに当たり、特に次の要素を考慮すべきである。

(a) 当該執行活動の目的を達成する上で両競争当局が有する能力に対して当該調整が及ぼす効果

(b) 当該執行活動に必要な情報を入手する上で両競争当局が有する相対的な能力

(c) いずれかの締約国政府の競争当局が、関連する反競争的行為に対して効果的な排除に係る措置を確保することができる程度

(d) 両締約国政府及び当該執行活動の対象者にとっての費用の削減可能性

(e) 排除に係る措置の調整が両締約国政府及び当該執行活動の対象者にもたらす潜在的な利益

3 一方の締約国政府の競争当局は、他方の締約国政府の競争当局に適切な通報を行うことを条件として、執行活動の調整をいつでも限定し、又は終了し、及び自己の執行活動を独自に行うことができる。

前条に規定する協力のために、一方の締約国政府の競争当局は、自国の法令及び自国政府の重要な利益に適合する限りにおいて、次のことを行う。

(a) 他方の締約国における競争に対しても悪影響を及ぼす可能性があると認める反競争的行為に関係する自己の執行活動について、当該他方の締約国政府の競争当局に通報すること。

(b) 他方の締約国政府の競争当局に対し、反競争的行為に関する重要な情報（自己が保有し、かつ、その注意の対象となっているものに限る。）であって、当該他方の締約国政府の競争当局の執行活動に関連し、又はその執行活動を正当化する可能性があると認めるものを提供すること。

(c) 要請があった場合には、この章の規定に従い、他方の締約国政府の競争当局に対し、自己が保有する情報であって、当該他方の締約国政府の競争当局の執行活動に関連するものを提供すること。

第三・六条　執行活動の調整

1 両締約国政府の競争当局（以下この章において「両競争当局」という。）が相互に関連する事案に関して執行活動を行う場合には、次のとおりとする。

(a) 両競争当局は、それぞれの執行活動の調整について検討する。

(f) 排除に係る措置であって、当該他方の締約国における行為を要求し、又は禁止するものを含む執行活動

3 1の規定に基づく通報は、一方の締約国政府の執行活動が他方の締約国政府の重要な利益に影響を及ぼす可能性があることを当該一方の締約国政府の競争当局が了知した場合には、当該一方の締約国の法令に反しないこと及び当該競争当局が実施している審査若しくは捜査に影響を及ぼさないことを条件として、できる限り速やかに行う。

4 この条の規定に基づく通報は、通報を受けた競争当局が自国政府の重要な利益への影響について当初の評価を行うことができるよう、十分詳細な内容を伴うものでなければならない。

第三・四条 執行活動における協力

一方の締約国政府の競争当局は、自国の法令及び自国政府の重要な利益に適合する限りにおいて、かつ、自己の合理的に利用可能な資源の範囲内で、他方の締約国政府の競争当局に対し自己の執行活動について支援を提供する。

第三・五条 情報の交換

2　一方の締約国政府の執行活動であって、他方の締約国政府の重要な利益に影響を及ぼす可能性があるものには、次の執行活動を含む。

(a)　当該他方の締約国政府の執行活動に関連する執行活動

(b)　当該他方の締約国の国民又は当該他方の締約国の関係法令に基づいて設立され、若しくは組織された企業に対して行う執行活動

(c)　企業結合（次の(i)又は(ii)に規定するものが、当該他方の締約国の関係法令に基づいて設立され、又は組織された企業である場合に限る。）に関する執行活動

(i)　当事者の一又は二以上

(ii)　当事者の一又は二以上を支配する企業

(d)　企業結合以外の反競争的行為であって、実質的に当該他方の締約国において行われるものに関する執行活動

(e)　当該一方の締約国政府の競争当局により、当該他方の締約国政府が要求し、奨励し、又は承認したと認められる行為に関係する執行活動

(i) 日本国については、私的独占の禁止及び公正取引の確保に関する法律（昭和二十二年法律第五十四号）（以下この章において「独占禁止法」という。）並びにその実施について定める命令及び規則並びにそれらの改正をいう。

(ii) モンゴル国については、二千十年六月十日の競争に関するモンゴル国の法律及びその実施について定める規則並びにそれらの改正をいう。

(c) 「執行活動」とは、締約国政府が自国の競争法の適用に関連して行う審査若しくは捜査又は手続をいい、次のものを含まない。

(i) 事業活動の監視又は通常の届出、報告若しくは申請の審査

(ii) 経済概況又は特定の産業分野における概況の調査を目的とする調査研究活動

第三・三条　通報

1　一方の締約国政府の競争当局は、自国の法令に適合する限りにおいて、他方の締約国政府の競争当局に対し、当該他方の締約国政府の重要な利益に影響を及ぼす可能性があると認める自国政府の執行活動について通報する。

する必要な専門知識を有する他の政府職員

2　小委員会は、両締約国政府の合意により、両締約国政府以外の関係団体の代表者であって、討議される問題に関連する必要な専門知識を有するものを招請することができる。

第三章　競争

第三・一条　目的

この章は、基本協定第十一・二条に規定する協力の実施に関する詳細及び手続を定めることを目的とする。

第三・二条　定義

この章の規定の適用上、

(a)　「競争当局」とは、

(i)　日本国については、公正取引委員会又はその後継機関をいう。

(ii)　モンゴル国については、公正競争・消費者保護庁又はその後継機関をいう。

(b)　「競争法」とは、

は、当該情報に対する要請を外交上の経路又は当該一方の締約国の法令に従って設けられたその他の経路を通じて当該一方の締約国政府に提出する。当該一方の締約国政府は、当該他方の締約国政府が示す合理的な期限内に迅速かつ好意的に回答を行うよう最善の努力を払う。

7　この章の他の規定にかかわらず、一方の締約国政府は、他方の締約国政府への情報の提供が自国の法令によって禁止されている場合又は自己の重要な利益と両立しないと認める場合には、当該提供を行うことを要しない。

第二・七条　税関手続及び貿易円滑化に関する小委員会

1　基本協定第四・八条の規定に基づき設置される税関手続及び貿易円滑化に関する小委員会（以下この条において「小委員会」という。）は、次の職員から成る。

(a)　共同議長として、日本国財務省又はその後継機関及びモンゴル国関税庁又はその後継機関の職員

(b)　日本国については、財務省及び外務省又はこれらの後継機関の職員並びに特例的な場合には討議される問題に関連する必要な専門知識を有する他の政府職員

(c)　モンゴル国については、関税庁又はその後継機関の職員及び特例的な場合には討議される問題に関連

する場合は、この限りでない。

2　一方の締約国政府は、情報の使用目的の制限に関し、自己が要請する保証を他方の締約国政府から得ることができない場合には、当該他方の締約国政府に提供する情報を限定することができる。

3　情報を要請する一方の締約国政府は、同様の要請が他方の締約国政府により行われたならば応ずることができない場合には、自己の要請においてその事実について注意を喚起する。当該要請に応ずるか否かについては、当該他方の締約国政府の裁量に委ねられる。

4　基本協定第四・七条及びこの章の規定に従って一方の締約国政府の税関当局から他方の締約国政府の税関当局に提供される情報については、当該他方の締約国の関税法令に基づく当該他方の締約国政府の税関当局の職務の遂行のためにのみ使用する。

5　基本協定第四・七条及びこの章の規定に従って提供される情報については、提供を受ける締約国政府は、裁判所又は裁判官が行う刑事手続において使用してはならない。

6　基本協定第四・七条及びこの章の規定に従って一方の締約国政府から他方の締約国政府に提供される情報を刑事手続において裁判所又は裁判官に提示することが必要とされる場合には、当該他方の締約国政府理手法の使用及び危険度に応じた管理手法に関する技術の向上を促進するよう努める。

3　両締約国政府の税関当局は、危険度に応じた管理手法に関する技術その他の取締りのための技術に関して最良の慣行を共有する。

第二・四条　不正取引への対応

1　両締約国政府の税関当局は、物品の不正取引への対応の分野において協力する。

2　両締約国政府は、物品の不正取引への対応の分野において、関税協力理事会の下での地域的な協力を促進するよう努める。

第二・五条　知的財産権

両締約国政府の税関当局は、知的財産権を侵害する疑いのある物品の輸入及び輸出への対応の分野において協力するよう努める。

第二・六条　情報の交換

1　一方の締約国政府は、他方の締約国政府が基本協定第四・七条及びこの章の規定に従って秘密のものとして提供するあらゆる情報の秘密性を保持する。ただし、当該他方の締約国政府が当該情報の開示に同意

1　両締約国政府は、関税法令の適正な適用を確保するため、並びに関税法令の違反及びその未遂を防止し、調査し、及び抑止するため、両締約国政府の税関当局を通じて相互に支援するよう努める。

2　両締約国政府は、必要かつ適当な場合には、両締約国政府の税関当局を通じて、研究、開発及び試験であって、新たな税関手続並びに取締りのための新たな装置及び技術に関するもの、税関職員の訓練活動並びに税関当局間の人的交流の分野において協力するよう努める。

第二・二条　情報通信技術

両締約国政府の税関当局は、その税関手続を改善することを目的として、その税関手続における情報通信技術の利用を促進するために協同の努力を払う（最良の慣行を共有することを含む。）。

第二・三条　危険度に応じた管理手法

1　両締約国間で取引される物品の通関を容易にするため、両締約国政府の税関当局は、危険度の高い物品の検査活動に集中することができる危険度に応じた管理手法の制度であって、危険度の低い物品の通関及び移動を簡素化するものを維持する。

2　両締約国政府は、セミナー、研修課程その他の措置を通じて、両締約国政府における危険度に応じた管

前文

日本国政府及びモンゴル国政府は、

経済上の連携に関する日本国とモンゴル国との間の協定（以下「基本協定」という。）第一・十二条の規定に従って、

次のとおり協定した。

第一章　総則

第一・一条　定義

この取極の適用上、

(a)　「両締約国」とは、日本国及びモンゴル国をいい、「締約国」とは、日本国又はモンゴル国をいう。

(b)　「両締約国政府」とは、日本国政府及びモンゴル国政府をいい、「締約国政府」とは、日本国政府又はモンゴル国政府をいう。

第二章　税関手続及び貿易円滑化

第二・一条　協力

第五・十四条　情報通信技術

第六章　最終規定

第六・一条　実施

第六・二条　目次及び見出し

第六・三条　改正

第六・四条　効力発生

第六・五条　紛争解決

第五・二条　製造業（基本協定第六章に規定する強制規格、任意規格及び適合性評価手続に関連する事項を含む。）

第五・三条　中小企業

第五・四条　貿易及び投資

第五・五条　公共基盤、建設及び都市開発

第五・六条　科学技術及び知的財産

第五・七条　金融サービス

第五・八条　教育及び人材養成

第五・九条　観光

第五・十条　環境

第五・十一条　鉱業及びエネルギー

第五・十二条　保健

第五・十三条　競争

経済上の連携に関する日本国とモンゴル国との間の協定第一・十二条の規定に基づく日本国政府とモンゴル国政府との間の実施取極

目次

３　正文の間に相違がある場合には、英語の本文による。

以上の証拠として、下名は、各自の政府から正当に委任を受けてこの協定に署名した。

二千十五年二月十日に東京で、日本語、モンゴル語及び英語により本書二通を作成した。

日本国のために

安倍晋三

モンゴル国のために

チメド・サイハンビレグ

とにより、この協定を終了させることができる。

第十七・六条　正文

1　この協定は、日本語、モンゴル語及び英語をひとしく正文とする。

2　1の規定にかかわらず、

(a)(i)　附属書一第二編は、ひとしく正文である日本語及び英語により作成される。

(ii)　附属書一第三編は、ひとしく正文であるモンゴル語及び英語により作成される。

(b)(i)　附属書六第一編A及び第二編は、ひとしく正文である日本語及び英語により作成される。

(ii)　附属書六第一編Bは、ひとしく正文であるモンゴル語及び英語により作成される。

(c)(i)　附属書七第一編は、ひとしく正文である日本語及び英語により作成される。

(ii)　附属書七第二編は、ひとしく正文であるモンゴル語及び英語により作成される。

(d)(i)　附属書八第一編及び附属書九第一編は、ひとしく正文である日本語及び英語により作成される。

(ii)　附属書八第二編及び附属書九第二編は、ひとしく正文であるモンゴル語及び英語により作成される。

府が交換することにより、両締約国が合意した日に効力を生ずる。

3　2の規定にかかわらず、次に掲げるもののみについての改正は、外交上の公文を両締約国政府が交換することにより行うことができる。

(a)　附属書一（ただし、統一システムの改正に伴う改正であって、附属書一の規定に従って一方の締約国により他方の締約国の原産品に適用される関税率の変更を伴わないものに限る。）

(b)　附属書二

(c)　附属書三

第十七・四条　効力発生

この協定は、この協定の効力発生に必要なそれぞれの国内法上の手続が完了した旨を通告する外交上の公文を両締約国政府が交換する日の後三十日目の日に効力を生ずる。この協定は、次条の規定に基づいて終了しない限り、効力を有する。

第十七・五条　終了

いずれの一方の締約国も、外交上の経路を通じて一年前に他方の締約国に対して書面による通告を行うこ約国が別段の合意をする場合を除くほか、仲裁裁判所のその他の費用は、両締約国が均等に負担する。

第十六・十四条　言語

全ての仲裁裁判手続並びに仲裁裁判所に提出される全ての文書及び情報は、英語によるものとする。

第十七章　最終規定

第十七・一条　目次及び見出し

この協定の目次並びにこの協定中の章、節及び条の見出しは、引用上の便宜のためにのみ付されたものであって、この協定の解釈に影響を及ぼすものではない。

第十七・二条　附属書及び注釈

この協定の附属書及びこの協定中の注釈は、この協定の不可分の一部を成す。

第十七・三条　改正

1　この協定は、両締約国間の書面による合意により改正することができる。

2　1に規定する改正は、両締約国によりそれぞれの国内法上の手続に従って承認されなければならず、その効力発生に必要なそれぞれの国内法上の手続が完了した旨を相互に通告する外交上の公文を両締約国政は、そのような要請を受領した日の後十日以内に協議を開始する。そのような要請が受領された日の後三十日以内に両締約国が問題を解決することができない場合には、被申立国は、その問題を仲裁裁判所に付託することができるものとし、当該仲裁裁判所は、当該条件が満たされているか否かを決定する。

7　この条の規定を適用するために設置される仲裁裁判所は、できる限り、裁定の対象となった問題を取り扱った仲裁裁判所の仲裁人により構成する。これが可能でない場合には、この条の規定を適用するために設置される仲裁裁判所の仲裁人は、第十六・七条2から4までの規定に従って任命する。両締約国が異なる期間について合意しない限り、この条の規定により設置される仲裁裁判所は、問題が付託された日の後六十日以内に決定を行う。当該決定は、最終的なものであり、かつ、両締約国を拘束する。

第十六・十二条　期間の変更

この章に定めるいかなる期間も、特定の紛争に関し、両締約国の相互の同意により変更することができる。

第十六・十三条　費用

各締約国は、自国が任命した仲裁人に係る費用及び自国が仲裁裁判手続に参加する費用を負担する。両締

4　申立国は、被申立国が1に規定する妥当な期間内に裁定を実施していないと認める場合において、被申立国が3(a)の規定に基づく協議を開始しなかったときは、三十日の予告をもって通告を行った後、被申立国に対するこの協定に基づく譲許その他の義務の適用を停止することができる。

5　3及び4に規定する譲許その他の義務の適用の停止は、次のことを条件とする。

(a)　当該譲許その他の義務の適用の停止に関連する紛争について協議又は仲裁裁判手続が進行している間においては、行わないこと。

(b)　一時的なものであり、かつ、相互に満足すべき解決が両締約国間で得られ、又は裁定が実施された時に解除されること。

(c)　裁定が実施されないことによる無効化又は侵害の程度と同等の程度に限定されること。

(d)　(c)に規定する無効化又は侵害に関連する分野と同一の分野に限定されること。もっとも、当該分野における譲許その他の義務の適用を停止することができず、又は効果的でない場合は、この限りでない。

6　被申立国は、申立国によるこの協定に基づく譲許その他の義務の適用の停止について3、4又は5に規定する条件が満たされていないと認める場合には、申立国に対して協議を要請することができる。申立国

1　両締約国が別段の合意をする場合を除くほか、被申立国は、第十六・八条及び第十六・九条の規定に従って下された仲裁裁判所の裁定を速やかに実施する。当該被申立国は、当該裁定を速やかに実施することができない場合には、当該裁定を妥当な期間内に実施する。

2　1に規定する妥当な期間は、適当な場合には仲裁裁判所の裁定に添付された当該裁定の実施の期間についての提案を考慮に入れ、両締約国の合意により決定される。両締約国が当該裁定が下された日の後四十五日以内に当該妥当な期間について合意することができない場合には、いずれの締約国も、その問題を仲裁裁判所に付託することができるものとし、当該仲裁裁判所は、当該妥当な期間を決定する。

3

(a)　被申立国は、1に規定する妥当な期間内に裁定を実施することができないと認める場合には、相互に満足すべき代償その他の代替措置の提供を図るため、当該妥当な期間の満了までに申立国と協議を開始する。

(b)　1に規定する妥当な期間の満了の日の後三十日以内に満足すべき代償その他の代替措置について合意されなかった場合には、申立国は、三十日の予告をもって通告を行った後、被申立国に対するこの協定に基づく譲許その他の義務の適用を停止することができる。

間内に両締約国に対して裁定案を提示することができないと認める場合には、両締約国の同意を得て、当該期間を延長することができる。ただし、いかなる場合にも、仲裁裁判所の設置の日から両締約国への裁定案の提示の日までの期間は、百五十日を超えないものとする。締約国は、裁定案が提示された日の後三十日以内に、仲裁裁判所に対して当該裁定案についての意見を書面により提出することができる。

8　仲裁裁判所は、裁定案が提示された日の後四十五日以内に裁定を両締約国に示す。

9　仲裁裁判所は、裁定その他の決定をコンセンサス方式によって行うよう努めるが、過半数による議決でこれを行うこともできる。

10　仲裁裁判所の裁定は、最終的なものであり、かつ、両締約国を拘束する。

第十六・十条　仲裁裁判手続の終了

両締約国は、両締約国に対して裁定が下される前であればいつでも、裁判長に対して共同で通報することにより、仲裁裁判手続の終了について合意することができる。この場合には、裁判長は、遅滞なく当該仲裁裁判手続を終了する。

第十六・十一条　裁定の実施

4　3の規定にかかわらず、いずれの一方の締約国も、紛争に関する見解について公に表明することができる。ただし、他方の締約国が秘密であると指定して仲裁裁判所に提出した情報又は意見書については、これを秘密のものとして取り扱う。一方の締約国が秘密のものとして情報又は意見書を提出した場合には、他方の締約国は、当該情報又は意見書について公開し得る秘密でない要約を提出するよう要請することができる。そのような要請を受けた当該一方の締約国は、当該要請を受け入れ、そのような要約を提出するか、又は理由を示すことを必要とすることなく当該要請を拒否することができる。

5　両締約国は、仲裁裁判手続における表明、陳述又は反論の場に出席する機会を与えられる。一方の締約国が仲裁裁判所に提出した情報又は意見書（裁定案の説明部分に関する意見及び仲裁裁判所の質問に対する回答を含む。）については、他方の締約国による利用を可能としなければならない。

6　仲裁裁判所の裁定の起草は、両締約国の参加なしに行うものとする。

7　仲裁裁判所は、両締約国が裁定案（説明部分並びに仲裁裁判所の認定及び結論から成る。）を検討することができるようにするため、その設置の日の後百二十日以内に、又は緊急の場合（腐敗しやすい物品に関する場合等）には六十日以内に、裁定案を提示する。仲裁裁判所は、当該百二十日又は当該六十日の期

３　仲裁裁判所は、いかなる関係者に対しても情報の提供を要請することができるものとし、また、問題の一定の側面についての意見を得るために専門家と協議することができる。仲裁裁判所は、いずれかの締約国が提起した科学上又は技術上の事項に関する事実に係る問題については、専門家に対して意見書の提出を要請することができる。

４　仲裁裁判所が３の規定により入手した情報については、両締約国による利用を可能としなければならない。

第十六・九条　仲裁裁判手続

１　仲裁裁判は、非公開とする。両締約国は、仲裁裁判所により出席するよう招請された場合に限り、その会合に出席する。

２　仲裁裁判手続の場所は、両締約国の合意により決定されるものとし、また、そのような決定が行われない場合には、仲裁裁判手続の第一回会合は被申立国の首都において行い、その後は両締約国において交互に行うものとする。

３　仲裁裁判所の評議及び仲裁裁判所に提出された文書は、秘密のものとして取り扱う。

第十六・八条　仲裁裁判所の任務

1　前二条の規定により設置される仲裁裁判所は、次のことを任務とする。

(a)　自己に付託された問題の客観的な評価（問題の事実関係、この協定の適用の可能性及びこの協定との適合性に関するものを含む。）を行うこと。

(b)　両締約国と定期的に協議を行うこと（当該協議の機会は、両締約国に均等に与えるものとする。）及び両締約国が相互に満足すべき解決を図るための十分な機会を与えること。

(c)　この協定及び適用可能な国際法の規則に従って裁定を下すこと。

(d)　裁定に法及び事実に関する認定並びに当該認定の理由を含めること。

(e)　締約国が要請する場合には、第十六・十一条の規定との関連において両締約国が考慮する裁定の実施方法（裁定の実施の期間を含む。）についての提案を裁定に添付すること。

2　仲裁裁判所は、必要かつ適当と認める関係情報の提供を両締約国に要請することができる。仲裁裁判所が必要かつ適当と認める情報の提供を要請する場合には、両締約国は、迅速かつ十分にこれに応ずるものとする。

人は、いずれかの締約国の国民であってはならず、いずれかの締約国に日常の住居を有してはならず、いずれかの締約国により雇用されてはならず、及びいかなる資格においても対象となる紛争を取り扱ったことがあってはならない。

3　両締約国は、仲裁裁判所の設置の要請が受領された日の後四十五日以内に、2の規定に従って提案した候補者を考慮して、第三の仲裁人を合意により任命するよう努める。

4　いずれかの締約国が2の規定により一人の仲裁人を任命しなかった場合又は両締約国が3の規定により第三の仲裁人について合意することができない場合には、いまだ任命されていない一人又は二人以上の仲裁人は、十日以内に、2の規定により提案された候補者の中からくじ引で選ばれる。

5　仲裁裁判所の設置の日は、裁判長が任命された日とする。

6　この条の規定により任命された仲裁人が辞任し、死亡し、又は職務を行うことができなくなった場合には、後任の仲裁人を最初の仲裁人の任命に係る規定と同様の方法で任命する。後任の仲裁人は、最初の仲裁人が有する全ての権限及び任務を有するものとする。仲裁裁判所が行う検討は、後任の仲裁人が任命される時まで停止されるものとする。

には二十日以内に、被申立国が第十六・四条の規定による協議を開始しない場合

(b) 協議の要請が受領された日の後六十日以内に、又は緊急の場合（腐敗しやすい物品に関する場合等）には三十日以内に、両締約国が第十六・四条の規定による協議により紛争を解決することができない場合

2 この条の規定による仲裁裁判所の設置の要請には、次の事項を含む当該要請の理由を明記する。

(a) 違反があったとされるこの協定の規定その他適用可能な国際法の関連する規定を含む申立ての法的根拠

(b) 事実に係る根拠

第十六・七条　仲裁裁判所の構成

1 仲裁裁判所は、三人の仲裁人から成るものとし、当該仲裁人は、適切な技術的又は法的知見を有するべきである。

2 各締約国は、仲裁裁判所の設置の要請が受領された日の後三十日以内に一人の仲裁人を任命し（自国民を任命することができる。）、及び裁判長となる第三の仲裁人の候補者を三人まで提案する。第三の仲裁

1　いずれの締約国も、あっせん、調停又は仲介をいつでも要請することができる。いずれの手続も、両締約国の合意により、いつでも開始することができるものとし、また、いずれかの締約国の要請により、いつでも終了することができる。

2　両締約国が合意する場合には、あっせん、調停又は仲介は、この章に定める仲裁裁判の進行中においても、継続することができる。

3　あっせん、調停又は仲介に係る手続及びこれらの手続において両締約国がとる立場は、秘密とされ、かつ、その後の手続においていずれの締約国の権利も害するものではない。

第十六・六条　仲裁裁判所の設置

1　申立国は、次のいずれかの場合には、被申立国に対して書面により仲裁裁判所の設置を要請することができる。ただし、申立国が、被申立国がこの協定に基づく義務の履行を怠った結果又は当該義務に反する措置をとった結果、この協定に基づいて直接又は間接に自国に与えられた利益が無効にされ、又は侵害されていると認めることを条件とする。

(a)　協議の要請が受領された日の後四十日以内に、又は緊急の場合（腐敗しやすい物品に関する場合等）

4　両締約国は、この条の規定による協議を通じて、問題についての相互に満足すべき解決に達するよう、全ての努力を払うものとする。両締約国は、当該協議が行われている間に、問題の十分な検討を可能とする十分な情報を相互に提供する。

5　両締約国は、この条の規定に基づく協議が行われている間、両締約国の関係する機関及び団体の職員であって協議の対象となる問題についての専門知識を有するものを関与させることを可能とするよう努める。

6　この条の規定に基づく協議は、秘密とされ、かつ、その後の手続においていずれの締約国の権利も害するものではない。

7　この条の規定に基づく協議は、両締約国の合意に基づき、対面して又は両締約国に利用可能なあらゆる技術的手段によって行うことができる。両締約国が協議を対面して行うことを合意する場合には、協議は両締約国が合意する場所において行われるものとし、場所についての合意がない場合には、被申立国の首都において行うものとする。

第十六・五条　あっせん、調停又は仲介

決するための場を選択することができる。

2　1の規定にかかわらず、申立国は、特定の紛争に関し、この章又は両締約国が締結している他の国際協定の規定に基づいて仲裁裁判所（世界貿易機関設立協定附属書二紛争解決に係る規則及び手続に関する了解の規定に基づく小委員会を含む。）の設置を要請した場合には、当該特定の紛争に関し選択されなかった仲裁裁判所又は小委員会の手続を利用してはならない。

第十六・四条　協議

1　一方の締約国は、この協定の解釈又は適用に関するいかなる問題についても、他方の締約国に対して書面により協議を要請することができる。

2　1に規定する協議の要請においては、申立国は、当該要請の理由（問題となっている措置の特定並びに申立てに関する法的根拠及び事実に係る根拠の記載を含む。）を示すものとする。

3　被申立国は、要請に書面により速やかに回答するものとし、要請を受領した日の後四十日以内に申立国との協議を誠実に開始する。緊急の場合（腐敗しやすい物品に関する場合等）には、被申立国は、要請を受領した日の後二十日以内に協議を開始する。

第十五・五条　次章の規定の不適用

次章の規定は、この章の規定については、適用しない。

第十六章　紛争解決

第十六・一条　適用範囲

この協定に別段の定めがある場合を除くほか、この章に定める紛争解決手続は、この協定の解釈又は適用から生ずる両締約国間の紛争の回避及び解決について適用する。

第十六・二条　一般原則

両締約国は、この協定の解釈及び適用について合意に達するよう常に努める。両締約国は、この協定の解釈又は適用に関するいかなる問題についても迅速かつ相互に満足すべき解決を得るために、協力、協議その他の手段を通じあらゆる努力を払う。

第十六・三条　紛争解決の場の選択

1　この章のいかなる規定も、両締約国が締結している他の国際協定（世界貿易機関設立協定を含む。）により利用可能な紛争解決手続を利用する両締約国の権利を害するものではない。申立国は、当該紛争を解

(e) この協定の規定に基づいて設置される他の小委員会が提出した協力に関する提案について討議すること。

(f) 適当な場合には、合同委員会に対し、この章の規定に基づく協力活動について勧告を行うこと。

(g) 合同委員会に対し、この章の規定の実施（両締約国がとるべき措置を含む。）に関する小委員会の所見及び討議の結果を報告すること。

(h) 合同委員会が委任するその他の任務を遂行すること。

3 小委員会は、適当な場合には、この協定の規定に基づく協力活動の適時の、効果的かつ効率的な実施を確保するため、政府開発援助その他の協力のための制度に関する両締約国の既存の協議の枠組みを認め、そのような枠組みとの間で情報を共有する。

4 小委員会は、両締約国政府の代表者から成る。小委員会は、両締約国政府以外の関係団体の代表者であって、討議される問題に関連する必要な専門知識を有するものを招請することができる。

5 小委員会は、両締約国が合意する時期及び場所において又は手段によって会合を開催する。小委員会は、この協定の効力発生の日の後一年以内に、第一回会合を開催するよう努める。

開始する。

2　両締約国は、それぞれ自国の法令に従い、この章の規定に基づく協力の実施のために、必要な資金その他の資源を利用可能なものとするよう努める。

3　この章の規定に基づく協力のための費用は、資金及び資源の効率的かつ効果的な利用により、両締約国が相互に合意する方法で負担する。

第十五・四条　協力に関する小委員会

1　この章の規定を効果的に実施し、及び運用するため、両締約国は、ここに協力に関する小委員会（以下この条において「小委員会」という。）を設置する。

2　小委員会は、次のことを任務とする。

(a)　この章の規定の効果的な実施及び運用について検討及び監視を行うこと。

(b)　第十五・一条に規定する各分野における協力に関する情報を交換すること。

(c)　両締約国間の更なる協力の方法を特定すること。

(d)　この章の規定に関連する問題について討議すること。

(h) 教育及び人材養成

(i) 観光

(j) 環境

(k) 鉱業及びエネルギー

(l) 保健

(m) 競争

(n) 情報通信技術

(o) 両締約国政府が相互に合意するその他の分野

第十五・二条　協力の範囲及び形態

この章の規定に基づく協力の範囲及び形態については、実施取極で定める。

第十五・三条　協力の費用

1 両締約国は、第十五・一条に規定する分野における潜在的な協力活動を検討し、及びこの章の規定に基づく協力活動の適時の、効率的かつ効果的な実施を確保するため、この協定の効力発生の日の後、討議を

第十五・一条　基本原則

両締約国は、それぞれ自国の法令に従い、両締約国間の物品及びサービスの貿易並びに投資を一層自由化し、及び円滑化し、並びに両締約国の国民の福祉及び持続可能な開発を促進することを目的として、この協定に基づく協力であって相互の利益に資するものを促進する。このため、両締約国は、次の分野において、両締約国政府間の協力を一層強化し、並びに両締約国の関係団体であって、その一方又は双方が両締約国政府以外の団体であるものの間の相互協力を奨励し、及び円滑にする。

(a)　農業、林業及び漁業（第五章に規定する衛生植物検疫措置に関連する事項を含む。）

(b)　製造業（第六章に規定する強制規格、任意規格及び適合性評価手続に関連する事項を含む。）

(c)　中小企業

(d)　貿易及び投資

(e)　公共基盤、建設及び都市開発

(f)　科学技術及び知的財産

(g)　金融サービス

(iv) 適当な場合には、当該他の小委員会に対し関連する問題を送付すること。

(g) 合同委員会に対し、(c)に規定する所見及び勧告を速やかに報告すること。

(h) 合同委員会が委任するその他の任務を遂行すること。

3 小委員会は、両締約国政府の代表者（小委員会において取り組まれる問題を所管する関係省庁の職員を含む。）から成る。小委員会は、両締約国政府以外の関係団体の代表者であって、小委員会において取り組まれる問題に関連する必要な専門知識を有するものを招請することができる。

4 小委員会は、両締約国が合意する時期及び場所において又は手段によって会合を開催する。

第十四・三条　連絡事務所

1 各締約国は、この章の目的のため、連絡事務所を指定し、及び維持する。

2 連絡事務所の任務その他の詳細については、実施取極で定める。

第十四・四条　第十六章の規定の不適用

第十六章の規定は、この章の規定については、適用しない。

第十五章　協力

(a) 次条の規定に従って各締約国により指定されるビジネス環境の整備に関する連絡事務所（以下この章において「連絡事務所」という。）が報告する所見を検討すること。

(b) 自己の発意により、又は連絡事務所が報告する所見に基づき、ビジネス環境に関連する問題に取り組み、及び速やかに当該問題を解決するための方法を追求すること。

(c) 両締約国に対して、小委員会の所見を報告し、及び勧告（両締約国がとるべき措置に関するものを含む。）を行うこと。

(d) 適当な場合には、(c)に規定する勧告に関し両締約国がとった措置について検討すること。

(e) (c)に規定する勧告及び(d)に規定する検討の結果を適当な方法で公に利用可能なものとすること。

(f) 作業の不必要な重複を避けるため、この協定に基づいて設置する他の小委員会と適当な方法で協力すること。その協力の形態には、次のことを含めることができる。

(i) 検討の結果を当該他の小委員会に報告すること。

(ii) 当該他の小委員会から意見を求めること。

(iii) 当該他の小委員会の構成員を小委員会に招請すること。

(e) 合同委員会が委任するその他の任務を遂行すること。

3 小委員会は、両締約国政府の代表者から成る。

4 小委員会は、両締約国が合意する時期及び場所において又は手段によって会合を開催する。

第十四章 ビジネス環境の整備

第十四・一条 基本原則

1 一方の締約国は、自国の法令に従い、自国において事業活動を遂行する他方の締約国の者のためのビジネス環境を一層整備するために適切な措置をとる。

2 両締約国は、それぞれ自国の法令に従い、それぞれの締約国におけるビジネス環境を一層整備するための協力を促進する。

第十四・二条 ビジネス環境の整備に関する小委員会

1 この章の規定を効果的に実施し、及び運用するため、両締約国は、ここにビジネス環境の整備に関する小委員会（以下この章において「小委員会」という。）を設置する。

2 小委員会は、次のことを任務とする。

第十三・四条　無差別待遇に関する交渉

一方の締約国は、この協定の効力発生の日の後、自国の政府調達市場へのアクセスに関する利益又は政府調達に関する措置についての有利な待遇を第三国に与える場合には、他方の締約国の要請に応じ、当該利益又は待遇を相互主義に基づき当該他方の締約国に対しても与えることを目的として当該他方の締約国との間で交渉するための機会を十分に与える。

第十三・五条　政府調達に関する小委員会

1　両締約国は、この章の規定を効果的に実施し、及び運用するため、ここに政府調達に関する小委員会（以下この条において「小委員会」という。）を設置する。

2　小委員会は、次のことを任務とする。

(a)　この章の規定の実施及び運用について検討及び監視を行うこと。

(b)　各締約国の政府調達市場に関する利用可能な情報を分析すること。

(c)　電子調達及び人材養成について協力すること。

(d)　合同委員会に対して小委員会の所見を報告すること。

各締約国は、成長及び雇用を促進するため生産及び貿易の拡大を推進する上で政府調達が有する重要性を認識し、自国の法令に従い、政府調達に関する措置の透明性を確保する。また、両締約国は、両締約国の開発上、資金上及び貿易上の要請を考慮する必要性を認める。各締約国は、政府調達に関する措置の公正かつ効果的な実施を確保する。

第十三・二条　情報の交換

両締約国は、それぞれ自国の法令に従い、適時にかつ可能な限り英語により、政府調達に関する自国の法令、政策及び慣行について並びに現行の政府調達制度の改革について、情報の交換を中央政府の間で行う。

第十三・三条　追加的な交渉

両締約国は、モンゴル国が世界貿易機関設立協定附属書四政府調達に関する協定（以下この条において「政府調達協定」という。）の締約国となる意思を表明したときに、政府調達に関する包括的な章を実現することを目的として、この章の規定を見直すための交渉を開始する。

注釈　この条の規定の適用上、政府調達協定が改正され、又は他の協定によって代替される場合には、「政府調達協定」とは、当該改正された政府調達協定又は当該他の協定をいうものとする。

(a) この章の規定の実施及び運用について検討及び監視を行うこと。

(b) この章の規定に従い、知的財産の保護及び知的財産権の行使を強化し、並びに知的財産に関する制度の効率的なかつ透明性のある運用を促進するため、知的財産に関連するあらゆる問題について討議すること。

(c) 合同委員会に対して小委員会の所見及び討議の結果を報告すること。

(d) 合同委員会が委任するその他の任務を遂行すること。

3 小委員会は、両締約国政府の代表者から成る。

4 小委員会は、両締約国が合意する時期及び場所において又は手段によって会合を開催する。

第十二・十九条　安全保障のための例外

この章の規定の適用上、貿易関連知的所有権協定第七十三条の規定は、必要な変更を加えた上で、この協定に組み込まれ、この協定の一部を成す。

第十三章　政府調達

第十三・一条　調達に関する原則

1　各締約国は、貿易関連知的所有権協定第六十一条の規定に従い、少なくとも故意による商業的規模の商標の不正使用及び著作物の違法な複製について適用される刑事上の手続及び刑罰を定める。

2　各締約国は、1に定める犯罪に関し、自国の権限のある当局が、自国の法令に従い、全ての侵害物品の没収又は廃棄を命ずる権限を有することについて定める。

第十二・十七条　デジタル環境における権利行使

各締約国の権利行使の手続は、デジタル通信網における著作権又は関連する権利の侵害（侵害の目的のため広範な頒布の手段を不法に使用することを含むことができる。）について適用する。このような手続は、電子商取引を含む正当な活動の新たな障害となることを回避し、かつ、表現の自由、公正な手続、プライバシーその他の基本原則が当該各締約国の法令に従って維持されるような態様で実施される。

第十二・十八条　知的財産に関する小委員会

1　両締約国は、この章の規定を効果的に実施し、及び運用するため、ここに知的財産に関する小委員会（以下この条において「小委員会」という。）を設置する。

2　小委員会は、次のことを任務とする。

て「侵害の疑いのある物品」という。）の解放を停止するために職権により行動することができる手続

(b) 権利者が自国の権限のある当局に対し侵害の疑いのある物品の解放を停止するよう申し立てることができる手続

2 各締約国は、1に定める手続の開始後合理的な期間内に自国の権限のある当局が侵害の疑いのある物品によって商標権又は著作権及び関連する権利が侵害されているか否かを認定することができる手続を採用し、又は維持する。

3 1の規定に基づき輸入貨物について解放を停止する場合には、輸入者及び権利者は、その停止について速やかに通知を受けるものとし、侵害の疑いのある物品に係る利用可能な全ての情報を提供される。

第十二・十五条 民事上の救済に係る権利行使

各締約国は、知的財産の権利者が、侵害活動を行っていることを知っていたか又は知ることができる合理的な理由を有していた侵害者に対し、知的財産権の侵害によって当該権利者が被った損害を補塡するために適当な賠償を請求する権利を有することを確保する。

第十二・十六条 刑事上の制裁に係る権利行使

3　この条の規定の適用上、「パリ条約」とは、千九百年十二月十四日にブラッセルで、千九百十一年六月二日にワシントンで、千九百二十五年十一月六日にハーグで、千九百三十四年六月二日にロンドンで、千九百五十八年十月三十一日にリスボンで及び千九百六十七年七月十四日にストックホルムで改正され、並びに千九百七十九年九月二十八日に修正された工業所有権の保護に関する千八百八十三年三月二十日のパリ条約をいう。

第十二・十三条　開示されていない情報の保護

各締約国は、貿易関連知的所有権協定第三十九条2の規定に従い、自国の法令において、開示されていない情報を十分かつ効果的に保護すること（開示されていない情報の保護期間であって私契約に規定するものを制限する措置又は開示されていない情報の開示を正当な理由なく強要する措置をとらないことを含む。）を確保する。

第十二・十四条　国境措置に係る権利行使

1　各締約国は、輸入貨物に関し、次の手続を採用し、又は維持する。

(a)　自国の税関当局が商標権又は著作権及び関連する権利を侵害する疑いのある物品（以下この条におい

２　各締約国は、放送機関に対し、当該放送機関の放送についてその同意なく行われる次に掲げる行為を禁止する権利を与える。

(a)　放送の再放送

(b)　放送の固定

(c)　放送の固定物の複製

３　各締約国は、自国の法令に従い、自国における著作権及び関連する権利を集中管理する団体が行う活動を促進するための適切な措置をとる。

第十二・十一条　地理的表示

各締約国は、自国の法令及び貿易関連知的所有権協定に従い、地理的表示の十分かつ効果的な保護を確保する。

第十二・十二条　不正競争

１　各締約国は、パリ条約第十条の二の規定に従い、不正競争行為からの効果的な保護を与える。

２　各締約国は、サービスについてパリ条約第十条の二の規定を準用することを確保する。

識されている商標と同一又は類似の商標が、不正な意図、特に、不正な利益を得る意図若しくは当該広く認識されている商標の所有者に損害を与える意図で使用される場合又はそのような使用の結果として混同を生じさせるおそれがある場合には、当該同一又は類似の商標の登録を拒絶し、又は取り消す。

注釈　各締約国は、商標が広く認識されている商標であるか否かを自国の法令に従って決定することができる。

2　各締約国は、合理的な理由があること及び手続上の要件に従うことを条件として、出願人が権限のある当局に対しその商標登録出願の審査を速やかに行うよう求める要請を提出することができることを確保する。このような要請が提出された場合において、適当なときは、権限のある当局は、当該商標登録出願の審査を速やかに行う。

第十二・十条　著作権及び関連する権利

1　各締約国は、著作者、実演家及びレコード製作者に対し、それぞれ、その著作物、レコードに固定された実演及びレコードについて、有線又は無線の方法により、公衆のそれぞれが選択する場所及び時期において利用が可能となるような状態に置くことを許諾する権利を付与する。

両締約国は、知的財産の保護についての啓発（知的財産の使用及び知的財産権の行使についての教育及び普及の計画を含む。）を促進するための必要な措置をとる。

第十二・七条　特許

1　各締約国は、特許出願に係る保護の対象がコンピュータ・プログラムに関連することのみを理由として、当該特許出願が拒絶されないことを確保する。もっとも、この条の規定は、自国の法令に従い、コンピュータ・プログラム自体を特許の対象から除外するか否かについての各締約国の自主性に影響を及ぼすものではない。

2　各締約国は、特許出願人が、自国の法令に定める期限内に、自己の発意により、二以上の発明を含む特許出願を一定の数の特許出願に分割することができることを確保する。

第十二・八条　意匠

各締約国は、物品の全体及び適当なときは部分について、意匠の十分かつ効果的な保護を与える。

第十二・九条　商標

1　各締約国は、いずれかの締約国においてその商標の所有者の商品又はサービスを示すものとして広く認

(ii) 登録の取消し又は無効を求めること。

第十二・五条 透明性

各締約国は、自国の知的財産に関する制度の運用における透明性を一層促進するため、自国の法令に従って可能な範囲において、次のことを行うために利用し得る適切な措置をとる。

(a) 少なくとも次の事項に関する情報を公開し、及びこれらに関する一件書類に含まれている関連する情報を要請に応じて少なくとも利害関係者に提供すること。

(i) 特許を付与する意図又は特許の出願及び付与

(ii) 実用新案の登録

(iii) 意匠権を付与する意図又は意匠の登録

(iv) 商標の登録又は登録出願

(b) 知的財産権の効果的な行使を確保するための自国の活動に関する情報その他の自国の知的財産に関する制度に係る情報について、公衆が利用することができるようにすること。

第十二・六条 知的財産の保護についての啓発の促進

５　各締約国は、弁理士制度又は知的財産権登録認定代理人制度を改善するよう努める。

６　各締約国は、知的財産権の取得について権利が登録され、又は付与される必要がある場合には、権利の取得のための実体的な条件が満たされていることを条件として、保護期間が不当に短縮されないように、権利の登録又は付与のための手続を合理的な期間内に行うことを確保する。この場合において、知的財産権の登録又は付与のための出願が、国内出願として行われるか、又は適用可能な国際協定に基づく国際出願として行われるかについては、問わないものとする。

７　各締約国は、次の事項を含む商標、意匠及び特許の登録のための制度を設ける。

(a)　出願人に対し、書面により（電磁的手段によることができる。）出願の拒絶の決定を理由を付して通知すること。

(b)　出願人が行政機関による拒絶に対して不服を申し立てる機会

(c)　出願人が行政機関による最終的な拒絶について司法上の審査を求める機会

(d)　利害関係者が次のことを行う機会（自国の法令に規定する場合に限る。）

(i)　出願又は登録に対して異議を申し立てること。

２　いずれの締約国も、特許、実用新案、意匠又は商標に関する出願手続その他の行政上の手続において、自国の権限のある当局に提出される書類（願書、優先権の主張の基礎となる先の出願の当該権限のある当局が受理する言語への翻訳文、委任状及び譲渡証書を含む。）上の署名その他書類を提出した者を特定する方法についての真正の証明を要求してはならない。

３　２の規定にかかわらず、各締約国は、次のものを要求することができる。

(a)　署名その他書類を提出した者を特定する方法が特許、実用新案登録、意匠登録又は商標登録の放棄に関するものである場合において、自国の法令が署名その他書類を提出した者を特定する方法についての真正の証明を要求する旨を定めるときは、その証明

(b)　自国の権限のある当局に提出された書類上の署名その他書類を提出した者を特定する方法が真正であることについて合理的な疑いがある場合には、証拠の提出（当該権限のある当局は、当該者に対して証拠の提出を要求することを通知するときは、その通知に証拠の提出を要求する理由を明記する。）

４　いずれの締約国も、出願日を認めるための条件として、委任状の提出が出願と同時に完了することを要求してはならない。

第十二・二条　定義

この章に規定する「知的財産」とは、貿易関連知的所有権協定に基づく全ての種類の知的財産をいう。

第十二・三条　内国民待遇

一方の締約国は、貿易関連知的所有権協定第三条及び第五条の規定に従い、知的財産の保護に関し、自国民に与える待遇よりも不利でない待遇を他方の締約国の国民に与える。

注釈　この条の規定の適用上、

(a)　「国民」とは、貿易関連知的所有権協定におけるものと同一の意味を有するものとする。

(b)　「保護」には、知的財産権の取得可能性、取得、範囲、維持及び行使に影響を及ぼす事項並びにこの章において特に取り扱われる知的財産権の使用に影響を及ぼす事項を含む。

(c)　「知的財産の保護」には、第十二・十二条に規定する不正競争の防止を含む。

第十二・四条　手続事項

1　各締約国は、知的財産に関する制度の効率的な運用を確保するため、知的財産権に関する自国の行政上の手続を改善するための適切な措置をとる。

第十一・五条　透明性

各締約国は、自国の競争法令及び競争政策の実施の透明性を促進する。

第十一・六条　第一・八条２及び第十六章の規定の不適用

第一・八条２及び第十六章の規定は、この章の規定については、適用しない。

第十二章　知的財産

第十二・一条　一般規定

１　両締約国は、この章の規定及び両締約国が締結している知的財産に関する国際協定に従い、知的財産の十分にして効果的かつ無差別な保護を与え、及び確保し、並びに知的財産権の侵害への対処として知的財産権を行使するための措置をとる。

２　両締約国は、また、知的財産に関する制度の運用における効率性及び透明性を促進する。

３　この章のいかなる規定も、貿易関連知的所有権協定その他の両締約国が締結している知的財産に関する国際協定に基づいて両締約国が有する現行の権利を害するものではなく、また、それらの協定に従って両締約国が負う現行の義務を免れさせるものではない。

を円滑にするため、反競争的行為に対して適当と認める措置をとる。

2 この章の規定の適用上、「反競争的行為」とは、それぞれの締約国の競争法令に基づき罰則又は排除に係る措置の対象とされる行動又は取引をいう。

第十一・二条 反競争的行為の規制に関する協力

1 両締約国は、それぞれ自国の法令に従い、かつ、自己の利用可能な資源の範囲内で、反競争的行為の規制に関して相互に協力し、及び支援する。

2 この条の規定に基づく協力の実施に関する詳細及び手続については、実施取極で定める。

第十一・三条 無差別待遇

各締約国は、同様の状況にある者の間で国籍を理由とした差別を行うことなく、自国の競争法令を適用する。

第十一・四条 手続の公正な実施

各締約国は、反競争的行為を規制するため、自国の関係法令に従い、行政上及び司法上の手続を公正な方法で実施する。

１　二国間投資協定第十七条２の規定にかかわらず、二国間投資協定は、この協定の効力発生の日に終了する。

２　両締約国は、二国間投資協定の終了の日の前に取得された投資財産及び収益に関しては、二国間投資協定第十七条３の規定に従い、二国間投資協定第一条から第十六条までの規定が二国間投資協定の終了の日から更に十五年の期間引き続き効力を有することを確認する。

３　２の規定の適用上、この協定のいかなる規定も、二国間投資協定の関連規定に基づく締約国の権利及び義務に影響を及ぼすものではない。

第十・二十条　有効期間及び終了

この協定の終了の日の前に取得された投資財産に関しては、この章の規定及びこの章に直接関係するこの協定の規定は、この協定の終了の日から更に十年の期間引き続き効力を有する。

第十一章　競争

第十一・一条　反競争的行為

１　各締約国は、自国の法令に従い、自国の市場の効率的な機能を通じて両締約国間の貿易及び投資の流れ

2　小委員会は、次のことを任務とする。

(a)　この章の規定の実施及び運用について検討及び監視を行うこと。

(b)　この章の規定に関連するあらゆる問題について情報を交換すること。

(c)　この章の規定に関連するあらゆる問題について討議すること。

(d)　合同委員会に対して小委員会の所見及び討議の結果を報告すること。

(e)　合同委員会が委任するその他の任務を遂行すること。

3　小委員会は、両締約国政府の代表者から成るものとする。

4　小委員会は、両締約国政府以外の関係団体の代表者であって討議される問題に関連する必要な専門知識を有するものを招請することができる。

5　小委員会は、両締約国が合意する時期及び場所において又は手段によって会合する。

6　この条の規定は、第十・五条、第十・六条又は第十・九条の規定が対象とする限りにおいて、租税に係る課税措置に関する事項について適用する。

第十・十九条　二国間投資協定との関係

反し、若しくは当該措置を阻害することとなるものを当該一方の締約国が採用し、又は維持する場合

2 一方の締約国は、他方の締約国の投資家であって当該他方の締約国の企業であるものが第三国の投資家によって所有され、又は支配されており、かつ、当該企業が当該他方の締約国の区域内において実質的な事業活動を行っていないときは、当該他方の締約国の投資家及びその投資財産に対し、この章の規定による利益を否認することができる。

第十・十七条　健康、安全及び環境に関する措置並びに労働基準

両締約国は、それぞれ自国の健康、安全及び環境に関する措置の緩和又は労働基準の引下げを通じて各締約国又は第三国の投資家による投資を奨励することを差し控える。各締約国は、自国の区域内における各締約国又は第三国の投資家による投資財産の設立、取得及び拡張を奨励する手段としてそのような措置又は基準の適用の免除その他の逸脱措置を行うべきではない。

第十・十八条　投資に関する小委員会

1 両締約国は、この章の規定を効果的に実施し、及び運用するため、ここに投資に関する小委員会（以下この条において「小委員会」という。）を設置する。

1　この章の他の規定にかかわらず、締約国は、信用秩序の維持のための金融サービスに関連する措置（投資家、預金者、保険契約者若しくは信託上の義務を金融サービスを提供する企業が負う者を保護し、又は金融システムの健全性及び安定性を確保するための措置を含む。）を採用し、又は維持することを妨げられない。

2　締約国が1の規定に基づいて採用し、又は維持する措置は、この章の規定に適合しない場合には、この章の規定に基づく当該締約国の義務を回避するための手段として用いてはならない。

第十・十六条　利益の否認

1　一方の締約国は、他方の締約国の投資家であって当該他方の締約国の企業であるものが第三国の投資家によって所有され、又は支配されており、かつ、次のいずれかの場合に該当するときは、当該他方の締約国の投資家及びその投資財産に対し、この章の規定による利益を否認することができる。

(a)　当該一方の締約国が当該第三国と外交関係を有していない場合

(b)　当該第三国に関する措置であって、当該他方の締約国の企業との取引を禁止するもの又は当該他方の締約国の企業若しくはその投資財産に対してこの章の規定による利益を与えることにより当該措置に違

それのある状況にある例外的な場合

2　1の制限的な措置は、次の全ての要件を満たすものとする。

(a)　内国民待遇及び最恵国待遇に基づいて適用されるものであること。

(b)　国際通貨基金協定に適合するものであること。

(c)　他方の締約国の商業上、経済上又は資金上の利益に対し不必要な損害を与えることを避けるものであること。

(d)　1に規定する状況に対処するために必要な限度を超えないものであること。

(e)　一時的なものであり、1に規定する状況が改善するに伴い漸進的に廃止されるものであること。

3　1の規定に基づいて課し、若しくは維持する制限又はその変更については、他方の締約国に対して速やかに通報する。

4　この条のいかなる規定も、国際通貨基金協定に基づく締約国の権利及び義務を変更するものと解してはならない。

第十・十五条　信用秩序の維持のための措置

ヨーク条約を含む。）に従って執行される。

21　いずれの一方の締約国も、他方の締約国及び当該一方の締約国の投資家が4の規定に従って仲裁に付託することに同意し、又は付託した投資紛争に関し、外交上の保護を与え、又は国家間の請求を行ってはならない。ただし、当該他方の締約国が当該投資紛争について下された裁定に従わなかった場合は、この限りでない。この21の規定の適用上、外交上の保護には、投資紛争の解決を容易にすることのみを目的とする非公式の外交交渉を含めない。

22　この条の規定は、第十・五条、第十・六条又は第十・九条の規定が対象とする限りにおいて、租税に係る課税措置に関する紛争について適用する。

第十・十四条　一時的なセーフガード措置

1　いずれの締約国も、次のいずれかの場合には、投資財産に関連する国境を越える資本取引並びに投資財産に関連する支払及び資金の移転に関する制限的な措置を採用し、又は維持することができる。

(a)　国際収支及び対外支払に関して重大な困難が生じている場合又は生ずるおそれのある場合

(b)　資金の移転が経済全般の運営、特に通貨及び外国為替政策に重大な困難をもたらし、又はもたらすお

(i) 損害賠償及び適当な利子

(ii) 原状回復。この場合の裁定においては、紛争締約国が原状回復に代えて損害賠償及び適当な利子を支払うことができることを定めるものとする。

仲裁裁判所は、この条及び適用される仲裁規則の規定に従い、費用及び弁護士の報酬についても裁定を下すことができる。

19 紛争締約国は、次に掲げる情報を除くほか、4の規定により設置される仲裁裁判所に提出され、又は当該仲裁裁判所が発する全ての文書（裁定を含む。）を時宜を失することなく公に利用可能なものにすることができる。

(a) 業務上の秘密の情報

(b) いずれかの締約国の関係法令により、特に秘密とされ、又は他の方法により開示から保護される情報

(c) 関連する仲裁規則に従って不開示としなければならない情報

20 仲裁裁判所の裁定は、最終的なものであり、かつ、紛争当事者を拘束する。当該裁定は、執行が求められている国における有効な裁定の執行に関する関係法令及び関連する国際法（ＩＣＳＩＤ条約及びニュー

はならない。

17 仲裁裁判所は、本案について決定する前に、当該仲裁裁判所の管轄権及び紛争投資家の請求の受理可能性に関する紛争締約国の異議について先決問題として取り扱い、及び、正当な理由があるときは、決定する。仲裁裁判所は、紛争締約国の異議について先決問題として決定するに当たり、正当な理由があるときは、主張を認められた一方の紛争当事者が異議の申立て又は異議に対する反論を行うに際して生じた合理的な費用及び弁護士の報酬を支払うよう命ずる裁定を下すことができる。仲裁裁判所は、そのような裁定が正当であるか否かを決定するに当たっては、紛争投資家の請求又は紛争締約国の異議に根拠がなかったか否かについて検討する。この検討を行う際、仲裁裁判所は、紛争当事者に対し意見を述べる合理的な機会を与える。

18 仲裁裁判所は、次の事項についてのみ裁定を下すことができる。

(a) 紛争締約国が、紛争投資家及びその投資財産に関し、この章の規定に基づく義務に違反したか否かに関する判断

(b) 違反があった場合には、次の(i)又は(ii)に規定する救済措置のいずれか一方又は双方

12　仲裁は、紛争当事者が別段の合意をする場合を除くほか、ニューヨーク条約を締結している国において行う。

13　４の規定により設置される仲裁裁判所は、この章の規定及びこの協定の関係する他の規定並びに関係する国際法の規則に従って、係争中の事案につき決定する。

14　紛争締約国は、他方の締約国に次のものを送付する。

(a)　仲裁に付託された投資紛争についての書面による通知（当該投資紛争が付託された日の後三十日以内に送付する。）

(b)　仲裁において提出された全ての主張書面の写し

15　紛争締約国でない締約国は、紛争当事者への書面による通知を行った場合には、この章の規定及びこの協定の関係する他の規定の解釈に関する問題につき仲裁裁判所に対して意見を提出することができる。

16　仲裁裁判所は、紛争投資家の権利を保全し、又は仲裁手続の進行を容易にするため、暫定的な保全措置（紛争当事者のいずれかが所持し、又は支配する証拠を保全するための命令を含む。）を命ずることができる。仲裁裁判所は、差押えを命じ、又は１(f)に規定する違反を構成するとされる措置の差止めを命じて

9　8の規定にかかわらず、4に規定する仲裁への投資紛争の付託は、紛争投資家が1(f)に規定する損失又は損害を被ったことを知った日又は知るべきであった最初の日のいずれか早い方の日から三年が経過した場合には、行うことができない。

10　4の規定により設置される仲裁裁判所は、紛争当事者が別段の合意をする場合を除くほか、紛争当事者それぞれが任命する各一人の仲裁人及び紛争当事者の合意により任命されて裁判長となる第三の仲裁人から成る三人の仲裁人により構成する。投資紛争が仲裁に付託された日から六十日以内に、紛争投資家又は紛争締約国が一人又は二人以上の仲裁人を任命しない場合には、紛争当事者のいずれも、11の規定の要件に従うことを条件として、4(a)又は(b)に規定する仲裁の場合には投資紛争解決国際センターの事務局長に対し、4(c)又は(d)に規定する仲裁の場合にはハーグの常設仲裁裁判所の事務総長に対し、いまだ任命されていない一人又は二人以上の仲裁人を任命するよう要請することができる。

11　第三の仲裁人は、紛争当事者が別段の合意をする場合を除くほか、いずれかの締約国の国民であってはならず、いずれかの締約国に日常の住居を有してはならず、紛争当事者のいずれによっても雇用されてはならず、及びいかなる資格においても対象となる投資紛争を取り扱ったことがあってはならない。

(a) 当該紛争投資家の氏名又は名称及び住所

(b) 当該紛争締約国の問題となる特定の措置並びに問題の所在を明確にする上で十分な当該投資紛争に関する事実に係る根拠及び法的根拠の簡潔な要約（この章の規定に基づくいずれの義務について違反があったとされるかについての特定を含む。）

(c) 4に規定する仲裁のうち当該紛争投資家が適用するために選択するもの

(d) 当該紛争投資家が求める救済手段及び損害賠償請求額の概算

8

(a) 各締約国は、紛争投資家が、投資紛争を4に規定する仲裁であって当該紛争投資家が選択するものに付託することに同意する。

(b) (a)の規定による同意及び紛争投資家による投資紛争の仲裁への付託は、次の(i)及び(ii)の規定の要件を満たさなければならない。

(i) ＩＣＳＩＤ条約第二章の規定又はＩＣＳＩＤに係る追加的な制度についての規則の規定であって、紛争の両当事者の書面による同意に関するもの

(ii) 書面による合意に関するニューヨーク条約第二条の規定

6
(a) 4及び8の規定にかかわらず、4に規定する仲裁への請求の付託は、次の(i)及び(ii)の場合に該当するときを除くほか、行うことができない。

(i) 紛争投資家が、1(f)に規定する違反を構成するとされる紛争締約国の措置に関し、いずれかの締約国の法律の下にある裁判所において訴訟を提起し、又は他の紛争解決手続(二国間投資協定に基づく投資紛争解決手続を含む。)において手続を開始する権利を放棄する旨の書面を当該紛争締約国に提出すること。

(ii) 紛争投資家が、1(f)に規定する違反を構成するとされる紛争締約国の措置に関し、二国間投資協定に基づく投資紛争解決手続においていかなる手続も開始していないこと。

(b) (a)の規定にかかわらず、紛争投資家は、紛争締約国の権限のある裁判所において、暫定的な差止めによる救済(損害賠償の支払を伴わないものに限る。)を申し立て、又はその申立てに係る手続を継続することができる。

7 4の規定に従い投資紛争を仲裁に付託しようとする紛争投資家は、紛争締約国に対し、当該投資紛争が付託される少なくとも九十日前に書面によりその旨の通報を行う。当該通報には、次の事項を明記する。

2　6(a)(i)の規定に従うことを条件として、この条のいかなる規定も、紛争投資家が紛争締約国の区域内において行政的又は司法的解決を求めることを妨げるものと解してはならない。

3　投資紛争は、可能な限り、紛争当事者の間の友好的な協議により解決する。

4　紛争投資家は、紛争締約国に対して書面による協議の要請を行った日から百二十日以内に当該協議により投資紛争が解決されない場合には、6の規定に従うことを条件として、当該投資紛争を次のいずれかの国際的な仲裁に付託することができる。

(a)　ＩＣＳＩＤ条約による仲裁。ただし、ＩＣＳＩＤ条約が両締約国間で効力を有する場合に限る。

(b)　ＩＣＳＩＤに係る追加的な制度についての規則による仲裁。ただし、いずれか一方の締約国のみがＩＣＳＩＤ条約の当事国である場合に限る。

(c)　国際連合国際商取引法委員会の仲裁規則による仲裁

(d)　紛争締約国と合意する場合には、他の仲裁規則による仲裁

5　適用される仲裁の規則は、この条の規定によって修正する部分を除くほか、4に規定する仲裁を規律する。

(a)　「紛争投資家」とは、投資紛争の当事者である投資家をいう。

(b)　「紛争締約国」とは、投資紛争の当事者である締約国をいう。

(c)　「紛争当事者」とは、紛争投資家及び紛争締約国をいう。

(d)　「ＩＣＳＩＤ条約」とは、千九百六十五年三月十八日にワシントンで作成された国家と他の国家の国民との間の投資紛争の解決に関する条約をいう。

(e)　「ＩＣＳＩＤに係る追加的な制度についての規則」とは、投資紛争解決国際センターの事務局が手続を実施するための追加的な制度を規律する規則をいう。

(f)　「投資紛争」とは、一方の締約国と他方の締約国の投資家との間の紛争であって、当該他方の締約国の投資家又は当該一方の締約国の区域内にある当該他方の締約国の投資家の投資財産について、この章の規定に基づく当該一方の締約国の義務の申し立てられた違反により損失又は損害が生じているものをいう。

(g)　「ニューヨーク条約」とは、千九百五十八年六月十日にニューヨークで作成された外国仲裁判断の承認及び執行に関する条約をいう。

(b) 証券の発行、交換又は取引

(c) 刑事犯罪

(d) 裁決手続における命令又は判決の履行の確保

第十・十二条　代位

一方の締約国又はその指定する機関が、自国の投資家に対し、他方の締約国の区域内にある当該投資家の投資財産に関連する損害の塡補に係る契約、保証契約又は保険契約に基づいて支払を行う場合には、当該他方の締約国は、当該支払の原因となった当該投資家の権利又は請求権の当該一方の締約国又はその指定する機関への譲渡を承認し、かつ、当該一方の締約国又はその指定する機関が、代位により、当該投資家の当初の権利又は請求権と内容及び範囲において同じ権利又は請求権を行使する権利を有することを承認する。当該権利又は請求権の譲渡に基づき当該一方の締約国又はその指定する機関に対して行われる支払及びこのようにして支払われた資金の移転については、前三条の規定を準用する。

第十・十三条　一方の締約国と他方の締約国の投資家との間の投資紛争の解決

1　この条の規定の適用上、

(a) 当初の資金及び投資財産を維持し、又は増大させるための追加的な資金
(b) 利益、利子、資本利得、配当、使用料、手数料その他の投資財産から生ずる収益
(c) 融資の返済その他の契約に基づいて行われる支払であって、投資財産に関連するもの
(d) 投資財産の全部又は一部の売却又は清算によって得られる収入
(e) 当該一方の締約国の区域内にある投資財産に関連する活動に従事する当該他方の締約国から赴任した従業員が得た収入その他の報酬
(f) 前二条の規定に従って行われる支払
(g) 第十・十三条の規定に基づく紛争の処理の結果として生ずる支払

2 各締約国は、1に規定する資金の移転が遅滞なく、かつ、自由利用可能通貨により移転の日の市場における為替相場で行われることを確保する。

3 1及び2の規定にかかわらず、締約国は、次の事項に関する自国の法令を衡平、無差別かつ誠実に適用する場合には、資金の移転を遅らせ、又は妨げることができる。

(a) 破産、支払不能又は債権者の権利の保護

件その他の緊急事態により、自国の区域内にある投資財産に関して損失又は損害を被った他方の締約国の投資家に対し、原状回復、損害賠償、補償その他の解決方法に関し、自国の投資家又は第三国の投資家に与える待遇のうち当該他方の締約国の投資家にとっていずれか有利なものよりも不利でない待遇を与える。

2　1に規定する解決方法の手段としての支払が行われる場合には、当該支払については、実際に換価すること、自由に移転すること並びに市場における為替相場により関係する投資家の締約国の通貨及び自由利用可能通貨に自由に交換することができるものとする。

3　第一・十条の規定にかかわらず、いずれの一方の締約国も、同条の規定に従ってとる措置を理由として、1の規定に基づく義務を免除されない。

第十・十一条　資金の移転

1　一方の締約国は、自国の区域に向けた又は自国の区域からの全ての資金の移転であって、自国の区域内にある他方の締約国の投資家の投資財産に関連するものが、遅滞なく、かつ、自由に行われることを確保する。この資金の移転には、特に次のものを含める。

に知られることにより生じた価格の変化を反映させてはならない。

3　補償については、遅滞なく支払うものとし、支払の時までの期間を考慮した商業的に妥当な利子を含める。当該補償については、実際に換価すること、自由に移転すること並びに収用の日の市場における為替相場により関係する投資家の締約国の通貨及び自由利用可能通貨に自由に交換することができるものとする。

4　収用の影響を受ける投資家は、当該投資家の事案及び補償の額に関し、この条に定める原則に従って速やかな審査を受けるため、収用を行う締約国の裁判所の裁判を受け、又はその行政機関に対して申立てをする権利を有する。ただし、第十・十三条の規定の適用を妨げない。

5　この条の規定は、租税に係る課税措置が収用を構成する限度において、当該課税措置について適用する。

6　この条の規定は、附属書十の規定に従って解釈する。

第十・十条　争乱からの保護

1　一方の締約国は、武力紛争又は自国の区域内における革命、暴動、国内争乱若しくはこれらに類する事あるいかなる措置についても、適用しない。

8　第十・三条、第十・四条及び前条の規定は、締約国が政府調達に関して採用し、又は維持するいかなる措置についても、適用しない。

第十・九条　収用及び補償

1　いずれの一方の締約国も、自国の区域内にある他方の締約国の投資家の投資財産の収用若しくは国有化又はこれに対する収用若しくは国有化と同等の措置（以下「収用」という。）を実施してはならない。ただし、次の全ての条件を満たす場合は、この限りでない。

(a)　公共の目的のためのものであること。

(b)　差別的なものでないこと。

(c)　2から4までの規定に従って迅速、適当かつ実効的な補償の支払を伴うものであること。

(d)　正当な法の手続及び第十・五条の規定に従って実施するものであること。

2　補償は、収用が公表された時又は収用が行われた時のいずれか早い方の時における収用された投資財産の公正な市場価格に相当するものでなければならない。公正な市場価格には、予定された収用が事前に公在する投資財産を売却その他の方法で処分することを要求してはならない。

5　一方の締約国は、この協定の効力発生の日の後に、附属書八の自国の表に記載する現行の適合しない措置を改正し、若しくは修正する場合又は附属書九の自国の表に記載する分野、小分野若しくは活動に関する新たな若しくは一層制限的な措置を採用する場合には、その改正若しくは修正又は当該新たな若しくは一層制限的な措置の実施の前に（例外的な状況においては実施の後できる限り速やかに）、次のことを行う。

(a)　当該改正若しくは修正又は当該措置の詳細な情報を他方の締約国に通報すること。

(b)　他方の締約国の要請があった場合には、相互の満足を確保することを目的として当該他方の締約国との間で誠実に協議を行うこと。

6　各締約国は、適当な場合には、附属書八及び附属書九の自国の表に掲げる適合しない措置を削減し、又は撤廃するよう努める。

7　第十・三条及び第十・四条の規定は、貿易関連知的所有権協定第三条及び第四条の規定に基づく義務の例外又は特別の取扱いとして貿易関連知的所有権協定第三条から第五条までに明示的に規定する範囲内に

締約国の表に記載するもの

(b) 締約国の地方政府により維持されるこれらの規定に適合しない現行の措置

(c) (a)及び(b)に規定する措置の継続又は即時の更新

(d) (a)及び(b)に規定する措置の改正又は修正（当該改正又は修正の直前における当該措置と第十・三条、第十・四条及び前条の規定との適合性の水準を低下させない場合に限る。）

2 一方の締約国は、1(b)に規定する適合しない措置であって、他方の締約国の都道府県又はウランバートル市若しくは県が採用し、又は維持するものが、当該一方の締約国の投資家が行う投資活動に障害をもたらすと認める場合には、当該措置の適用に関し相互に満足すべき解決を得るために協議を要請することができる。

3 第十・三条、第十・四条及び前条の規定は、締約国が附属書九の自国の表に記載する分野、小分野又は活動に関して採用し、又は維持する措置については、適用しない。

4 いずれの一方の締約国も、附属書九の自国の表の対象となる措置をこの協定の効力発生の日の後に採用する場合には、他方の締約国の投資家に対し、その国籍を理由として、当該措置が効力を生じた時点で存を提供し、労働者を訓練し、若しくは雇用し、特定の施設を建設し、若しくは拡張し、又は研究開発を行うことを要求し、これに従うことを求めることを妨げるものと解してはならない。

(b) 1(k)の規定は、反競争的行為を規制する法律の違反に係る救済措置として裁判所又は競争当局が、1(k)に規定する事項の採用の要求を課し、又は当該事項の採用を約束し、若しくは履行することを強制する場合には、適用しない。

(c) 1(a)から(c)まで並びに2(a)及び(b)の規定は、対外援助に関する計画に関連して物品又はサービスについて必要とされる要件については、適用しない。

(d) 2(a)及び(b)の規定は、輸入締約国が物品の内容に関して課する要件であって、特恵的な関税又は特恵的な割当ての適用を受けるために必要なものについては、適用しない。

4 1及び2の規定は、これらの規定に定める要求以外のいかなる要求についても、適用しない。

第十・八条　適合しない措置

1 第十・三条、第十・四条及び前条の規定は、次のものについては、適用しない。

(a) 締約国の中央政府により維持されるこれらの規定に適合しない現行の措置であって、附属書八の当該

2　いずれの締約国も、自国の区域内における締約国又は第三国の投資家の投資活動に関し、利益の享受又はその継続のための条件として、次の事項を要求し、これに従うことを求めてはならない。

(a)　一定の水準又は割合の現地調達を達成すること。

(b)　自国の区域内において生産された物品若しくは提供されたサービスを購入し、利用し、若しくは優先し、又は自国の区域内の者から物品若しくはサービスを購入すること。

(c)　輸入数量又は輸入価額を、輸出数量若しくは輸出価額と又は当該投資家の投資財産に関連する外国為替の流入の量と何らかの形で関連付けること。

(d)　当該投資家の投資財産により生産される物品又は提供されるサービスの自国の区域内における販売を、輸出数量若しくは輸出価額と又は外国為替収入と何らかの形で関連付けることにより制限すること。

(e)　輸出又は輸出のための販売を制限すること。

3
(a)　2のいかなる規定も、締約国が、自国の区域内における締約国又は第三国の投資家の投資活動に関し、利益の享受又はその継続のための条件として、自国の区域内において、生産拠点を設け、サービス

(g) 特定の国籍を有する者を役員、理事又は取締役に任命すること。

(h) 自国の区域内に当該投資家の特定地域又は世界市場に向けた事業本部を設置すること。

(i) 一定の数又は割合の自国民を雇用すること。

(j) 当該投資家が生産する物品又は当該投資家が提供するサービスの一又は二以上を、特定地域又は世界市場に向けて自国の区域のみから供給すること。

(k) 当該投資家と自国の区域内の者との間で任意に締結されるライセンス契約（既に締結されたものかどうかを問わない。）について次の事項を採用すること。ただし、当該締約国が政府の権限の行使として、次の事項を採用することの要求を課し、又は次の事項を採用することを約束し、若しくは履行することを強制する場合に限る。

(i) 当該ライセンス契約の下での使用料に係る一定の率又は額

(ii) 当該ライセンス契約の有効期間に係る一定の期間

注釈　この(k)に規定する「ライセンス契約」とは、技術、製造工程その他の財産的価値を有する知識の移転に関するライセンス契約をいう。

第十・七条　特定措置の履行要求の禁止

1　いずれの締約国も、自国の区域内における締約国又は第三国の投資家の投資活動に関し、次の事項の要求を課し、又は強制してはならず、また、当該事項を約束し、又は履行することを強制してはならない。

(a)　一定の水準又は割合の物品又はサービスを輸出すること。

(b)　一定の水準又は割合の現地調達を達成すること。

(c)　自国の区域内において生産された物品若しくは提供されたサービスを購入し、利用し、若しくは優先し、又は自国の区域内の者から物品若しくはサービスを購入すること。

(d)　輸入数量又は輸入価額を、輸出数量若しくは輸出価額と又は当該投資家の投資財産に関連する外国為替の流入の量と何らかの形で関連付けること。

(e)　当該投資家の投資財産により生産される物品又は提供されるサービスの自国の区域内における販売を、輸出数量若しくは輸出価額と又は外国為替収入と何らかの形で関連付けることにより制限すること。

(f)　輸出又は輸出のための販売を制限すること。

規定又は他の国際協定に対する違反があった旨の決定が行われることは、この1の規定に対する違反があったことを証明するものではない。

注釈2　「公正かつ衡平な待遇」には、法の正当な手続の原則に従った刑事上若しくは民事上の訴訟手続又は行政上の裁決手続における裁判を行うことを拒否しないとの締約国の義務を含む。

2　一方の締約国が他方の締約国の投資家の特定の投資財産に関して書面により義務を負うこととなった場合において、当該投資家が当該投資財産の設立、取得又は拡張の際に当該一方の締約国による当該義務の履行を求めることが可能であったときは、当該一方の締約国は、当該義務を遵守する。

3　この条の規定は、租税に係る課税措置に適用する。

第十・六条　裁判所の裁判を受ける権利

1　一方の締約国は、自国の区域内において、投資家の権利の行使及び擁護のため全ての審級にわたり裁判所の裁判を受け、及び行政機関に申立てをする権利に関し、他方の締約国の投資家に対し、同様の状況において自国の投資家又は第三国の投資家に与える待遇よりも不利でない待遇を与える。

2　この条の規定は、租税に係る課税措置に適用する。

２　１の規定は、一方の締約国が、自国の区域内における他方の締約国の投資家の投資活動に関して特別な手続を定める措置を採用し、又は維持することを妨げるものと解してはならない。ただし、当該手続は、この章の規定に基づく当該投資家の権利を実質的に害するものであってはならない。

第十・四条　最恵国待遇

一方の締約国は、自国の区域内において、投資活動に関し、他方の締約国の投資家及びその投資財産に対し、同様の状況において第三国の投資家及びその投資財産に与える待遇よりも不利でない待遇を与える。

第十・五条　一般的待遇

１　一方の締約国は、自国の区域内において、他方の締約国の投資家の投資財産に対し、国際法に基づく待遇（公正かつ衡平な待遇並びに十分な保護及び保障を含む。）を与える。

注釈１　この１の規定は、他方の締約国の投資家の投資財産に与えられるべき待遇の最低限度の基準として、外国人の待遇に関する国際慣習法上の最低基準を用いることについて定めたものである。「公正かつ衡平な待遇」及び「十分な保護及び保障」の概念は、外国人の待遇に関する国際慣習法上の最低基準が要求する待遇以上の待遇を与えることを求めるものではない。この協定の他の

(b)
(i) 企業が投資家によって「所有」されるとは、当該投資家が当該企業の五十パーセントを超える持分を所有する場合をいう。
(ii) 企業が投資家によって「支配」されるとは、当該投資家が当該企業の役員の過半数を指名し、又は当該企業の活動につき法的に指示する権限を有する場合をいう。

(c) 「現行の」とは、この協定の効力発生の日において効力を有することをいう。

(d) 「自由利用可能通貨」とは、国際通貨基金協定に定義する自由利用可能通貨をいう。

(e) 「投資活動」とは、投資財産の設立、取得、拡張、運営、経営、維持、使用、享有及び売却その他の処分をいう。

(f) 「措置」とは、あらゆる措置（法令、規則、手続、決定、行政上の行為その他のいずれの形式であるかを問わない。）をいう。

第十・三条　内国民待遇

1　一方の締約国は、自国の区域内において、投資活動に関し、他方の締約国の投資家及びその投資財産に対し、同様の状況において自国の投資家及びその投資財産に与える待遇よりも不利でない待遇を与える。

注釈２　この章の規定は、この協定の効力発生の前に生じた事態に起因する請求については、適用しない。

２　この章の規定と第七章の規定とが抵触する場合には、次のとおりとする。

(a)　第十・三条、第十・四条及び第十・七条の規定の対象となっている事項に関しては、この章の規定と第七章の規定とが抵触する限度において、同章の規定が優先する。

(b)　(a)に規定する事項以外の事項に関しては、この章の規定と第七章の規定とが抵触する限度において、この章の規定が優先する。

３　この章のいかなる規定も、出入国管理に関する法令に基づく措置に関して締約国に義務を課するものではない。

第十・二条　定義

この章の規定の適用上、

(a)　「二国間投資協定」とは、二千一年二月十五日に東京で署名された投資の促進及び保護に関する日本国とモンゴル国との間の協定をいう。

3　小委員会は、両締約国政府の代表者から成る。

4　小委員会は、両締約国が合意する時期及び場所において又は手段によって会合を開催する。

第十章　投資

第十・一条　適用範囲

1　この章の規定は、締約国が採用し、又は維持する措置であって、次の事項に関するものについて適用する。

(a)　他方の締約国の投資家

(b)　当該締約国の区域内にある他方の締約国の投資家の投資財産

(c)　第十・七条及び第十・十七条の規定の適用の対象となる全ての投資財産であって、当該締約国の区域内にあるもの

注釈1　この章の規定は、一方の締約国が採用し、又は維持する措置であって、この協定の効力発生の前に他方の締約国の投資家により当該一方の締約国の区域内において投資された投資財産に関連するものについても適用する。

5　両締約国は、活発な電子商取引の環境に不可欠な要素として、国境を越える情報の流れの維持を図ることの重要性を認識する。

6　両締約国は、デジタル・プロダクトの貿易を更に促進することの重要性を認識する。

第九・十三条　電子商取引に関する小委員会

1　この章の規定を効果的に実施し、及び運用するため、両締約国は、ここに電子商取引に関する小委員会（以下この条において「小委員会」という。）を設置する。

2　小委員会は、次のことを任務とする。

(a)　この章の規定の実施及び運用について検討及び監視を行うこと。

(b)　この章の規定に関連する問題（適当な場合には、第九・四条の規定の見直しを含む。）について討議すること。

(c)　デジタル・プロダクトの貿易を更に促進するための新たな機会を追求すること。

(d)　合同委員会に対して小委員会の所見を報告すること。

(e)　合同委員会が委任するその他の任務を遂行すること。

の自国の区域内における輸入、頒布、販売又は利用の条件として、当該ソフトウェアのソース・コードの移転又は当該ソース・コードへのアクセスを要求してはならない。

2　この条の規定の適用上、1の規定の対象となるソフトウェアは、大量販売用ソフトウェア又は当該ソフトウェアを含む製品に限定するものとし、中枢的な基盤のために利用されるソフトウェアを含まない。

第九・十二条　協力

1　両締約国は、適当な場合には、電子商取引の発展を促進するため、二国間で協力し、並びに地域的な及び多数国間の場に積極的に参加する。

2　両締約国は、適当な場合には、情報及び経験（電子商取引に関する法令及び最良の慣行についてのものを含む。）であって、特に、消費者の信頼、サイバーセキュリティ、要求されていない商業上の電子メールの防止、知的財産、電子政府及び個人情報の保護に関連するものを共有する。

3　両締約国は、中小企業が電子商取引を利用するに当たって直面する障害を克服するために協力する。

4　各締約国は、自国が利用することができる現存の手段により、自国における非営利団体による電子商取引の促進を目的とした活動（情報及び意見の交換を含む。）を奨励する。

第九・十条　コンピュータ関連設備の所在地に関する要求の禁止

1　いずれの一方の締約国も、次に掲げるものが自国の区域内における事業を遂行するための条件として、当該区域内に所在するコンピュータ関連設備を利用し、又は当該区域内にコンピュータ関連設備を設置することを要求してはならない。

(a)　他方の締約国のサービス提供者

(b)　他方の締約国の投資家

(c)　当該一方の締約国の区域内における他方の締約国の投資家の投資財産

2　1の規定にかかわらず、この条のいかなる規定も、締約国が正当な公共政策の目的を達成するために必要な措置であってコンピュータ関連設備の利用及び設置に影響を及ぼすものを採用し、又は維持することを妨げるものと解してはならない。ただし、それらの措置を、恣意的若しくは不当な差別の手段となるような態様で、又は貿易に対する偽装した制限となるような態様で適用しないことを条件とする。

第九・十一条　ソース・コード

1　いずれの一方の締約国も、他方の締約国の者が所有するソフトウェア又は当該ソフトウェアを含む製品各締約国は、宣伝を目的とする要求されていない商業上の電子メールを規制するために適切かつ必要な措置をとるよう努める。

第九・八条　貿易実務に係る文書の電子化

1　各締約国は、貿易実務に係る文書の全てについて、公衆による電子的な形式での利用を可能なものとするよう努める。

2　各締約国は、電子的に提出される貿易実務に係る文書について、当該文書が書面により提出された場合と法的に同等なものとして受理するよう努める。

3　両締約国は、電子的に提出される貿易実務に係る文書の受理を促進するため、二国間で、及び国際的な場において協力する。

第九・九条　国内規制

各締約国は、電子商取引に影響を及ぼす自国の全ての措置が、透明性のある、客観的、合理的かつ公平な態様で実施され、及び正当な政策目的を実現するために必要な水準以上に大きな負担とならないことを確保する。

を満たすこと又は自国の国内法令に従って認定され、若しくは承認された認証サービスの提供者によって発行される特定の電子証明書に基づくものであることを要求することができる。ただし、次の要件を満たすことを条件とする。

(a) その要求が、正当な政策目的に資するものであること。

(b) その要求が、(a)に規定する目的の達成に実質的に関連するものであること。

第九・六条　消費者の保護

1 両締約国は、電子商取引のための透明性のある、かつ、効果的な措置であって、消費者の保護に関するもの及び消費者の信頼の向上に資する措置を採用し、及び維持する重要性を認識する。

2 両締約国は、消費者の保護を促進するため、電子商取引に関連する活動に関し、消費者の保護について責任を有するそれぞれの権限のある当局の間における協力の重要性を認識する。

3 両締約国は、それぞれ自国の国内法令に従い、電子商取引の利用者の個人情報を保護するための措置を採用し、又は維持する。

第九・七条　要求されていない商業上の電子メール

のような決定は、透明性のある、客観的、合理的かつ公正な態様で行う。

4　一方の締約国は、1の規定に基づく自国の義務を履行するに当たりデジタル・プロダクトの原産地を決定する場合において、他方の締約国の要請があるときは、当該デジタル・プロダクトの原産地を決定するための方法について説明する。

5　両締約国は、デジタル・プロダクトの原産地を決定するための基準をこの協定に組み入れることを検討することを目的として当該基準の作成を促進するため、国際機関及び国際的な場において協力する。

第九・五条　電子署名

1　いずれの締約国も、電子署名を規制する措置であって次のものを採用し、又は維持してはならない。

(a)　電子的な取引の当事者が当該取引のための適切な電子署名の方式を相互に決定することを禁止する措置

(b)　電子的な取引の当事者に対し当該取引が法的な要件を満たしていることを裁判所において証明する機会を与えることを妨げる措置

2　1の規定にかかわらず、各締約国は、電子的な取引の特定の種類について、電子署名が特定の実施基準

りも不利な待遇を与える措置

2　1の規定は、次のものについては、適用しない。

(a)　政府調達

(b)　締約国又は公的企業が交付する補助金（贈与、公的に支援される借款、保証及び保険を含む。）

(c)　第七・四条2の規定に基づいて締約国が維持する措置

(d)　第七・三条及び第七・五条の規定の範囲内で締約国が採用し、又は維持する措置であって、次のいずれかに該当するもの

(i)　附属書六に定める当該締約国の特定の約束に係る表において約束していない分野に関する措置

(ii)　附属書六に定める当該締約国の特定の約束に係る表において合意され、及び特定される条件及び制限に反しない措置

(e)　第十・八条の規定に基づいて締約国が採用し、又は維持する適合しない措置

3　一方の締約国は、1の規定に基づく自国の義務を履行するに当たり、必要な場合には、デジタル・プロダクトが自国、他方の締約国又は第三国のいずれのデジタル・プロダクトであるかを誠実に決定する。そ

(c)　「電子署名」とは、電磁的記録に記録することができる情報についてとられる措置であって、次の(i)及び(ii)の要件を満たすものをいう。

(i)　当該情報が当該措置をとった者により承認されていることを示す措置であること。

(ii)　当該情報が改変されていないことを確認する措置であること。

(d)　「貿易実務に係る文書」とは、締約国が発行し、又は管理する様式であって、物品の輸入又は輸出に関連して、輸入者若しくは輸出者により、又はこれらの者のために作成される必要があるものをいう。

第九・三条　関税

各締約国は、両締約国間における電子的な送信に対して関税を賦課しないという慣行を維持する。

第九・四条　デジタル・プロダクトの無差別待遇

1　一方の締約国は、次の措置を採用し、又は維持してはならない。

(a)　他方の締約国のデジタル・プロダクトに対し、自国の同種のデジタル・プロダクトに与える待遇よりも不利な待遇を与える措置

(b)　他方の締約国のデジタル・プロダクトに対し、第三国の同種のデジタル・プロダクトに与える待遇よ

2　この章は、電子商取引の利用に対する信用及び信頼の環境を醸成することに寄与すること、両締約国間における電子商取引を促進すること並びに世界的に電子商取引の一層広範な利用を促進することを目的とする。

3　両締約国は、電子商取引における技術的中立性の原則を認識する。

4　この章の規定と第二章、第七章、次章又は第十二章の規定とが抵触する場合には、その抵触の限度において、この章以外の章の規定が優先する。

第九・二条　定義

この章の規定の適用上、

(a)　「デジタル・プロダクト」とは、コンピュータ・プログラム、文字列、ビデオ、映像、録音物その他のものであってデジタル式に符号化されたもの（キャリアメディアに固定されるものであるか電子的に送信されるものであるかを問わない。）をいう。

(b)　「電子証明書」とは、利用者が電子署名を行ったことを確認するために用いられる物が、当該利用者に係るものであることを証明するために作成される電磁的記録をいう。

第八・七条　紛争解決

1　第十六章に定める紛争解決手続は、次の(a)及び(b)の要件を満たす場合を除くほか、この章の規定については、適用しない。

(a)　事案に一定の実行の類型が含まれること。

(b)　当該事案によって影響を受ける一方の締約国の自然人が他方の締約国の行政上の救済措置を可能な限り尽くしたこと。

2　他方の締約国の権限のある当局による特定の事案に関する最終的な決定が、1(b)に規定する行政上の救済措置に係る手続の開始の日の後一年以内に行われず、かつ、当該決定が行われないことが1(b)に規定する自然人に起因する遅延によるものでないときは、当該行政上の救済措置は、尽くされたものとみなす。

第九章　電子商取引

第九・一条　一般規定

1　両締約国は、電子商取引によって経済的な成長及び機会がもたらされることを認識し、また、電子商取引の利用及び発展に対する不必要な障害を回避することの重要性を認識する。

1　この章の規定を効果的に実施し、及び運用するため、両締約国は、ここに自然人の移動に関する小委員会（以下この条において「小委員会」という。）を設置する。

2　小委員会は、次のことを任務とする。

(a)　この章の規定の実施及び運用について検討及び監視を行うこと。

(b)　自然人の入国及び一時的な滞在を相互主義に基づいて一層促進するための措置の立案について検討すること。

(c)　附属書七に規定する自然人の入国及び一時的な滞在に影響を及ぼす措置に関する情報を交換すること。

(d)　この章の規定に関連する問題であって両締約国が合意するものについて討議すること。

(e)　合同委員会に対して小委員会の所見を報告すること。

(f)　合同委員会が委任するその他の任務を遂行すること。

3　小委員会は、両締約国政府の代表者から成る。

4　小委員会は、両締約国が合意する時期及び場所において又は手段によって会合を開催する。

(e) 当該一方の締約国における一時的な滞在に係る資格の変更

2 一方の締約国は、他方の締約国の自然人から要請があった場合には、1に規定する要件及び手続に関する情報を提供するよう努める。

3 一方の締約国は、1(a)から(e)までに掲げる入国、一時的な滞在又は許可について、他方の締約国の自然人が効果的な申請を行うことに影響を及ぼす新たな要件及び手続の導入又は1に規定する現行の要件及び手続の変更を、当該他方の締約国に速やかに通報するよう努める。

4 一方の締約国は、自国の権限のある当局が1に規定する申請について徴収する手数料自体がこの章の規定に基づく他方の締約国の自然人の入国及び一時的な滞在に対して不当な障害とならないことを確保する。

5 一方の締約国は、自国の法令の範囲内で、他方の締約国の自然人の入国及び一時的な滞在に関する要件を簡素化し、並びに他方の締約国の自然人の入国及び一時的な滞在に関する手続を円滑化し、及び迅速化するための措置をとるよう可能な限り努める。

第八・六条　自然人の移動に関する小委員会

２　１に規定する区分の対象となる自然人については、附属書七に定める条件に従って入国及び一時的な滞在が許可される。ただし、当該自然人が、入国及び一時的な滞在について適用される出入国管理に関する法令であってこの章の規定に反しないものに従うことを条件とする。

３　いずれの締約国も、１に規定する自然人であって入国及び一時的な滞在を許可するものの数について制限を課し、又は維持してはならない。

第八・五条　要件及び手続

１　一方の締約国は、附属書七に定める自国の特定の約束の対象となる自然人に関し、他方の締約国の自然人が次に掲げる事項について効果的な申請を行うために必要な要件及び手続に関する情報を、この協定の効力発生の日に公表し、又は当該他方の締約国に利用可能なものとする。

(a)　当該一方の締約国への入国

(b)　当該一方の締約国における当初の一時的な滞在

(c)　当該一方の締約国における一時的な滞在の更新

(d)　適用がある場合には、当該一方の締約国における就労の許可われているとはみなさない。

第八・三条　定義

この章の規定の適用上、「締約国の自然人」とは、締約国内に居住しているか否かを問わず、当該締約国の法律の下で当該締約国の国民である自然人をいう。

第八・四条　特定の約束

1　一方の締約国は、次の者について行う特定の約束を附属書七に定める。

(a)　他方の締約国の短期の商用訪問者

(b)　他方の締約国の企業内転勤者

(c)　他方の締約国の投資家

(d)　自由職業サービスに従事する他方の締約国の自然人

(e)　当該一方の締約国にある公私の機関との間の契約に基づいて高度の水準の技術又は知識を必要とするサービスの提供に従事する他方の締約国の自然人

(f)　(b)から(e)までに規定する自然人に同行する配偶者及び子

第八・二条　適用範囲

1　この章の規定は、第八・四条1に定める区分のいずれかに該当する一方の締約国の自然人であって、他方の締約国に入国するものの入国及び一時的な滞在に影響を及ぼす措置について適用する。

2　この章の規定は、一方の締約国の自然人であって、他方の締約国の雇用市場へのアクセスを求めるものに影響を及ぼす措置及び国籍、市民権又は永続的な居住若しくは雇用に関する措置については、適用しない。

3　この章の規定は、一方の締約国が他方の締約国の自然人の入国及び一時的な滞在を規制するための措置（自国の国境を保全し、及び自国の国境を越える自然人の秩序ある移動を確保するために必要な措置を含む。）を適用することを妨げるものではない。ただし、附属書七に定める特定の約束の条件に従って当該他方の締約国に与えられる利益を無効にし、又は損なうような態様で当該措置を適用しないことを条件とする。

注釈　他方の締約国の自然人に対しては査証を要求し、特定の第三国の自然人に対しては要求しないという事実のみをもって、附属書七に定める特定の約束の条件に基づく利益が無効にされ、又は損なな時期に検討する。

2　一方の締約国が自国のサービスの分野、小分野又は活動についてこの協定の効力発生の日の後に自主的に更なる自由化を行った場合には、当該一方の締約国は、そのような自主的な自由化をこの協定に組み込むよう求める他方の締約国の要請を適当な時期に検討する。

第八章　自然人の移動

第八・一条　一般原則

1　この章の規定は、両締約国間の特恵的な貿易関係、自然人の入国及び一時的な滞在を互恵主義に基づいて促進し、並びに入国及び一時的な滞在のための透明性のある基準及び手続を定めたいという両締約国の希望並びに国境の安全を確保し、並びに各締約国の国内労働力及び永続的な雇用を保護する必要性を反映したものである。

2　各締約国は、1に規定する一般原則に従ってこの章の規定に関連する措置をとるものとし、特に、この協定に基づく物品若しくはサービスの貿易又は投資活動を不当に妨げ、又は遅らせることのないよう迅速にこれらの措置をとる。

第七・十六条　サービスの貿易に関する小委員会

1　両締約国は、この章の規定を効果的に実施し、及び運用するため、ここにサービスの貿易に関する小委員会（以下この条において「小委員会」という。）を設置する。

2　小委員会は、次のことを任務とする。

(a)　この章の規定の実施及び運用について検討及び監視を行うこと。

(b)　この章の規定に関連する問題について討議すること。

(c)　合同委員会に対して小委員会の所見を報告すること。

(d)　合同委員会が委任するその他の任務を遂行すること。

3　小委員会は、両締約国政府の代表者から成る。

4　小委員会は、両締約国が合意する時期及び場所において又は手段によって会合を開催する。

第七・十七条　約束の見直し

1　両締約国間のサービスの貿易の更なる自由化（約束の形式を再交渉する可能性を含む。）のため、両締約国は、この章の規定及びこの章に規定する附属書の見直しを両締約国が合意する機会に行うことを適当

1　一方の締約国は、他方の締約国のサービス提供者であって当該他方の締約国の法人であるものが第三国の者によって所有され、又は支配されており、かつ、次のいずれかの場合に該当すると認めるときは、当該サービス提供者に対し、この章の規定による利益を否認することができる。

(a)　当該一方の締約国が当該第三国と外交関係を有していない場合

(b)　当該一方の締約国が、当該第三国に関する措置であって次のいずれかに該当するものを採用し、又は維持する場合

(i)　当該法人との取引を禁止するもの

(ii)　当該法人に対してこの章の規定による利益を与えることにより当該措置に違反し、又は当該措置を阻害することとなるもの

2　一方の締約国は、他方の締約国のサービス提供者であって当該他方の締約国の法人であるものが第三国の者によって所有され、又は支配されており、かつ、当該法人が当該他方の締約国の区域内において実質的な事業活動を行っていないと認めるときは、事前の通報及び協議を行うことを条件として、当該サービス提供者に対し、この章の規定による利益を否認することができる。

第七・十四条　透明性

各締約国は、全ての分野において、第七・三条から第七・五条までの規定に基づく義務に影響を及ぼす全ての関係する措置を記載した法的拘束力のない表を作成する。当該表は、この協定の効力発生の日から五年以内に他方の締約国と交換され、及び公に利用可能なものとされるものとし、また、必要に応じ又は両締約国の合意に基づき、将来の見直し及び改定の対象となる。当該表には、次の要素を含める。

(a)　分野及び小分野又は事項

(b)　適合しない規定（内国民待遇、最恵国待遇又は市場アクセスに係るもの）の種類

(c)　当該措置の法的根拠その他の根拠

(d)　当該措置の簡潔な説明

注釈　この条の規定に基づく表は、透明性のためにのみ作成されるものであり、この章の規定に基づく締約国の権利及び義務に影響を及ぼすものと解してはならない。この条の規定に基づくいかなる見直し又は改定も、当該表を更新することのみを目的とする。

第七・十五条　利益の否認

は維持することができる。

2　1に規定する制限は、次の全ての要件を満たすものとする。

(a)　内国民待遇及び最恵国待遇に基づいて適用されるものであること。

(b)　国際通貨基金協定に適合するものであること。

(c)　他方の締約国の商業上、経済上又は資金上の利益に対し不必要な損害を与えることを避けるものであること。

(d)　1に規定する状況に対処するために必要な限度を超えないものであること。

(e)　一時的なものであり、1に規定する状況が改善するに伴い漸進的に廃止されるものであること。

3　締約国は、1に規定する制限を決定するに当たり、自国の経済又は開発の計画にとって一層重要なサービスの提供を優先させることができる。ただし、特定のサービスの分野を保護するために当該制限を課してはならず、また、これを維持してはならない。

4　1の規定に基づいて一方の締約国が課し、若しくは維持する制限又はその変更については、他方の締約国に対して速やかに通報する。

事項に関連する秘密でない情報であって公に利用可能なものを提供することによって協力する。当該要請を受けた締約国は、また、自国の法令に従い、かつ、要請を行った締約国による情報の秘密の保護に関し適切な協定が締結されることを条件として、利用可能な他の情報を当該要請を行った締約国に提供する。

第七・十二条　支払及び資金の移転

1　締約国は、次条に規定する場合を除くほか、サービスの貿易に関連する経常取引のための資金の国際的な移転及び支払に対して制限を課してはならない。

2　この章のいかなる規定も、国際通貨基金協定に適合する為替の利用を含め、同協定に基づく国際通貨基金の加盟国としての両締約国の権利及び義務に影響を及ぼすものではない。ただし、締約国は、次条の規定に基づく場合又は国際通貨基金の要請による場合を除くほか、資本取引に関する自国の特定の約束に反するような制限を資本取引に対して課してはならない。

第七・十三条　国際収支の擁護のための制限

1　国際収支及び対外支払に関して重大な困難が生じている場合又は生ずるおそれがある場合には、締約国は、サービスの貿易に対する制限（取引のための支払又は資金の移転に対するものを含む。）を課し、又締約国は、当該独占的なサービス提供者が自国の区域内において第七・三条及び第七・五条の規定に基づく当該特定の約束に反する態様で活動するために自己の独占的地位を濫用しないことを確保する。

3　一方の締約国は、他方の締約国の独占的なサービス提供者が１又は２の規定に反する態様で活動していると信ずるに足りる理由がある場合には、当該他方の締約国に対し、関連業務に関する特定の情報の提供を要請することができる。

4　この条の規定は、排他的なサービス提供者の場合、すなわち、締約国が法令上又は事実上、(a)少数のサービス提供者を許可し、又は設立し、かつ、(b)自国の区域内でこれらのサービス提供者の間の競争を実質的に妨げる場合についても適用する。

第七・十一条　商慣習

1　両締約国は、サービス提供者の一定の商慣習（前条の規定に該当するものを除く。）が競争を抑制し、及びこれによりサービスの貿易を制限することがあることを認める。

2　一方の締約国は、他方の締約国の要請に応じ、１に規定する商慣習を撤廃することを目的として協議する。要請を受けた締約国は、当該要請に対して十分かつ好意的な考慮を払うものとし、問題となっているならない。

(b) 当該一方の締約国は、他方の締約国に対し、当該協定若しくは取決めへの当該他方の締約国の加入について交渉し、又はこれと同等の協定若しくは取決めについて両締約国間で交渉するための機会を十分に与える。

(c) 当該一方の締約国は、承認を一方的に行う場合には、他方の締約国に対し、当該他方の締約国において得られた教育若しくは経験、満たされた要件又は与えられた免許若しくは資格証明も承認されるべきであることについて意見を表明するための機会を十分に与える。

第七・十条　独占及び排他的なサービス提供者

1 締約国は、自国の区域内の独占的なサービス提供者が関連する市場において独占的なサービスを提供するに当たり、第七・三条から第七・五条までの規定に基づく自国の義務に反する態様で活動しないことを確保する。

2 締約国の特定の約束の対象となっている分野において当該締約国の独占的なサービス提供者が自己の独占権の範囲外のサービスを提供するに当たって直接に又は提携する会社を通じて競争する場合には、当該

(b) サービスの質を確保するために必要である以上に大きな負担とならないこと。

(c) サービスの提供に対する偽装した制限とならないこと。

第七・九条　承認

1　一方の締約国は、他方の締約国のサービス提供者に対して許可、免許又は資格証明を与えるに当たり、自国の基準の全部又は一部を満たすために、当該他方の締約国において得られた教育若しくは経験、満たされた要件又は与えられた免許若しくは資格証明を承認することができる。

2　1に規定する承認であって調和その他の方法により行うことができるものは、両締約国間の協定若しくは取決めに基づいて又は一方的に行うことができる。

3　一方の締約国が、第三国において得られた教育若しくは経験、満たされた要件又は与えられた免許若しくは資格証明を、当該一方の締約国と当該第三国との間の協定若しくは取決めに基づいて、又は一方的に、承認することとする場合には、次のとおりとする。

(a) 第七・四条のいかなる規定も、当該一方の締約国に対し、他方の締約国において得られた教育若しくは経験、満たされた要件又は与えられた免許若しくは資格証明を承認することを求めるものと解してはならない。

合には、その記載は、第七・三条の規定についての条件又は制限でもあるとみなす。

第七・八条　国内規制

1　各締約国は、一般に適用される全ての措置であってサービスの貿易に影響を及ぼすものが合理的、客観的かつ公平な態様で実施されることを確保する。

2　締約国の権限のある当局は、サービスの提供のために当該締約国の許可が必要な場合には、当該締約国の法令に基づき不備がないと認められる申請が提出された後合理的な期間内に、当該申請に関する決定を申請者に通知する。当該締約国の権限のある当局は、当該申請者の要請に応じ、当該申請の処理状況に関する情報を不当に遅滞することなく提供する。

3　一方の締約国は、サービス分野において当該一方の締約国が採用し、又は維持する措置であって他方の締約国のサービス提供者に対する許可、資格要件、資格の審査に係る手続、技術上の基準及び免許要件に関連するものがサービスの貿易に対する不必要な障害とならないことを確保するため、当該措置が次の基準に適合することを確保する。

(a)　客観的なかつ透明性のある基準（例えば、サービスを提供する能力）に基づくこと。

ビスの貿易に影響を及ぼす措置（資格、基準又は免許についての事項に関するものを含む。）に関する約束について交渉することができる。当該約束については、附属書六の自国の特定の約束に係る表に記載する。

第七・七条　特定の約束に係る表

1　各締約国は、第七・三条及び前二条の規定に基づいて行う特定の約束を表に記載する。附属書六のそれぞれの特定の約束に係る表は、当該特定の約束を行った分野又は小分野に関し、次の事項を特定する。

(a)　市場アクセスの条件及び制限

(b)　内国民待遇についての条件及び制限

(c)　追加的な約束

(d)　適当な場合には、当該特定の約束の履行のための期間

2　特定の約束を行い、かつ、「SS」と記載した分野又は小分野に関し、1(a)及び(b)に規定する条件及び制限（出入国管理に関する法令に基づく措置によるものを除く。）は、第七・三条又は第七・五条の規定に適合しない現行の措置に基づくものに限る。

3　第七・三条及び第七・五条のいずれの規定にも適合しない措置は、同条に関する欄に記載する。この場

(c) サービスの事業の総数又は指定された数量単位によって表示されたサービスの総産出量の制限（数量割当てによるもの又は経済上の需要を考慮するとの要件によるもの）

注釈 この(c)に規定する制限には、サービスの提供のための投入を制限する締約国の措置を含まない。

(d) 特定のサービスの分野において雇用され、又はサービス提供者が雇用する自然人であって、特定のサービスの提供に必要であり、かつ、当該提供に直接関係するものの総数の制限（数量割当てによるもの又は経済上の需要を考慮するとの要件によるもの）

(e) サービス提供者がサービスを提供するに当たり、法定の事業体又は合弁企業について特定の形態を制限し、又は要求する措置

(f) 外国資本の参加の制限（外国資本による株式保有の比率の上限を定めるもの又は外国資本による個別若しくは全体の投資総額の比率の上限を定めるもの）

第七・六条 追加的な約束

両締約国は、第七・三条及び前条の規定に基づく特定の約束に係る表への記載の対象となっていないサー

特定した条件及び制限に基づく待遇よりも不利でない待遇を与える。

注釈　締約国は、第七・二条(m)(i)に規定する提供の態様によるサービスの提供に関し市場アクセスに係る約束を行う場合において、国境を越える資本の移動が当該サービス自体の重要な部分であるときは、当該約束をもって当該資本の移動を認めることを約束したこととする。締約国は、同条(m)(iii)に規定する提供の態様によるサービスの提供に関し市場アクセスに係る約束を行う場合には、当該約束をもって自国の区域への関連する資本の移動を認めることを約束したこととする。

2　締約国は、市場アクセスに係る約束を行った分野において、附属書六の自国の特定の約束に係る表において別段の定めをしない限り、小地域を単位とするか自国の区域の全体を単位とするかを問わず、次の措置を維持し、又は採用してはならない。

(a)　サービス提供者の数の制限（数量割当て、独占、排他的なサービス提供者又は経済上の需要を考慮するとの要件のいずれによるものであるかを問わない。）

(b)　サービスの取引総額又は資産総額の制限（数量割当てによるもの又は経済上の需要を考慮するとの要件によるもの）

定の義務を履行することができる。

3　一方の締約国が他方の締約国のサービス又はサービス提供者に対して与える形式的に同一の又は形式的に異なる待遇により競争条件が当該他方の締約国の同種のサービス又はサービス提供者と比較して自国のサービス又はサービス提供者にとって有利となる場合には、当該待遇は、自国のサービス又はサービス提供者に与える待遇よりも不利であると認める。

第七・四条　最恵国待遇

1　一方の締約国は、他方の締約国のサービス及びサービス提供者に対し、第三国の同種のサービス及びサービス提供者に与える待遇よりも不利でない待遇を与える。

2　各締約国は、1の規定に合致しない措置であっても、当該措置が附属書六の最恵国待遇の免除に係る表に掲げられ、かつ、同表に定める要件を満たす場合においては、当該措置を維持することができる。

第七・五条　市場アクセス

1　一方の締約国は、第七・二条(m)に規定するサービスの提供の態様による市場アクセスに関し、他方の締約国のサービス及びサービス提供者に対し、附属書六の自国の特定の約束に係る表において合意し、及びはその上空において、運航し、又は有償若しくは貸切りで旅客、貨物若しくは郵便物を運送する定期又は不定期の航空運送サービスに係る権利（運航地点、運営路線、運送するものの種類、提供する輸送力、運賃及びその条件並びに数、所有、支配その他航空企業を指定するための基準を含む。）をいう。

第七・三条　内国民待遇

1　一方の締約国は、附属書六の自国の特定の約束に係る表に記載する分野において、かつ、当該表に定める条件及び制限に従い、サービスの提供に影響を及ぼす全ての措置に関し、他方の締約国のサービス及びサービス提供者に対し、自国の同種のサービス及びサービス提供者に与える待遇よりも不利でない待遇を与える。

注釈　この条の規定に基づいて行われる特定の約束は、いずれの締約国に対しても、関連するサービス又はサービス提供者が自国のものでないことにより生ずる競争上の固有の不利益を補償することを要求するものと解してはならない。

2　一方の締約国は、他方の締約国のサービス及びサービス提供者に対し自国の同種のサービス及びサービス提供者に与える待遇と形式的に同一の待遇を与えるか形式的に異なる待遇を与えるかを問わず、1の規用される条件を含まない。

(k) 「政府の権限の行使として提供されるサービス」とは、商業的な原則に基づかず、かつ、一又は二以上のサービス提供者との競争を行うことなく提供されるサービスをいう。

(l) 「サービスの提供」には、サービスの生産、流通、マーケティング、販売及び納入を含む。

(m) 「サービスの貿易」とは、次に規定する態様のサービスの提供をいう。

(i) 一方の締約国の区域から他方の締約国の区域へのサービスの提供（越境の態様による提供）

(ii) 一方の締約国の区域内におけるサービスの提供であって他方の締約国のサービス消費者に対して行われるもの（海外消費の態様による提供）

(iii) 一方の締約国のサービス提供者によるサービスの提供であって他方の締約国の区域内の業務上の拠点を通じて行われるもの（業務上の拠点を通ずる態様による提供）

(iv) 一方の締約国のサービス提供者によるサービスの提供であって他方の締約国の区域内において当該一方の締約国の自然人の存在を通じて行われるもの（自然人の存在を通ずる態様による提供）

(n) 「運輸権」とは、いずれかの締約国内の地点を出発地若しくは目的地として又は当該締約国内若しく

て、採用し、又は維持する措置

(g)「サービスの貿易に影響を及ぼす締約国の措置」には、次の措置を含む。

(i) サービスの購入、支払又は利用に係る措置

(ii) サービスの提供に関連して、当該締約国が公衆一般に提供されることを要求しているサービスへのアクセス及び当該サービスの利用に係る措置

(iii) 当該締約国の区域内におけるサービスの提供のための他方の締約国の者の存在（業務上の拠点を含む。）に係る措置

(h)「独占的なサービス提供者」とは、締約国が自国の関連市場におけるサービスの唯一の提供者として法令上又は事実上許可し、又は設立する者（公私を問わない。）をいう。

(i)「締約国の自然人」とは、締約国の法律に基づく当該締約国の国民をいう。

(j)「航空運送サービスの販売及びマーケティング」とは、関係する航空運送人が自己の航空運送サービスの販売及びマーケティング（市場調査、広告、流通その他マーケティングの全ての側面を含む。）を自由に行う機会をいう。ただし、これらの活動には、航空運送サービスの価格の決定及びサービスに適

(c)「現行の」とは、この協定の効力発生の日において効力を有することをいう。

(d)「他方の締約国の法人」とは、次のいずれかの法人をいう。

(i) 他方の締約国の法律に基づいて設立され、又は組織される法人

(ii) 業務上の拠点を通じてサービスが提供される場合には、次のいずれかの者が所有し、又は支配する法人

(A) 他方の締約国の自然人

(B) (i)に規定する他方の締約国の法人

(e)「措置」とは、あらゆる措置（法令、規則、手続、決定、行政上の行為その他のいずれの形式であるかを問わない。）をいう。

注釈「措置」には、サービス貿易一般協定が対象とする範囲内の租税に係る課税措置を含める。

(f)「締約国が採用し、又は維持する措置」とは、次の措置をいう。

(i) 締約国の全ての段階の政府又は機関が採用し、又は維持する措置

(ii) 非政府機関が、締約国の全ての段階の政府又は機関によって委任された権限を行使するに当たっ

3　2(b)の規定にかかわらず、この章の規定は、次の事項に影響を及ぼす措置について適用する。

(a)　航空機の修理及び保守のサービス

(b)　航空運送サービスの販売及びマーケティング

(c)　コンピュータ予約システムのサービス

4　附属書四は、金融サービスに関し、この章の補足規定（適用範囲及び定義を含む。）を定める。

5　附属書五は、電気通信サービスに関し、この章の補足規定（適用範囲及び定義を含む。）を定める。

第七・二条　定義

この章の規定の適用上、

(a)　「航空機の修理及び保守のサービス」とは、航空機がサービスを提供していない間に当該航空機又はその一部に対して行われる活動をいい、いわゆるライン・メンテナンスを含まない。

(b)　「コンピュータ予約システムのサービス」とは、航空機の発着予定、空席状況、運賃及び運賃規則に関する情報が組み込まれたコンピュータ・システムを通じて予約を受け付け、又は発券を行うことにより提供するサービスをいう。

第七・一条　適用範囲

1　この章の規定は、締約国が採用し、又は維持する措置であって、サービスの貿易に影響を及ぼすものについて適用する。

2　この章の規定は、次のものについては、適用しない。

(a) 海上運送サービスのうち内航海運に係るもの

(b) 航空運送サービスに関し、運輸権（いかなる方法で与えられるものであるかを問わない。）に影響を及ぼす措置又は運輸権の行使に直接関係するサービスに影響を及ぼす措置

(c) 政府調達

(d) 締約国又は公的企業により交付される補助金（贈与、公的に支援される借款、保証及び保険を含む。）

(e) 出入国管理に関する法令に基づく措置

(f) 一方の締約国の雇用市場へのアクセスを求める他方の締約国の自然人に影響を及ぼす措置及び国籍、市民権又は永続的な居住若しくは雇用に関する措置

(g) 政府の権限の行使として提供されるサービス

(f) この章の規定に関連する事項に関する両締約国間の技術的な協力について討議すること。

(g) 相互に受け入れることができる解決を得ることを目的として、この章の規定に関連するあらゆる問題(両締約国間に紛争を引き起こす可能性がある問題を含む。)について討議すること。

(h) 関係機関に対し小委員会の所見を報告すること。

(i) 合同委員会が委任するその他の任務を遂行すること。

3 小委員会は、両締約国政府の代表者から成る。

4 小委員会は、両締約国が合意する時期及び場所において又は手段によって会合を開催する。

5 この条の規定の適用上、小委員会は、次のものによって調整される。

(a) 日本国については、外務省又はその後継機関

(b) モンゴル国については、産業省又はその後継機関

第六・十条 第十六章の規定の不適用

第十六章の規定は、この章の規定については、適用しない。

第七章 サービスの貿易

一方の締約国は、強制規格、任意規格及び適合性評価手続に関する他方の締約国からの全ての妥当な照会に応じ、並びに適当な場合には他方の締約国が知るべきであると考えるその他の関連する情報を当該他方の締約国に提供する照会所を指定する。

第六・九条　強制規格、任意規格及び適合性評価手続に関する小委員会

1　両締約国は、この章の規定を効果的に実施し、及び運用するため、ここに強制規格、任意規格及び適合性評価手続に関する小委員会（以下この条において「小委員会」という。）を設置する。

2　小委員会は、次のことを任務とする。

(a)　この章の規定の実施及び運用について検討及び監視を行うこと。

(b)　強制規格、任意規格及び適合性評価手続の作成及び改善において協力を強化すること。

(c)　強制規格、任意規格及び適合性評価手続に関する情報の交換を行うこと。

(d)　強制規格、任意規格及び適合性評価手続に関連する事項について協議すること。

(e)　強制規格、任意規格及び適合性評価手続に関する活動に従事する地域的な場及び多国間の場での活動に関する情報の交換を行うこと。

し、適用される強制規格又は任意規格に適合していることについて、当該他方の締約国の適合性評価手続が自国の適合性評価手続と同等の保証を与えるものであると当該一方の締約国が認めることを条件とする。

3　一方の締約国は、他方の締約国において行われた適合性評価手続の結果を受け入れない場合には、当該他方の締約国の要請に応じ、かつ、自国の法令に従い、当該他方の締約国が適当なときに是正手段をとることができるようにその理由について説明する。

4　一方の締約国は、可能な場合には、自国の区域内における適合性評価機関に与えられる条件よりも不利でない条件で、他方の締約国における適合性評価機関を認定し、指定し、又は承認する。一方の締約国は、自国の区域において特定の強制規格又は任意規格について適合性を評価する機関の認定、指定又は承認を行うが、他方の締約国における機関であって当該強制規格又は任意規格について適合性を評価するものの認定、指定又は承認を拒否する場合には、当該他方の締約国の要請に応じ、その理由について説明する。

第六・八条　照会所

報（研究及び文書を含む。ただし、秘密の情報を除く。）を実行可能な範囲内で提供する。

2　一方の締約国は、他方の締約国の強制規格が自国の強制規格と異なる場合であっても、当該他方の締約国の強制規格を同等なものとして受け入れることに積極的な考慮を払う。ただし、当該他方の締約国の強制規格が当該一方の締約国の強制規格の目的を十分に達成することを当該一方の締約国が認めることを条件とする。

3　一方の締約国は、他方の締約国の強制規格を自国の強制規格と同等なものとして受け入れない場合には、当該他方の締約国の要請に応じ、その理由について説明する。

第六・七条　適合性評価手続の結果の受入れ

1　両締約国は、一方の締約国が他方の締約国において行われた適合性評価手続の結果を受け入れることを促進するための広範な仕組みが存在することを認識する。一方の締約国は、他方の締約国の要請があった場合には、自国の区域内において用いられている当該仕組みの範囲に関する情報を提供する。

2　一方の締約国は、他方の締約国における適合性評価手続が自国の適合性評価手続と異なる場合においても、可能なときは、当該他方の締約国における適合性評価手続の結果を受け入れることを確保する。ただ

(b) 貿易の技術的障害に関する協定附属書一に定める用語及び定義を適用する。

第六・四条　権利及び義務の再確認

両締約国は、貿易の技術的障害に関する協定に基づく強制規格、任意規格及び適合性評価手続に関する権利及び義務を再確認する。

第六・五条　国際規格

1 各締約国は、貿易の技術的障害に関する協定2.4及び5.4の規定が定める範囲内で、関連する国際規格及び指針又は勧告を自国の強制規格及び適合性評価手続の基礎として用いる。

2 一方の締約国は、国際標準化の活動において、自国の国内標準化機関が他方の締約国の関連する国内標準化機関と協力するよう奨励する。その協力は、両締約国が構成員である地域標準化機関又は国際標準化機関において行うことができる。

第六・六条　強制規格

1 一方の締約国が他方の締約国の強制規格と類似の強制規格を作成することに関心を有する場合には、当該他方の締約国は、当該一方の締約国の要請に応じ、自国の強制規格の作成に当たって利用した関連の情

(a) 政府機関が政府機関の生産又は消費の必要上作成する購入仕様

(b) 衛生植物検疫措置の適用に関する協定附属書Aに定義する衛生植物検疫措置

第六・二条　目的

この章の目的は、次のとおりとする。

(a) 貿易の技術的障害に関する協定の実施の改善を通じて、両締約国間の貿易を増大し、及び促進すること。

(b) 強制規格、任意規格及び適合性評価手続が貿易に不必要な障害をもたらすことのないようにすることを確保すること。

(c) 両締約国間の協力を促進すること。

第六・三条　定義

この章の規定の適用上、

(a) 「貿易の技術的障害に関する協定」とは、世界貿易機関設立協定附属書一A貿易の技術的障害に関する協定をいう。

む。）について討議すること。

(e) この章の規定に関連するその他の問題について討議すること。

(f) 関係機関に対して小委員会の所見を報告すること。

(g) 合同委員会が委任するその他の任務を遂行すること。

3 小委員会は、両締約国政府の代表者から成るものとし、関連する専門家の適切な参加を得る。

4 小委員会は、両締約国が合意する時期及び場所において又は手段によって会合を開催する。

第五・七条　第十六章の規定の不適用

第十六章の規定は、この章の規定については、適用しない。

第六章　強制規格、任意規格及び適合性評価手続

第六・一条　適用範囲

1 この章の規定は、貿易の技術的障害に関する協定に定義する強制規格、任意規格及び適合性評価手続であって、両締約国間の物品の貿易に影響を及ぼす可能性があるものについて適用する。

2 この章の規定は、次のものについては、適用しない。

合には関連する情報を当該他方の締約国に提供する照会所を指定する。

第五・六条　衛生植物検疫措置に関する小委員会

1　両締約国は、この章の規定を効果的に実施し、及び運用するため、ここに衛生植物検疫措置に関する小委員会（以下この条において「小委員会」という。）を設置する。

2　小委員会は、次のことを任務とする。

(a)　この章の規定の実施及び運用について検討及び監視を行うこと。

(b)　両締約国の衛生植物検疫に関する規制及び基準の変更又は導入、両締約国の区域内における衛生植物検疫に係る事件の発生その他の事項（両締約国間の物品の貿易に直接又は間接に影響を及ぼす可能性があるものに限る。）について情報の交換を行うこと。

(c)　相互に受け入れることができる解決を得ることを目的として、衛生植物検疫措置の適用に関する協定に規定する措置の調和、措置の同等、地域的な状況に対応した調整並びに管理、検査及び承認の手続に関する事項に取り組むため、科学に立脚した技術的な協議を行うこと。

(d)　衛生植物検疫措置に関する両締約国間の技術的な協力（能力の開発、技術援助及び専門家の交流を含

第五・三条　措置の調和

両締約国は、衛生植物検疫措置の適用に関する協定第三条に規定するところにより、衛生植物検疫措置の調和に関連する事項について、できるだけ広い範囲にわたり協力するよう努める。その協力は、各締約国が衛生植物検疫措置の適用に関する協定第五条の規定に従って決定した人、動物又は植物の生命又は健康に関する自国の適切な保護の水準を変更することを求められることなく行われる。

第五・四条　措置の同等

1　輸入締約国は、輸出締約国が当該輸入締約国に対し当該輸出締約国の衛生植物検疫措置が当該輸入締約国の衛生植物検疫上の適切な保護の水準を達成することを客観的に証明するときは、当該輸出締約国の衛生植物検疫措置を同等なものとして認める。

2　一方の締約国は、他方の締約国の要請に応じ、特定の衛生植物検疫措置の同等の認定について二国間で取決めを行うために協議を行う。

第五・五条　照会所

一方の締約国は、衛生植物検疫措置に関する他方の締約国からの全ての妥当な照会に応じ、及び適当な場

(b)　この章の規定に関連する分野であって、両締約国間の貿易を円滑化するために改善されるべきものを特定すること。

(c)　合同委員会に対し小委員会の所見を報告すること。

(d)　合同委員会が委任するその他の任務を遂行すること。

3　小委員会の組織については、実施取極で定める。

4　小委員会は、両締約国が合意する時期及び場所において又は手段によって会合を開催する。

第五章　衛生植物検疫措置

第五・一条　適用範囲

この章の規定は、両締約国間の物品の貿易に直接又は間接に影響を及ぼす可能性がある両締約国の全ての衛生植物検疫措置であって、衛生植物検疫措置の適用に関する協定に基づくものについて適用する。

第五・二条　権利及び義務の再確認

両締約国は、衛生植物検疫措置の適用に関する協定に基づく衛生植物検疫措置に関する権利及び義務を再確認する。

(a) 当該物品の関税分類

(b) 当該物品の関税評価

(c) 当該物品が前章の規定に基づき輸出締約国の原産品に当たるか否か。

第四・七条　協力及び情報の交換

1 両締約国は、税関手続（禁制品の取引並びに知的財産権を侵害する疑いのある物品の輸入及び輸出への対応を含む。）の分野において相互に協力し、及び情報を交換する。

2 そのような協力及び情報の交換は、実施取極で定めるところによって実施される。

3 第一・八条2の規定は、この条の規定に基づく情報の交換については、適用しない。

第四・八条　税関手続及び貿易円滑化に関する小委員会

1 両締約国は、この章の規定を効果的に実施し、及び運用するため、ここに税関手続及び貿易円滑化に関する小委員会（以下この条において「小委員会」という。）を設置する。

2 小委員会は、次のことを任務とする。

(a) この章の規定の実施及び運用について検討及び監視を行うこと。

(a)「物品の一時輸入のための通関手帳」とは、次の条約におけるものと同一の意味を有する。

(i) 日本国については、千九百六十一年十二月六日にブリュッセルで作成された物品の一時輸入のための通関手帳に関する通関条約

(ii) モンゴル国については、千九百九十年六月二十六日にイスタンブールで作成された一時輸入に関する条約

(b)「一時輸入」とは、関税の納付につき全額の又は部分的な免除を受けて物品を関税領域に条件付で持ち込むことができる税関手続をいう。当該物品は、特定の目的のために輸入されなければならず、かつ、当該物品を使用することによる通常の価値の低下を除くほか、いかなる変更も加えられることなく、一定の期間内に再輸出することが予定されていなければならない。

第四・六条 事前教示

輸入締約国は、自国が採用し、又は維持する関係法令又は手続に基づく書面による申請があり、かつ、教示を拒むべき合理的な理由を欠く場合には、物品の輸入に先立ち、次の事項について、事前の教示を書面により行うよう努める。

(ii) 自国の貿易関係者

(iii) 第三国の税関当局

3 各締約国は、影響を受ける当事者に対し、自国による税関に係る事項についての行為に関する司法上又は行政上の審査手続であって容易に利用可能なものを提供する。これらの審査は、当該行為の行政上の実施に責任を有する当局から独立したものとし、及び公平かつ公正に実施する。

第四・五条　一時輸入及び通過物品

1 各締約国は、自国の法令及び国際的な義務に従い、両締約国間で取引される物品の一時輸入のための手続を引き続き容易にする。

2 一方の締約国は、千九百九十四年のガット第五条3の規定に従い、他方の締約国からの通過物品又は他方の締約国への通過物品の通関を引き続き円滑に行う。

3 両締約国は、セミナー、研修課程その他の措置を通じて、物品の一時輸入のための通関手帳の国際的な義務に基づく使用及び両締約国又は第三国における通過物品の通関の円滑化を促進するよう努める。

4 この条の規定の適用上、

も併せて提供する。

4　各締約国は、税関に係る事項に関する両締約国の利害関係者からの妥当な照会に応ずる一又は二以上の照会所を指定し、特に自国のウェブサイトにより、当該照会所の名称及び住所を公に利用可能なものとする。

第四・四条　通関

1　両締約国は、予見可能であり、かつ、一貫性及び透明性がある方法でそれぞれの税関手続を適用する。

2　各締約国は、両締約国間で取引される物品の速やかな通関のため、次のことを行う。

(a)　情報通信技術を利用すること。

(b)　自国の税関手続を簡素化すること。

(c)　関税協力理事会の主催の下で作成される標準規定及び勧告規定その他の関連する国際的な基準及び勧告された慣行に自国の税関手続を可能な限り調和させること。

(d)　適当な場合には、自国の税関当局と次のものとの間の協力を促進すること。

(i)　自国の他の国内当局

第四・二条　定義

この章の規定の適用上、「関税法令」とは、物品の輸入、輸出及び通過に関して各締約国の税関当局が運用し、及び執行する法令であって、関税、手数料及び他の税に関するもの又は各締約国の関税領域の境界を越える規制物品の移動の禁止、制限その他これらに類する規制に関するものをいう。

第四・三条　透明性

1　各締約国は、自国の関税法令に関して一般に利用される全ての関連情報を、いかなる利害関係者についても、容易に利用可能なものとすることを確保する。

2　各締約国は、利用可能なものとされた情報を自国の関税法令の改正により修正しなければならない場合には、利害関係者が当該改正を考慮に入れることができるよう、修正された情報を可能な限り当該改正の効力発生に先立って容易に利用可能なものとする。

3　各締約国は、両締約国の利害関係者の要請があった場合には、当該利害関係者が提起した個別的な税関に係る事項であって自国の関税法令に関するものについての情報をできる限り迅速かつ正確に提供する。各締約国は、特に要請された情報のみでなく、利害関係者が知るべきであると考えるその他の適切な情報

4　小委員会は、両締約国が合意する時期及び場所において又は手段によって会合を開催する。

第三・二十六条　原産地規則のための運用上の手続規則

合同委員会は、この協定の効力発生の日に、原産地規則のための運用上の手続規則を採択する。両締約国の税関当局、権限のある政府当局その他の関係当局は、同手続規則に定める詳細な規則に従って、この章の規定に基づく任務を遂行する。

第四章　税関手続及び貿易円滑化

第四・一条　適用範囲及び目的

1　この章の規定は、両締約国間で取引される物品の通関に必要な税関手続について適用する。

2　この章の規定は、両締約国により、各締約国の法令に従って、かつ、各締約国の税関当局の利用可能な資源の範囲内で実施される。

3　この章は、両締約国間の物品の貿易を円滑化するため、透明性、関税法令の適正な適用及び物品の速やかな通関を確保する枠組みを確立すること並びに税関手続の分野における協力を促進することを目的とする。

輸入締約国と輸出締約国との間の連絡については、英語により行う。

第三・二十五条　原産地規則に関する小委員会

1　両締約国は、この章の規定を効果的に実施し、及び運用するため、ここに原産地規則に関する小委員会（以下この条において「小委員会」という。）を設置する。

2　小委員会は、次のことを任務とする。

(a)　次のものに関し、検討を行い、及び必要な場合には合同委員会に対して適当な勧告を行うこと。

(i)　この章の規定の実施及び運用

(ii)　いずれかの締約国が提案する附属書二又は附属書三の改正

(iii)　次条に規定する原産地規則のための運用上の手続規則

(b)　この章の規定に関連する他のあらゆる問題であって両締約国が合意するものについて検討すること。

(c)　合同委員会に対して小委員会の所見を報告すること。

(d)　合同委員会が委任するその他の任務を遂行すること。

3　小委員会は、両締約国政府の代表者から成る。

局又はその指定団体に提出した場合には、自国の法令に従って、当該輸出者及び生産者に対して適当な罰則その他の制裁を定め、又は維持する。

2 各締約国は、原産地証明書の発給を受けた輸出者又は輸出締約国に所在する第三・十六条8(b)に規定する生産者が、原産地証明書が発給された後に当該原産地証明書の発給を受けた産品が当該輸出締約国の原産品でないことを知ったにもかかわらず、当該輸出締約国の権限のある政府当局又はその指定団体に対して書面により遅滞なく通報することを怠った場合には、自国の法令に従って、当該輸出者及び生産者に対して適当と認める措置をとる。

注釈 原産地証明書の発給を受けた輸出者又は輸出締約国に所在する第三・十六条8(b)に規定する生産者は、原産地証明書が発給された後に当該原産地証明書の発給を受けた産品が当該輸出締約国の原産品でないことを知った後、当該輸出締約国の権限のある政府当局又はその指定団体に対して書面により遅滞なく通報した場合には、各締約国の法令に従い、この2に規定する措置の対象とならない。

第三・二十四条 雑則

2　輸入締約国の税関当局がこの章の規定に従って入手した情報については、

(a)　この章の規定の実施のために、当該輸入締約国の税関当局のみが使用することができる。

(b)　当該輸入締約国が裁判所又は裁判官の行ういかなる刑事手続においても使用してはならない。ただし、外交上の経路又は輸出締約国の関係法令に従って設けられたその他の経路を通じて、当該情報の提供が当該輸出締約国に要請され、かつ、当該情報が当該輸入締約国に提供された場合は、この限りでない。

第三・二十二条　軽微な誤り

輸入締約国の税関当局は、軽微な誤り（例えば、軽微な表現の相違又は語句の欠落、タイプの誤り、指定された欄からのはみ出し）を考慮しないものとする。ただし、当該軽微な誤りが原産地証明書に含まれる情報の正確性に疑いを生じさせるようなものではないことを条件とする。

第三・二十三条　虚偽申告に対する罰則及び措置

1　各締約国は、原産地証明書の発給を受けた輸出者又は輸出締約国に所在する第三・十六条8(b)に規定する生産者が、原産地証明書が発給される前に虚偽の申告書その他の文書を輸出締約国の権限のある政府当

(b) 当該輸出締約国が訪問の実施を拒否する場合又は前条2の規定による書面による要請に対し同条4に規定する期間内に回答しない場合

(c) 前二条の規定に従い当該輸入締約国の税関当局に提供された情報が当該産品が当該輸出締約国の原産品であることを証明するために十分でない場合

4 輸入締約国の税関当局は、場合に応じて前二条に規定する手続を実施した後、輸出締約国の権限のある政府当局に対し、産品が当該輸出締約国の原産品であるか否かについての書面による決定（当該決定に係る事実認定及び法的根拠を含む。）を送付する。当該輸出締約国の権限のある政府当局は、その施設が前条に規定する訪問の対象となった輸出者又は当該輸出締約国に所在する産品の生産者に対して、当該決定を通報する。

第三・二十一条　秘密性

1 各締約国は、自国の法令に従い、この章の規定に従って自国に秘密のものとして提供される情報の秘密性を保持するものとし、また、当該情報をその提供者の競争的地位を害するおそれがある開示から保護する。

意するその他の期間内に、1の規定に基づいて収集した情報を輸入締約国の税関当局に提供する。

第三・二十条　原産品であるか否かについての決定及び関税上の特恵待遇に係る決定

1　輸入締約国の税関当局は、輸入者が産品について関税上の特恵待遇を要求する場合において、当該産品が輸出締約国の原産品でないとき又は当該輸入者がこの章に規定する関連する要件を満たさないときは、当該産品に関税上の特恵待遇を与えないことができる。

2　輸入締約国の税関当局は、第三・十六条12の規定に従って輸出締約国の権限のある政府当局から原産地証明書の発給の決定を取り消すとの通報を受領したときは、産品が当該輸出締約国の原産品でないと決定し、関税上の特恵待遇を与えないことができる。

3　輸入締約国の税関当局は、次のいずれかの場合には、産品が輸出締約国の原産品でないと決定し、関税上の特恵待遇を与えないことができるものとし、当該輸出締約国の権限のある政府当局に対して書面によりその旨の決定を送付する。

(a)　当該輸出締約国の権限のある政府当局が要請に対して第三・十八条3又は前条5に規定する期間内に情報を提供しない場合

より当該輸出締約国に送付する。当該輸出締約国の権限のある政府当局は、その施設に訪問を受ける輸出者又は当該輸出締約国に所在する産品の生産者に対し、訪問を受けることについて同意するか否かの書面による回答を求める。

3　2に規定する要請を行う書面には、次の事項に関する情報を含める。

(a)　当該書面を作成する輸入締約国の税関当局を特定する事項

(b)　その施設への訪問が要請される輸出者又は輸出締約国に所在する産品の生産者の氏名又は名称

(c)　訪問の実施を希望する日及び場所

(d)　要請する訪問の目的及び実施の範囲（原産地証明書に記載された産品であって、確認の対象となっているものについての明記を含む。）

(e)　訪問に立ち会う輸入締約国の税関当局の職員の氏名及び官職

4　輸出締約国は、1の規定に基づいて要請された訪問の実施を受諾するか否かを、2に規定する要請を行う書面を受領した日の後三十日以内に輸入締約国に対して書面により回答する。

5　輸出締約国の権限のある政府当局は、自国の法令に従い、訪問の最終日の後四十五日以内又は相互に同

第三・十九条　原産品であるか否かについての確認のための訪問

1　輸入締約国の税関当局は、前条の規定に基づく確認の要請の結果に満足しない場合には、次のことを行うことができる。

(a)　輸出締約国の権限のある政府当局が当該輸入締約国の税関当局の立会いの下に原産地証明書の発給を受けた輸出者又は当該輸出締約国に所在する第三・十六条8(b)に規定する産品の生産者の施設を訪問することを通じて、産品が当該輸出締約国の原産品であるか否かに関する情報を収集し、及び提供することと並びにそのため当該産品の生産に使用された設備の確認を行うことを、当該輸出締約国に対して要請すること。

(b)　産品が輸出締約国の原産品であるか否かに関する情報であって、当該輸出締約国の権限のある政府当局又はその指定団体が所持するものを提供することを、当該輸出締約国に対し(a)に規定する訪問の間又はその後に要請すること。

2　輸入締約国の税関当局は、1の規定に基づく訪問の実施を輸出締約国に対して要請する場合には、そのような要請を行う書面を、訪問の実施を希望する日の少なくとも四十日前までに受領の確認を伴う方法に原産地証明書に関する情報を確認するために相互に支援する。

2　輸入締約国の税関当局は、関税上の特恵待遇を与えられるものとして輸出締約国から輸入される産品が当該輸出締約国の原産品であるか否かを決定するため、当該輸出締約国の権限のある政府当局に対し、当該産品が当該輸出締約国の原産品であるか否かに関する情報を原産地証明書に基づいて要請することができる。

3　輸出締約国の権限のある政府当局は、2の規定の実施のために、自国の法令に従い、要請された情報を当該要請の受領の日の後四箇月を超えない期間内に提供する。輸入締約国の税関当局は、必要と認める場合には、産品が輸出締約国の原産品であるか否かに関する追加の情報を要請することができる。輸出締約国の権限のある政府当局は、輸入締約国の税関当局が追加の情報を要請する場合には、自国の法令に従い、要請された情報を当該要請の受領の日の後二箇月を超えない期間内に提供する。

4　輸出締約国の権限のある政府当局は、3の規定の実施のために、原産地証明書の発給を受けた輸出者又は当該輸出締約国に所在する第三・十六条8(b)に規定する産品の生産者に対し、輸入締約国の税関当局から要請された情報を当該政府当局に提供するよう要請することができる。

輸出締約国の原産品であることを証明するために提示された全ての補助的な文書を含む。

12　輸出締約国の権限のある政府当局は、原産地証明書の発給の決定を取り消す場合には、当該原産地証明書が当該権限のある政府当局に返却された場合を除くほか、当該原産地証明書の発給を受けた輸出者及び輸入締約国の税関当局に対して速やかにその取消しを通報する。

第三・十七条　輸出に関する義務

各締約国は、自国の法令に従い、原産地証明書の発給を受けた輸出者又は輸出締約国に所在する前条８(b)に規定する産品の生産者が、次のことを行うことを確保する。

(a)　当該原産地証明書の発給を受けた産品が当該輸出締約国の原産品でないことを知ったときは、当該輸出締約国の権限のある政府当局又はその指定団体に対して書面により遅滞なく通報すること。

(b)　当該原産地証明書の発給の日の後五年間、産品が輸出締約国の原産品であることに関する記録を保管すること。

第三・十八条　原産地証明書に基づく確認の要請

1　両締約国は、この章の規定の適正な適用を確保するため、この協定及びそれぞれの国内の法令に従い、

8　産品の輸出者が輸出締約国に所在する当該産品の生産者でない場合には、当該輸出者は、次のいずれかの申告書に基づいて原産地証明書の発給を申請することができる。

(a)　当該輸出者が権限のある政府当局又はその指定団体に提出する申告書であって、当該産品の生産者が当該輸出者に提供する情報に基づくもの

(b)　当該輸出者の要請により、当該産品の生産者が権限のある政府当局又はその指定団体に直接かつ任意に提出する申告書

9　原産地証明書は、当該原産地証明書の発給を申請する輸出者又は輸出締約国に所在する8(b)に規定する産品の生産者が、輸出締約国の権限のある政府当局又はその指定団体に対し、輸出される産品が当該輸出締約国の原産品であることを証明した後にのみ発給される。

10　輸出締約国の権限のある政府当局は、当該権限のある政府当局又はその指定団体が使用する署名の見本及び印章の図案を輸入締約国に提供する。

11　各締約国は、自国の法令に従い、自国の権限のある政府当局又はその指定団体がその発給した原産地証明書についての記録を当該原産地証明書の発給の日の後五年間保管することを確保する。当該記録には、

づき、輸出締約国の権限のある政府当局が発給する。当該原産地証明書には、附属書三に定める事項についての記載を必ず含めるものとする。

2　輸出締約国の権限のある政府当局は、この条の規定の実施のために、自国の関係法令により与えられた権限に基づき、原産地証明書の発給について責任を負う他の団体（以下この章において「指定団体」という。）を指定することができる。

3　輸出締約国の権限のある政府当局が指定団体を指定する場合には、当該輸出締約国は、輸入締約国に対し書面によりその指定団体を通報する。

4　両締約国は、この章の規定の実施のために、この協定の効力発生の日に第三・二十六条に規定する原産地規則のための運用上の手続規則において英語による各締約国の原産地証明書の様式を定める。

5　原産地証明書は、英語で記入する。

6　原産地証明書は、印刷によるもの又は両締約国が合意する他の媒体によるものとする。

7　発給された原産地証明書は、輸入締約国への輸出締約国の原産品の一回限りの輸入について適用され、かつ、当該原産地証明書が発給された日から十二箇月間有効なものとする。

産地証明書の提出を要求しない。ただし、当該輸入が原産地証明書に関する義務を回避することを目的として行われたと合理的に認め得る輸入の一部を構成しないことを条件とする。

(b) 自国の法令に従い、原産地証明書に関する義務を免除することができる。

3 輸入締約国は、適当な場合には、輸入者に対し、産品が輸出締約国の原産品であることを示す他の証拠の提出を要求することができる。

4 輸出締約国の原産品が一又は二以上の第三国を経由して輸入される場合には、輸入締約国は、当該原産品について関税上の特恵待遇を要求する輸入者に対して、次のものの提出を要求することができる。

(a) 通し船荷証券の写し

(b) 当該第三国の税関当局その他関連する団体が提供する証明書その他の情報であって、当該第三国において積卸しその他産品を良好な状態に保存するために必要な作業以外の作業が当該原産品について行われていないことを証明するもの

第三・十六条　原産地証明書

1 前条1に規定する原産地証明書は、輸出者又は権限を与えられたその代理人によって行われる申請に基

われていること。

２　産品が原産資格割合の要件の対象となる場合には、当該産品の原産資格割合を算定するに当たり、当該産品の小売用の包装材料及び包装容器の価額を、場合に応じて当該産品が生産される締約国の原産材料又は非原産材料の価額として考慮する。

第三・十四条　輸送用及び船積み用のこん包材料及びこん包容器

産品の輸送用及び船積み用のこん包材料及びこん包容器については、当該産品が原産品であるか否かを決定するに当たって考慮しない。

第三・十五条　関税上の特恵待遇の要求

１　輸入締約国は、輸出締約国の原産品について、この協定に従い、原産地証明書に基づき関税上の特恵待遇を与える。

２　１の規定にかかわらず、輸入締約国は、

(a)　課税価額の総額が千五百アメリカ合衆国ドル若しくは輸入締約国の通貨によるその相当額又は輸入締約国が設定するこれよりも高い額を超えない輸出締約国の原産品の輸入については、輸入者に対して原

いこと。

(b) 当該産品と共に納入される附属品、予備部品又は工具の数量及び価額が当該産品について慣習的なものであること。

2 産品が原産資格割合の要件の対象となる場合には、当該産品の原産資格割合を算定するに当たり、附属品、予備部品又は工具の価額を、場合に応じて当該産品が生産される締約国の原産材料又は非原産材料の価額として考慮する。

第三・十三条　小売用の包装材料及び包装容器

1 産品を小売用に包装するための包装材料及び包装容器については、統一システムの解釈に関する通則5の規定に従って当該産品に含まれるものとして分類される場合には、当該産品が締約国の原産品であるか否かを決定するに当たって考慮しない。ただし、当該産品が次のいずれかに該当することを条件とする。

(a) 完全に得られ、又は生産される産品であって、第三・二条(a)に定めるものであること。

(b) 原産材料のみから生産される産品であって、第三・二条(b)に定めるものであること。

(c) 当該産品について附属書二に定める関連する関税分類の変更又は特定の製造若しくは加工の作業が行

において、これらの産品が在庫において混在している締約国において輸出に先立っていかなる生産工程も経ず、又はいかなる作業（積卸しその他これらの産品を良好な状態に保存するために必要な作業を除く。）も行われないときは、これらの産品が当該締約国の原産品であるか否かについては、当該締約国における一般的に認められている会計原則に基づく在庫管理方式に従って決定することができる。

第三・十一条　間接材料

間接材料については、生産される場所のいかんを問わず、産品が生産される締約国の原産材料とみなす。

第三・十二条　附属品、予備部品及び工具

1　産品の生産に使用された全ての非原産材料について附属書二に定める関連する関税分類の変更又は特定の製造若しくは加工の作業が行われたか否かを決定するに当たり、当該産品と共に納入される附属品、予備部品又は工具であって、当該産品の標準的な附属品、予備部品又は工具の一部を成すものについては、次の(a)及び(b)の要件を満たす場合には、考慮しない。

(a)　当該産品と共に納入される附属品、予備部品又は工具が仕入書において当該産品と別に記載されるか否かにかかわらず、当該附属品、予備部品又は工具に係る仕入書が当該産品の仕入書と別立てにされな方の締約国に他方の締約国から輸入される場合であっても、当該他方の締約国の原産品とみなす。

2　締約国において組み立ててないか又は分解してある産品の材料から組み立てられる産品であって、当該材料が統一システムの解釈に関する通則２(a)の規定に従って完成品として分類される産品として当該締約国に輸入されたものについては、当該締約国の原産品とみなす。ただし、組み立ててないか又は分解してある産品の非原産材料が組み立ててないか又は分解してある形態でなく個別に当該締約国に輸入されていたならば、当該産品が第三・二条から第三・七条までの関連規定の適用される要件を満たしていたであろう場合に限る。

第三・十条　代替性のある産品及び材料

1　在庫において混在している代替性のある締約国の原産材料及び当該原産材料と代替性のある非原産材料が産品の生産に使用される場合において、当該産品が当該締約国の原産品であるか否かを決定するときは、これらの材料が当該締約国の原産材料であるか否かについては、当該締約国における一般的に認められている会計原則に基づく在庫管理方式に従って決定することができる。

2　代替性のある締約国の原産品及び当該原産品と代替性のある非原産品が在庫において混在している場合

2　1の規定は、附属書二に定める品目別規則に優先する。

第三・八条　積送基準

1　他方の締約国の原産品であって、次のいずれかの条件を満たすものは、積送基準を満たす原産品とする。

(a)　当該他方の締約国から直接輸送されること。

(b)　積替え又は一時蔵置のために一又は二以上の第三国を経由して輸送される場合にあっては、当該第三国において積卸しその他産品を良好な状態に保存するために必要な作業以外の作業が行われていないこと。

2　他方の締約国の原産品が1に定める積送基準を満たさない場合には、当該原産品については、当該他方の締約国の原産品とみなさない。

第三・九条　組み立ててないか又は分解してある産品

1　第三・二条から第三・七条までの関連規定の要件を満たし、かつ、統一システムの解釈に関する通則2(a)の規定に従って完成品として分類される産品については、組み立ててないか又は分解してある状態で一料については、適用しない。ただし、当該非原産材料が、この条の規定に従って原産品とされる産品と異なる号に掲げられる場合を除く。

第三・七条　原産資格を与えることとならない作業

1　産品は、次の作業が行われたことのみを理由として締約国の原産品としてはならない。

(a)　輸送又は保管の間に産品を良好な状態に保存することを確保する作業（乾燥、冷凍、塩水漬け等）その他これに類する作業

(b)　改装及び仕分

(c)　組み立てられたものを分解する作業

(d)　瓶、ケース及び箱に詰めることその他の単純な包装作業

(e)　統一システムの解釈に関する通則２(a)の規定に従って一の産品として分類される部品及び構成品の収集

(f)　物品を単にセットにする作業

(g)　(a)から(f)までに規定する作業の組合せ

とができる。ただし、当該産品の最後の生産工程が輸出国である当該一方の締約国において行われ、かつ、当該生産工程が第三・七条に規定する作業を超える水準のものである場合に限る。

(a) 当該一方の締約国において当該産品を生産するための材料として使用される他方の締約国の原産品を当該一方の締約国の原産材料とみなすこと。

(b) 他方の締約国において行われた生産を当該一方の締約国において行われた生産とみなすこと。

(c) 当該産品が非原産材料を使用して生産される産品であるときは、当該一方の締約国又は他方の締約国において一又は二以上の生産者により行われる異なる段階における生産を考慮すること。

第三・六条　僅少の非原産材料

1　附属書二に定める品目別規則の適用上、特定の産品について適用される品目別規則において当該産品の価額、重量又は容積による特定の割合が定められ、かつ、当該産品の生産に使用される非原産材料が全体として当該割合を超えない場合には、当該非原産材料が当該産品について適用される規則を満たしているか否かは考慮しない。

2　1の規定は、統一システムの第一類から第二四類までの各類に掲げる産品の生産に使用される非原産材で当該材料を輸送するために当該締約国において要する運賃、保険料、こん包費その他の全ての費用及び当該輸送に関して当該締約国において要する他の費用（一般的に認められており、かつ、確認可能なものに限る。）を除外することができる。

4　産品が締約国の原産品であるか否かを決定するため原産資格割合を算定するに当たり、

(a)　1(a)に規定する当該産品のVNMには、当該産品の生産に当たって使用される当該締約国の原産材料の生産において使用される非原産材料の価額を含めない。

(b)　1(b)に規定する当該産品のVOMには、当該産品の生産に当たって使用される当該締約国の原産材料の生産において使用される非原産材料の価額を含める。

5　2(b)又は3(a)の規定において産品又は材料の価額を決定するために関税評価協定を適用するに当たり、関税評価協定は、必要な変更を加えて、国内取引の場合又は当該産品若しくは材料の取引が存在しない場合について適用する。

第三・五条　累積

産品が一方の締約国の原産品であるか否かを決定するに当たり、当該一方の締約国は、次のことを行うこ

注釈　産品の原産資格割合の算定に当たり、輸出締約国における一般的に認められている会計原則を適用する。

2(a)　産品の本船渡しの価額は存在するが、その価額が不明で確認することができない場合には、1に規定するＦＯＢは、当該産品の買手から当該産品の生産者への確認可能な最初の支払に係る価額に調整される価額とする。

(b)　産品の本船渡しの価額が存在しない場合には、1に規定するＦＯＢは、関税評価協定第一条から第八条までの規定に従って決定される価額とする。

3　1の規定に従って原産資格割合を算定するに当たり、締約国における産品の生産において使用される材料の価額は、次のいずれかの価額とする。

(a)　関税評価協定に従って決定される価額であって、当該産品の生産者が所在する締約国の輸入港に当該材料を輸送するために要する運賃、適当な場合の保険料、こん包費その他の全ての費用を含むもの

(b)　当該材料の価額が不明で確認することができない場合には、当該材料についての当該締約国における確認可能な最初の支払に係る価額。ただし、当該材料の供給者の倉庫から当該産品の生産者の所在地ま

(a) 非原産材料の価額に基づく計算式（控除方式）

$$\mathrm{QVC} = \frac{\mathrm{FOB} - \mathrm{VNM}}{\mathrm{FOB}} \times 100$$

(b) 原産材料の価額に基づく計算式（積上げ方式）

$$\mathrm{QVC} = \frac{\mathrm{VOM} + \text{直接労務費} + \text{直接経費} + \text{利益}}{\mathrm{FOB}} \times 100$$

この場合において、

「ＱＶＣ」とは、百分率で表示される産品の原産資格割合をいう。

「ＦＯＢ」とは、２に規定する場合を除くほか、輸送の方法を問わず、産品の買手から当該産品の売手に支払われる当該産品の本船渡しの価額をいう。ただし、当該産品が輸出される際に軽減され、免除され、又は払い戻された内国税を含まない。

「ＶＮＭ」とは、産品の生産において使用される全ての非原産材料の価額をいう。

「ＶＯＭ」とは、産品の生産において使用される全ての原産材料の価額をいう。

(f) 当該締約国の船舶により、両締約国の領海外の海から得られる水産物その他の産品

(g) 両締約国の領海外における当該締約国の工船上で(f)に規定する産品から生産される産品

(h) 当該締約国の領海外の海底又はその下から得られる産品。ただし、当該締約国が、国連海洋法条約に基づき、当該海底又はその下を開発する権利を有することを条件とする。

(i) 当該締約国において収集される産品であって、当該締約国において本来の目的を果たすことができず、回復又は修理が不可能であり、かつ、処分又は部品若しくは原材料の回収にのみ適するもの

(j) 当該締約国における製造若しくは加工の作業又は消費から生ずるくず及び廃品であって、処分又は原材料の回収にのみ適するもの

(k) 本来の目的を果たすことができず、かつ、回復又は修理が不可能な産品から、当該締約国において回収される部品又は原材料

(l) 当該締約国において(a)から(k)までに規定する産品のみから得られ、又は生産される産品

第三・四条 原産資格割合

1 第三・二条(c)の規定の適用上、産品の原産資格割合は、次のいずれかの計算式により算定する。

(a) 当該締約国において完全に得られ、又は生産される産品であって、次条に定めるもの

(b) 当該締約国の原産材料のみから当該締約国において完全に生産される産品

(c) 非原産材料を使用して当該締約国において完全に生産される産品であって、附属書二に定める品目別規則（関税分類の変更、原産資格割合又は特定の製造若しくは加工の作業に関する要件を定める規則）及びこの章の他の全ての関連する要件を満たすもの

第三・三条　完全に得られる産品

前条(a)の規定の適用上、次に定める産品は、締約国において完全に得られ、又は生産される産品とする。

(a) 生きている動物であって、当該締約国において生まれ、かつ、成育されたもの

(b) 当該締約国において狩猟、わなかけ、漁ろう、採集又は捕獲により得られる動物

(c) 当該締約国において生きている動物から得られる産品

(d) 当該締約国において収穫され、採取され、又は採集される植物及び植物性生産品

(e) 当該締約国において抽出され、又は得られる鉱物その他の天然の物質（(a)から(d)までに規定するものを除く。）

使用が当該生産の一部であると合理的に示すことができるもの

(h) 「材料」とは、他の産品の生産に使用される産品をいう。

(i) 「非原産材料」とは、この章の規定に従って原産品とされない材料をいう。

(j) 「原産材料」とは、この章の規定に従って原産品とされる材料をいう。

(k) 「輸送用及び船積み用のこん包材料及びこん包容器」とは、産品を輸送中に保護するために使用される産品であって、第三・十三条に規定する小売用の包装材料及び包装容器以外のものをいう。

(l) 「関税上の特恵待遇」とは、第二・四条1の規定に従って輸出締約国の原産品について適用する関税率をいう。

(m) 「生産者」とは、産品又は材料の生産に従事する者をいう。

(n) 「生産」とは、産品を得る方法をいい、製造、組立て、加工、成育、栽培、繁殖、採掘、抽出、収穫、漁ろう、わなかけ、採集、収集、狩猟及び捕獲を含む。

第三・二条　原産品

この章に別段の定めがある場合を除くほか、次のいずれかの産品は、締約国の原産品とする。

(f)「輸入者」とは、輸入締約国に産品を輸入する者をいう。

(g)「間接材料」とは、他の産品の生産、試験若しくは検査に使用される産品（当該他の産品に物理的に組み込まれないものに限る。）又は他の産品の生産に関連する建物の維持若しくは設備の稼働のために使用される産品をいい、次のものを含む。

(i) 燃料及びエネルギー

(ii) 工具、ダイス及び鋳型

(iii) 設備及び建物の維持のために使用される予備部品及び産品

(iv) 生産の過程で使用され、又は設備及び建物の稼働のために使用される潤滑剤、グリース、コンパウンド材その他の産品

(v) 手袋、眼鏡、履物、衣類並びに安全のための設備及び備品

(vi) 他の産品の試験又は検査に使用される設備、装置及び備品

(vii) 触媒及び溶剤

(viii) その他の産品であって、他の産品に組み込まれておらず、かつ、当該他の産品の生産におけるその

(ii) 当該締約国の旗を掲げて航行すること。

(iii) 次のいずれかの条件を満たすこと。

(A) 両締約国の国民が五十パーセント以上の持分を所有していること。

(B) いずれかの締約国に本店及び主たる営業所を有する法人であって、第三国において登録されている工船又は船舶を所有していないものが所有していること。

(d) 「代替性のある締約国の原産品」又は「代替性のある締約国の原産材料」とは、それぞれ、商取引において相互に交換することが可能な締約国の原産品又は原産材料であって、それらの特性が本質的に同一のものをいう。

(e) 「一般的に認められている会計原則」とは、資産又は負債として記録すべき財産又は債務、記録すべき資産及び負債の変化、資産及び負債並びにそれらの変化についての算定方法、開示すべき情報の範囲及び開示の方法並びに作成すべき財務書類につき、締約国において特定の時に、一般的に認められている会計原則又は十分に権威のある支持を得ている会計原則をいう。それらの規準は、一般に適用される概括的な指針をもって足りるが、詳細な手続及び慣行であることを妨げない。

第二・二十一条　輸出についての協力

両締約国は、第十五章の規定に従い、輸出締約国から輸入締約国に輸出される中古の四輪自動車の分野において相互に協力する。

第三章　原産地規則

第三・一条　定義

この章の規定の適用上、

(a)「権限のある政府当局」とは、各締約国の法令に従い、原産地証明書の発給又はその発給を行う団体の指定について責任を負う当局をいう。

(b)「輸出者」とは、輸出締約国に所在する者であって、当該輸出締約国から産品を輸出するものをいう。

(c)「当該締約国の工船」又は「当該締約国の船舶」とは、それぞれ、次の(i)から(iii)までの全ての要件を満たす工船又は船舶をいう。

(i)　当該締約国において登録されていること。

（以下この条において「小委員会」という。）を設置する。

2　小委員会は、次のことを任務とする。

(a)　この章の規定の実施及び運用について検討及び監視を行うこと。

(b)　この章の規定に関連する他の問題であって両締約国が合意するものについて検討すること。

(c)　次条に規定する物品の貿易のための運用上の手続規則に関し、見直しを行い、及び必要な場合には合同委員会に対し適当な勧告を行うこと。

(d)　合同委員会に対し小委員会の所見を報告すること。

(e)　合同委員会が委任するその他の任務を遂行すること。

3　小委員会は、両締約国政府の代表者から成る。

4　小委員会は、両締約国が合意する時期及び場所において又は手段によって会合を開催する。

第二・二十条　物品の貿易のための運用上の手続規則

合同委員会は、この協定の効力発生の日に、物品の貿易のための運用上の手続規則を採択する。両締約国の関係当局は、同手続規則に定める詳細な規則に従って、この章の規定に基づく任務を遂行する。

第三節　他の規定

第二・十七条　ダンピング防止措置及び相殺措置

この章のいかなる規定も、締約国が千九百九十四年のガット第六条、ダンピング防止協定及び補助金及び相殺措置に関する協定の規定に基づいて措置をとることを妨げるものと解してはならない。

第二・十八条　国際収支の擁護のための措置

1　この章のいかなる規定も、締約国が国際収支上の目的のために措置をとることを妨げるものと解してはならない。当該措置をとる締約国は、千九百九十四年のガット第十二条及び世界貿易機関設立協定附属書一Ａ千九百九十四年の関税及び貿易に関する一般協定の国際収支に係る規定に関する了解に規定する条件に従うものとする。

2　この章のいかなる規定も、締約国が国際通貨基金協定に基づく為替管理又は為替制限を実施することを妨げるものではない。

第二・十九条　物品の貿易に関する小委員会

1　両締約国は、この章の規定を効果的に実施し、及び運用するため、ここに物品の貿易に関する小委員会

3　一方の締約国が、他方の締約国の原産品の輸入に対し、千九百九十四年のガット第十九条の規定及びセーフガード協定又は農業協定第五条の規定に従ってセーフガード措置をとるに先立ちこの節の規定に基づく二国間セーフガード措置をとっている場合には、当該セーフガード措置の適用期間は、当該二国間セーフガード措置の適用期間に算入される。一方の締約国は、千九百九十四年のガット第十九条の規定及びセーフガード協定又は農業協定第五条の規定に従ってとられたセーフガード措置の終了後は、当該輸入に対し、当該二国間セーフガード措置の残存期間を上限として当該二国間セーフガード措置の適用を再開することができる。

第二・十五条　両締約国間の連絡

第二・十一条1及び第二・十三条2に規定する書面による通報その他のこの節の規定に基づく両締約国間の連絡については、英語により行う。

第二・十六条　見直し

両締約国は、この協定の効力発生の日から十年を経過した後、必要に応じ、この節の規定について見直しを行う。

二・九条1に規定する適用期間に算入される。

4　第二・九条3から5までの規定は、暫定的な二国間セーフガード措置について準用する。暫定的な二国間セーフガード措置の結果として課された関税は、その後行われる第二・十条1に規定する調査により原産品の輸入の増加が国内産業に重大な損害を与えているとの決定又は与えるおそれがあるとの決定が行われない場合には、払い戻される。

第二・十四条　世界貿易機関設立協定に基づくセーフガード措置との関係

1　この節のいかなる規定も、一方の締約国が、次のいずれかの規定に従い他方の締約国の原産品に対してセーフガード措置をとることを妨げるものではない。

(a)　千九百九十四年のガット第十九条及びセーフガード協定の規定

(b)　農業協定第五条の規定

2　千九百九十四年のガット第十九条の規定及びセーフガード協定又は農業協定第五条の規定に従って一方の締約国が他方の締約国の原産品の輸入に対してセーフガード措置をとる場合には、当該輸入に対してこの節の規定に基づく二国間セーフガード措置を同時にとってはならない。

の適用を停止する権利を有する締約国は、実質的に同等の効果を達成するために必要な最小限度の期間であり、かつ、当該二国間セーフガード措置が適用されている期間に限り、当該権利を行使することができる。

第二・十三条　暫定的な二国間セーフガード措置

1　遅延すれば回復し難い損害を与えるような危機的な事態が存在する場合には、一方の締約国は、他方の締約国の原産品の輸入の増加が自国の国内産業に重大な損害を与えていること又は与えるおそれがあることについての明白な証拠があるという仮の決定に基づき、第二・八条２(a)又は(b)に規定する措置の形態をとる暫定的な二国間セーフガード措置をとることができる。

2　一方の締約国は、暫定的な二国間セーフガード措置をとる前に、他方の締約国に対し書面による通報を行う。当該暫定的な二国間セーフガード措置の適用については、これがとられた後速やかに両締約国間の協議を開始する。

3　暫定的な二国間セーフガード措置の適用期間は、二百日を超えてはならない。当該適用期間中、第二・十条に定める関連する要件が満たされるものとする。暫定的な二国間セーフガード措置の適用期間は、第重大な損害又は重大な損害のおそれがあることについての証拠、とろうとする二国間セーフガード措置の対象となる原産品の正確な説明及び当該原産品が分類される統一システムの号、当該二国間セーフガード措置の正確な説明並びに当該二国間セーフガード措置を導入しようとする日付及び予定適用期間

3　二国間セーフガード措置をとろうとし、又は延長しようとする一方の締約国は、前条1に規定する調査から得られる情報を検討し、当該二国間セーフガード措置に関し意見を交換し、及び次条に規定する補償について合意に達するため、他方の締約国に対し、事前の協議を行うための十分な機会を与える。

第二・十二条　補償

1　二国間セーフガード措置をとろうとし、又は延長しようとする一方の締約国は、他方の締約国に対し、当該二国間セーフガード措置の結果生ずると予想される関税の増大分と実質的に等価値の対応を関税に関する譲許について講ずることによる貿易上の補償の適切な方法について合意することができる。

2　両締約国が前条3の規定に従って協議を開始した後三十日以内に補償について合意することができない場合には、原産品について二国間セーフガード措置がとられた締約国は、この協定に基づく関税に関する譲許であって当該二国間セーフガード措置と実質的に等価値のものの適用を停止することができる。譲許

当局が調査を行った後においてのみ二国間セーフガード措置をとることができる。

2　1に規定する調査については、特別な場合を除くほか、当該調査の開始の日の後一年以内に完了させなければならず、かつ、いかなる場合においても、当該調査の開始の日の後十八箇月を超えてはならない。

第二・十一条　通報及び協議

1　一方の締約国は、次の場合には、他方の締約国に対し直ちに書面による通報を行う。

(a)　重大な損害又は重大な損害のおそれ及びその理由に関する前条1に規定する調査を開始する場合

(b)　二国間セーフガード措置をとり、又は延長する決定を行う場合

2　1に規定する書面による通報を行う一方の締約国は、全ての関連する情報を他方の締約国に提供する。当該情報には、次の事項を含める。

(a)　1(a)に規定する場合における書面による通報については、調査の開始の理由、調査の対象となる原産品についての正確な説明及び当該原産品が分類される統一システムの号、調査の対象となる期間並びに調査の開始の日付

(b)　1(b)に規定する場合における書面による通報については、原産品の輸入の増加により引き起こされた

を漸進的に緩和する。

2　二国間セーフガード措置の対象とされた原産品の輸入については、当該二国間セーフガード措置がとられた期間と等しい期間又は一年のうちいずれか長い期間が経過するまで、二国間セーフガード措置を再度とってはならない。

3　二国間セーフガード措置の対象とされた原産品について、当該二国間セーフガード措置の適用期間の終了後における関税率は、当該二国間セーフガード措置がとられなかったとしたならば適用したであろう税率とする。

4　二国間セーフガード措置は、輸入締約国によるある物品の輸入において輸出締約国の原産品の輸入の割合が当該物品の総輸入量の三パーセントを超えない場合には、当該原産品についてとられてはならない。

5　各締約国は、二国間セーフガード措置に関し、公平な、時宜を得た、透明性のある、かつ、効果的な手続を採用し、又は維持する。

第二・十条　調査

1　締約国は、セーフガード協定第三条及び第四条2に定める手続と同様の手続に従い、自国の権限のある

2　締約国は、二国間セーフガード措置として次のいずれかの措置をとることができる。
(a)　この章に定める関税の引下げの対象となる1に規定する原産品の関税の更なる引下げを停止すること。
(b)　次の税率のうちいずれか低いものを超えない水準まで1に規定する原産品の関税を引き上げること。
(i)　二国間セーフガード措置をとる日における実行最恵国税率
(ii)　この協定の効力発生の日の前日における実行最恵国税率

第二・九条　条件及び制限

1　二国間セーフガード措置は、重大な損害を防止し、又は救済し、かつ、調整を容易にするために必要な限度及び期間を超えて維持されてはならず、また、当該二国間セーフガード措置の適用期間は、三年を超えてはならない。ただし、極めて例外的な状況においては、二国間セーフガード措置の適用期間を延長することができるが、延長を含めた合計の適用期間は、六年を超えないものとする。二国間セーフガード措置の予定適用期間が一年を超える場合には、調整を容易にするため、当該二国間セーフガード措置を維持している締約国は、当該二国間セーフガード措置の適用期間中一定の間隔で当該二国間セーフガード措置は、自国の国内法令に適合する方法により、その新設の前に、又はその後できる限り速やかに、当該他方の締約国に対して関連する情報を利用可能なものとし、又は通報するよう努める。この2の規定は、当該情報の共有について当該一方の締約国が公共の利益に反すると認めるときは、適用しない。

注釈　一方の締約国は、世界貿易機関設立協定に基づく関連する手続を通じて他方の締約国に対して関連する情報を提供することにより、この2の規定を履行することができる。

第二節　セーフガード措置

第二・八条　二国間セーフガード措置の適用

1　一方の締約国は、第二・四条の規定に従って他方の締約国の原産品の関税を撤廃し、又は引き下げた結果として、当該原産品が絶対量又は国内生産量に比較しての相対量において増加した数量で自国に輸入されている場合において、当該増加した数量が自国の国内産業に対する重大な損害又は重大な損害のおそれを引き起こす原因となっているときは、この節の規定に従うことを条件として、自国の国内産業に対する重大な損害を防止し、又は救済し、かつ、調整を容易にするために必要な最小限度の範囲において、二国間セーフガード措置をとることができる。

の規定に従って適用される税率より低くなる場合には、各締約国は、当該産品について、その低い税率を適用する。

第二・五条　関税上の評価

関税評価協定第一部の規定は、両締約国間で取引される物品の課税価額の決定について準用する。

第二・六条　輸出補助金

いずれの締約国も、農業協定附属書一に掲げる農産品について、世界貿易機関設立協定に基づく義務に適合しないいかなる輸出補助金も新設し、又は維持してはならない。

第二・七条　輸入及び輸出の制限

1　いずれの一方の締約国も、他方の締約国の産品の輸入について、又は他方の締約国に仕向けられる産品の輸出若しくは輸出のための販売について、関税以外の禁止又は制限であって関連する世界貿易機関設立協定の規定に基づく義務に適合しないいかなるものも新設し、又は維持してはならない。

2　一方の締約国は、両締約国が合意する産品の他方の締約国からの輸入又は当該他方の締約国への輸出について関税以外の禁止又は制限であって世界貿易機関設立協定に適合してとられるものを新設する場合に書一の自国の表に従って、関税を撤廃し、又は引き下げる。

2 両締約国は、いずれかの締約国の要請に基づき、附属書一の自国の表において交渉の対象として指定した原産品に関する市場アクセスの改善その他の事項について、当該表に定める条件に従って交渉する。

3 両締約国間で取引される物品は、千九百九十四年のガット第二条1(b)の規定に従い、輸入について又は輸入に関連して課せられるその他の全ての種類の租税又は課徴金を免除される。

4 この条のいかなる規定も、一方の締約国が他方の締約国の産品の輸入について、第二・一条(f)(i)から(iii)までにそれぞれ規定する内国税に相当する課徴金、ダンピング防止税若しくは相殺関税又は手数料その他の課徴金を随時課することを妨げるものではない。

5 特定の産品に関する最恵国待遇に基づく自国の関税の撤廃又は引下げの結果として、当該産品の実行最恵国税率が、当該産品と同じ関税品目に分類される原産品について1の規定に従って適用される税率に等しくなり、又はこれより低くなる場合には、一方の締約国は、他方の締約国に対し、その撤廃又は引下げを遅滞なく通報する。

6 特定の産品に関する自国の実行最恵国税率が、当該産品と同じ関税品目に分類される原産品について1

(i)「暫定的な二国間セーフガード措置」とは、第二・十三条1に規定する暫定的な二国間セーフガード措置をいう。

(j)「重大な損害」とは、国内産業の状態の著しい全般的な悪化をいう。

(k)「重大な損害のおそれ」とは、事実に基づき、明らかに差し迫った重大な損害と認められるものをいい、申立て、推測又は希薄な可能性にのみ基づくものを含まない。

第二・二条　物品の分類

両締約国間で取引される物品の分類は、統一システムに適合したものとする。

第二・三条　内国民待遇

一方の締約国は、千九百九十四年のガット第三条の規定の例により、他方の締約国の産品に対して内国民待遇を与えるものとし、このため、同条の規定は、必要な変更を加えた上で、この協定に組み込まれ、この協定の一部を成す。

第二・四条　関税の撤廃又は引下げ

1　この協定に別段の定めがある場合を除くほか、一方の締約国は、他方の締約国の原産品について、附属

(d)「補助金及び相殺措置に関する協定」とは、世界貿易機関設立協定附属書一A補助金及び相殺措置に関する協定をいう。

(e)「二国間セーフガード措置」とは、第二・八条2に規定する二国間セーフガード措置をいう。

(f)「関税」とは、産品の輸入に関連して課される関税及び輸入税をいう。ただし、次のものを含まない。

(i) 千九百九十四年のガット第二条2及び第三条2の規定に適合して課される内国税に相当する課徴金

(ii) 締約国の法令により、かつ、千九百九十四年のガット第六条、ダンピング防止協定及び補助金及び相殺措置に関する協定の規定に適合して課されるダンピング防止税又は相殺関税

(iii) 提供された役務の費用に応じた手数料その他の課徴金

(g)「物品の課税価額」とは、従価による関税の賦課のための輸入物品の価額をいう。

(h)「国内産業」とは、締約国内で活動する同種の若しくは直接に競合する産品の生産者の全体又は当該生産者のうち当該産品の生産高の合計が当該産品の国内総生産高の相当な部分を占めている生産者をいう。

(m) 第十五・四条に規定する協力に関する小委員会

2 小委員会は、1に規定する各条において特定する任務を遂行する。

第一・十五条　両締約国間の連絡

各締約国は、この協定に関する全ての事項について両締約国間の連絡を円滑にするため、連絡部局を指定する。

第二章　物品の貿易

第一節　一般規則

第二・一条　定義

この章の規定の適用上、

(a) 「農業協定」とは、世界貿易機関設立協定附属書一A農業に関する協定をいう。

(b) 「ダンピング防止協定」とは、世界貿易機関設立協定附属書一A千九百九十四年の関税及び貿易に関する一般協定第六条の実施に関する協定をいう。

(c) 「セーフガード協定」とは、世界貿易機関設立協定附属書一Aセーフガードに関する協定をいう。

1　この協定の効力発生の日に、次の小委員会を設置する。

(a)　第二・十九条に規定する物品の貿易に関する小委員会

(b)　第三・二十五条に規定する原産地規則に関する小委員会

(c)　第四・八条に規定する税関手続及び貿易円滑化に関する小委員会

(d)　第五・六条に規定する衛生植物検疫措置に関する小委員会

(e)　第六・九条に規定する強制規格、任意規格及び適合性評価手続に関する小委員会

(f)　第七・十六条に規定するサービスの貿易に関する小委員会

(g)　第八・六条に規定する自然人の移動に関する小委員会

(h)　第九・十三条に規定する電子商取引に関する小委員会

(i)　第十・十八条に規定する投資に関する小委員会

(j)　第十二・十八条に規定する知的財産に関する小委員会

(k)　第十三・五条に規定する政府調達に関する小委員会

(l)　第十四・二条に規定するビジネス環境の整備に関する小委員会

(c) この協定に基づいて設置される全ての小委員会の作業を監督し、及び調整すること。

(d) 次のものを採択すること。

(i) 第二・二十条及び第三・二十六条にそれぞれ規定する物品の貿易のための運用上の手続規則及び原産地規則のための運用上の手続規則

(ii) 必要な決定

(e) 両締約国が合意するその他の任務を遂行すること。

3

(a) 合同委員会は、両締約国政府の代表者から成る。

(b) 合同委員会は、次条に規定するもの以外の小委員会を設置することができる。

(c) 合同委員会は、小委員会に対して自己の任務の遂行を委任することができる。

4 合同委員会は、その規則及び手続を定める。

5 合同委員会は、この協定の効力発生の日に第一回会合を開催するものとし、その後は、両締約国が合意する時期及び場所において又は手段によって会合を開催する。

第一・十四条　小委員会

2　この協定と世界貿易機関設立協定とが抵触する場合には、その抵触の限度において、世界貿易機関設立協定が優先する。

3　この協定と両締約国が締結している協定（世界貿易機関設立協定を除く。）とが抵触する場合には、両締約国は、国際法の一般原則を考慮しつつ、相互に満足すべき解決を得るために直ちに相互に協議する。

第一・十二条　実施取極

両締約国政府は、この協定を実施するための詳細及び手続を定める別の取極であって、この協定を補完するもの（以下「実施取極」という。）を締結する。

第一・十三条　合同委員会

1　両締約国は、この協定に基づき合同委員会を設置する。

2　合同委員会は、次のことを任務とする。

(a)　この協定の実施及び運用について検討及び監視を行い、必要な場合には、両締約国に対して適当な勧告を行うこと。

(b)　この協定の改正について検討し、及び両締約国に勧告すること。

要な変更を加えた上で、この協定に組み込まれ、この協定の一部を成す。

3　両締約国は、次に掲げる場合に関連する事項について相互に協議することができる。

(a)　少数の一次産品の輸出に経済が依存する締約国の輸出収入が、当該産品の販売又は国際価格の低下により、著しく減少する場合

(b)　締約国の特定の産業の確立を促進することが、その国民の一般的生活水準を引き上げるために求められる場合

注釈　この条の規定の適用上、千九百九十四年のガット第二十条(b)及びサービス貿易一般協定第十四条(b)の規定は、人、動物又は植物の生命又は健康の保護のために必要な環境上の措置を含むこと並びに千九百九十四年のガット第二十条(g)の規定は、生物資源であるか否かを問わず、有限天然資源の保存に関する措置に適用することが了解される。

第一・十一条　他の協定との関係

1　両締約国は、世界貿易機関設立協定又は両締約国が締結しているその他の協定に基づく権利及び義務を再確認する。

であって、その開示が、法令の実施を妨げ、その他公共の利益に反することとなり、又は公私の特定の企業の正当な商業上の利益を害することとなるものの提供を要求するものではない。

第一・九条　租税

1　この協定に別段の定めがある場合を除くほか、この協定の規定は、租税に係る課税措置については、適用しない。

2　この協定のいかなる規定も、租税条約に基づく締約国の権利及び義務に影響を及ぼすものではない。この協定と当該租税条約とが抵触する場合には、その抵触の限度において、当該租税条約が優先する。

3　第一・三条及び前条の規定は、この協定の規定が租税に係る課税措置に適用される限度において、当該措置について適用する。

第一・十条　例外

1　この協定（第七章、第八章及び第十二章を除く。）の適用上、千九百九十四年のガット第二十条及び第二十一条の規定は、必要な変更を加えた上で、この協定に組み込まれ、この協定の一部を成す。

2　第七章から第十章までの規定の適用上、サービス貿易一般協定第十四条及び第十四条の二の規定は、必

(a) 当事者それぞれの立場を裏付ける主張を行い、又は自己の立場を防御するための適当な機会が与えられること。

(b) 証拠及び記録される意見に基づく決定が行われること。

3 各締約国は、自国の法令によって定められる上訴又は更なる審査の手続に従うことを条件として、問題となっている行政上の行為に関し、当該行政上の行為に関する決定が関係当局によって実施されることを確保する。

第一・七条 腐敗行為の防止に関する措置

各締約国は、自国の法令に従い、この協定の対象となる事項に関する自国の公務員による腐敗行為を防止し、及び阻止するために、適当な措置をとる。

第一・八条 秘密の情報

1 一方の締約国は、自国の法令に従い、他方の締約国がこの協定に従って秘密のものとして提供した情報の秘密性を保持する。

2 この協定に別段の定めがある場合を除くほか、この協定のいかなる規定も、締約国に対し、秘密の情報

４　締約国の権限のある当局は、ある者に対して義務を課し、又は法的な権利を制限する最終的な決定を行う前に、時間的にかつ措置の性格上許容され、及び公共の利益に反することとならないときは、自国の法令に従って、その者に対して次の通知及び機会を与えるよう努める。

(a)　適当な通知（当該措置の性格、当該措置の根拠となる法令の条項及び当該措置の原因となる事実の記載を含む。）

(b)　その者の立場を裏付ける事実及び主張を提示するための適当な機会

第一・六条　審査及び上訴

１　各締約国は、この協定の対象となる事項に関する行政上の行為について、速やかな審査及び正当な理由がある場合にはその是正が行われるために、裁判所又は手続を維持する。当該裁判所又は手続は、公平なものとし、及びそのような行為の行政上の実施について責任を有する当局から独立していなければならない。

２　各締約国は、１に規定する裁判所又は手続において、当事者に対し次のことを要求する権利が与えられることを確保する。

る者によって提出された申請を受理した場合には、自国の法令に従って、次のことを行う。

(a) 3に規定する定められた標準的な期間を考慮して、自国の法令に基づき不備がないと認められる申請が提出された後合理的な期間内に、当該申請に関する決定を申請者に通知すること。

(b) 申請者の要請があった場合には、申請の処理状況に関する情報を合理的な期間内に提供すること。

2　締約国の権限のある当局は、自国の法令に従い、1に規定する申請を審査する基準を定めるものとし、また、次のことを行う。

(a) 当該基準をできる限り具体的なものとすること。

(b) 当該基準を公に利用可能なものとすること（公に利用可能なものとすることが当該締約国にとって行政上特別の支障を来すこととなる場合を除く。）。

3　締約国の権限のある当局は、1に規定する申請の審査を行うため、自国の法令に従って、次のことを行う。

(a) 申請の受理と当該申請に対して行う行政上の決定との間の標準的な期間を定めるよう努めること。

(b) 標準的な期間が定められたときは、当該期間を公に利用可能なものとすること。

２　各締約国は、１に規定する法令について責任を有する権限のある当局の名称及び住所を容易に公に利用可能なものとする。

３　一方の締約国は、他方の締約国の要請があった場合には、１に規定する事項に関して、合理的な期間内に、可能な範囲において英語で、当該他方の締約国の個別の質問に応じ、及び当該他方の締約国に情報を提供する。

４　各締約国は、この協定の実施及び運用に重大な影響を及ぼす法令を導入し、又は変更する場合には、緊急の場合を除き、かつ、国内法の対象となる範囲内で、当該法令が公表され、又は公に利用可能なものとされる時と当該法令の導入又は変更が効力を生ずる時との間に適当な期間を置くよう努める。

第一・四条　公衆による意見提出の手続

各締約国は、自国の法令に従い、かつ、実施可能な範囲内で、この協定の対象となる事項に関する公衆による意見提出の手続を維持する。

第一・五条　行政上の措置に関連する手続

１　締約国の権限のある当局は、この協定の実施及び運用に関連し、又は影響を及ぼす行政上の決定を求める締約国の区域外に所在する当該サービス提供者の部分に及ぼされる必要はない。

(s) 「衛生植物検疫措置の適用に関する協定」とは、世界貿易機関設立協定附属書一A衛生植物検疫措置の適用に関する協定をいう。

(t) 「公的企業」とは、締約国が所有し、又は支配している法人をいう。

(u) 「貿易関連知的所有権協定」とは、世界貿易機関設立協定附属書一C知的所有権の貿易関連の側面に関する協定をいう。

(v) 「国連海洋法条約」とは、千九百八十二年十二月十日にモンテゴ・ベイで作成された海洋法に関する国際連合条約をいう。

(w) 「世界貿易機関設立協定」とは、千九百九十四年四月十五日にマラケシュで作成された世界貿易機関を設立するマラケシュ協定をいう。

第一・三条　透明性

1 各締約国は、法令、一般に適用される司法上の決定及び自国が締結している国際協定であって、この協定の対象となる事項に関するものを速やかに公表し、又は公に利用可能なものとする。

企業、個人企業及び団体を含む。）をいう。

(n)

(i) 法人がいずれかの者によって「所有」されるとは、当該者が当該法人の五十パーセントを超える持分を受益者として所有する場合をいう。

(ii) 法人がいずれかの者によって「支配」されるとは、当該者が当該法人の役員の過半数を指名し、又は当該法人の活動につき法的に指示する権限を有する場合をいう。

(o) 「原産品」とは、第三章の規定に従って原産品とされる産品をいう。

(p) 「両締約国」とは、日本国及びモンゴル国をいい、「締約国」とは、日本国又はモンゴル国をいう。

(q) 「者」とは、場合に応じて、自然人又は企業若しくは法人をいう。

(r) 「サービス提供者」とは、サービスを提供し、又は提供しようとする者をいう。

注釈　法人がサービスを直接ではなく、支店、代表事務所その他の形態の業務上の拠点を通じて提供し、又は提供しようとする場合には、サービス提供者（すなわち、当該法人）に対し、第七章の規定に基づいてサービス提供者に与えられる待遇が当該業務上の拠点を通じて与えられる。当該待遇は、当該業務上の拠点に及ぼされるものとし、サービスが提供され、又は提供されようとす

(vii) 法令又は契約によって与えられる権利（例えば、特許、免許、承認、許可。金融サービス及び電気通信サービスの提供、原子力の生産並びに天然資源の探査及び採掘のための権利を含む。）

(viii) 他の全ての資産（有体であるか無体であるかを問わず、また、動産であるか不動産であるかを問わない。）及び賃借権、抵当権、先取特権、質権その他の関連する財産権

注釈　投資財産には、投資財産から生ずる価値、特に、利益、利子、資本利得、配当、使用料及び手数料を含む。投資される資産の形態の変更は、その投資財産としての性質に影響を及ぼすものではない。

(l) 「締約国の投資家」とは、次の者であって、他方の締約国の区域内において、投資を行おうとし、行っており、又は既に行ったものをいう。

(i) 締約国の法律の下で当該締約国の国民である自然人

(ii) 締約国の企業

(m) 「法人」とは、営利目的であるか否かを問わず、また、民間又は政府のいずれが所有しているかを問わず、関係の法律に基づいて適正に設立され、又は組織される法定の事業体（社団、信託、組合、合弁

の解釈に係る注釈を含む。

(j)「統一システム」とは、商品の名称及び分類についての統一システムに関する国際条約附属書に定める商品の名称及び分類についての統一システムであって、両締約国によりそれぞれの国内法の下で採用され、及び実施されるものをいう。

(k)「投資財産」とは、投資家により直接又は間接に所有され、又は支配されている全ての種類の資産をいい、次のものを含む。

(i) 企業及び企業の支店

(ii) 株式、出資その他の形態の企業の持分（その持分から派生する権利を含む。）

(iii) 債券、社債、貸付金その他の貸付債権（その貸付債権から派生する権利を含む。）

(iv) 契約（完成後引渡し、建設、経営、生産又は利益配分に関する契約を含む。）に基づく権利

(v) 金銭債権及び金銭的価値を有する契約に基づく給付の請求権

(vi) 知的財産

注釈　「知的財産」とは、第十二・二条に規定するものをいう。

(d)「税関当局」とは、各締約国又は第三国の法令に従い、関税法令の運用及び執行について責任を負う当局をいう。

(i) 日本国については、財務省又はその後継機関

(ii) モンゴル国については、関税庁又はその後継機関

(e)「日」とは、暦日をいい、週末及び休日を含む。

(f)「企業」とは、営利目的であるか否かを問わず、また、民間又は政府のいずれが所有し、又は支配しているかを問わず、関係法令に基づいて適正に設立され、又は組織される法人その他の事業体（社団、信託、組合、個人企業、合弁企業、団体、組織及び会社を含む。）をいう。

(g)「締約国の企業」とは、締約国の関係法令に基づいて設立され、又は組織される企業をいう。

(h)「サービス貿易一般協定」とは、世界貿易機関設立協定附属書一Bサービスの貿易に関する一般協定をいう。

(i)「千九百九十四年のガット」とは、世界貿易機関設立協定附属書一A千九百九十四年の関税及び貿易に関する一般協定をいう。この協定の適用上、千九百九十四年のガットの条項を引用する場合には、そ

(a)「関税評価協定」とは、世界貿易機関設立協定附属書一A千九百九十四年の関税及び貿易に関する一般協定第七条の実施に関する協定をいう。

(b)「区域」とは、

(i) 日本国については、日本国の領域並びに日本国が国際法に基づき主権的権利又は管轄権を行使する排他的経済水域及び大陸棚をいう。

(ii) モンゴル国については、モンゴル国の領域をいう。

注釈　この(b)の規定は、国連海洋法条約を含む国際法に基づく両締約国の権利及び義務に影響を及ぼすものではない。

(c)「業務上の拠点」とは、業務を行うため又は自由職業のための事業所をいい、これらの事業所には、サービスの提供を目的として締約国の区域内で行われる次のいずれかの行為により置かれるものを含む。

(i) 法人の設立、取得又は維持

(ii) 支店又は代表事務所の設置又は維持

第一・一条　目的

この協定は、両締約国の発展段階及び経済上の必要性を考慮しつつ、次に掲げる手段を通じて、両締約国間の新たな経済的な活力を作り出すことを目的とする。

(a) 両締約国間の物品及びサービスの貿易を自由化し、及び円滑化すること。

(b) 両締約国間の自然人の移動を円滑化すること。

(c) 両締約国における投資の機会を増大させ、並びに投資財産及び投資活動の保護を強化すること。

(d) 知的財産の保護を強化すること。

(e) 各締約国における競争法の効果的な執行のための協力及び調整を促進すること。

(f) 貿易及び投資に関連する全ての分野における両締約国間の協力並びにビジネス環境の整備を更に強化し、拡大し、及び深めるための枠組みを設定すること。

(g) この協定の実施及び運用並びに紛争の防止及び解決のための効果的な手続を創設すること。

第一・二条　一般的定義

この協定に別段の定めがある場合を除くほか、この協定の適用上、とし、両締約国間の貿易及び投資の一層の拡大のための予見可能な通商上の環境を確保し、並びに両締約国の経済効率の向上及び経済成長に貢献することを希望し、

両締約国間の通商上及び経済上の関係を一層強化するための民間部門の重要な役割に留意し、並びにこの協定がそのような民間部門のための新たな貿易及び投資の機会を創出することを信じ、

この協定の実施が、人材養成を通じて新たな、かつ、より良い雇用の機会を創出することに貢献し、両締約国の国民の生活水準（消費者の福祉を含む。）を向上させることを信じ、

この協定が、両締約国間の既存の政治的及び経済的なきずなの強化に貢献するのみならず、日本国とモンゴル国との間の「戦略的パートナーシップ」の構築における重要な段階の一つとなるとの見解を再確認し、

千九百九十四年のガット第二十四条及びサービス貿易一般協定第五条を想起し、

この協定が両締約国間の関係において新たな時代を開くものとなるであろうことを確信し、

両締約国間の経済上の連携の強化のための法的枠組みを設定することを決意して、

次のとおり協定した。

第一章　総則

前文

日本国及びモンゴル国は、

貿易及び投資の増大並びに両締約国間の互恵的な協力を通じて発展を遂げてきた良好な関係並びに強固な経済的及び政治的きずなを意識し、

国際化及び世界経済の一層緊密な統合によってもたらされる活発なかつ急速に変化する国際環境が、新たな多数の経済上の課題及び機会を両締約国に提示していることを理解し、

両締約国の経済がお互いを補完する条件に恵まれていること並びにその補完性が両締約国間の貿易及び投資の活動を通じたそれぞれの経済力の利用により両締約国における持続可能な経済的発展を一層促進することに寄与するものであることを認識し、

経済発展の水準における両締約国間の相違を理解し、

両締約国間の貿易及び投資を規律する互恵的な規則を通じて貿易及び投資に関する明確かつ強固な枠組みを創設することを希望し、

さらに、両締約国の経済の競争力及び供給の能力を強化し、両締約国の市場をより効率的かつ活発なもの

附属書七（第八章関係）　自然人の移動に関する特定の約束

附属書八（第十章関係）　第十・八条１に規定する措置に関する留保

附属書九（第十章関係）　第十・八条３に規定する措置に関する留保

附属書十（第十章関係）　収用

第十六・二条　一般原則
第十六・三条　紛争解決の場の選択
第十六・四条　協議
第十六・五条　あっせん、調停又は仲介
第十六・六条　仲裁裁判所の設置
第十六・七条　仲裁裁判所の構成
第十六・八条　仲裁裁判所の任務
第十六・九条　仲裁裁判手続
第十六・十条　仲裁裁判手続の終了
第十六・十一条　裁定の実施
第十六・十二条　期間の変更
第十六・十三条　費用
第十六・十四条　言語

第十四章　ビジネス環境の整備
第十四・一条　基本原則
第十四・二条　ビジネス環境の整備に関する小委員会
第十四・三条　連絡事務所
第十四・四条　第十六章の規定の不適用

第十五章　協力
第十五・一条　基本原則
第十五・二条　協力の範囲及び形態
第十五・三条　協力の費用
第十五・四条　協力に関する小委員会
第十五・五条　次章の規定の不適用

第十六章　紛争解決
第十六・一条　適用範囲

第十二章　知的財産

第十二・一条　一般規定
第十二・二条　定義
第十二・三条　内国民待遇
第十二・四条　手続事項
第十二・五条　透明性
第十二・六条　知的財産の保護についての啓発の促進
第十二・七条　特許
第十二・八条　意匠
第十二・九条　商標
第十二・十条　著作権及び関連する権利
第十二・十一条　地理的表示
第十二・十二条　不正競争

第十・二条　定義
第十・三条　内国民待遇
第十・四条　最恵国待遇
第十・五条　一般的待遇
第十・六条　裁判所の裁判を受ける権利
第十・七条　特定措置の履行要求の禁止
第十・八条　適合しない措置
第十・九条　収用及び補償
第十・十条　争乱からの保護
第十・十一条　資金の移転
第十・十二条　代位
第十・十三条　一方の締約国と他方の締約国の投資家との間の投資紛争の解決
第十・十四条　一時的なセーフガード措置

第七・十六条　サービスの貿易に関する小委員会

第七・十七条　約束の見直し

第八章　自然人の移動

第八・一条　一般原則

第八・二条　適用範囲

第八・三条　定義

第八・四条　特定の約束

第八・五条　要件及び手続

第八・六条　自然人の移動に関する小委員会

第八・七条　紛争解決

第九章　電子商取引

第九・一条　一般規定

第九・二条　定義

第七・三条　内国民待遇
第七・四条　最恵国待遇
第七・五条　市場アクセス
第七・六条　追加的な約束
第七・七条　特定の約束に係る表
第七・八条　国内規制
第七・九条　承認
第七・十条　独占及び排他的なサービス提供者
第七・十一条　商慣習
第七・十二条　支払及び資金の移転
第七・十三条　国際収支の擁護のための制限
第七・十四条　透明性
第七・十五条　利益の否認

第三・六条　僅少の非原産材料
第三・七条　原産資格を与えることとならない作業
第三・八条　積送基準
第三・九条　組み立ててないか又は分解してある産品
第三・十条　代替性のある産品及び材料
第三・十一条　間接材料
第三・十二条　附属品、予備部品及び工具
第三・十三条　小売用の包装材料及び包装容器
第三・十四条　輸送用及び船積み用のこん包材料及びこん包容器
第三・十五条　関税上の特恵待遇の要求
第三・十六条　原産地証明書
第三・十七条　輸出に関する義務
第三・十八条　原産地証明書に基づく確認の要請

[TEXT IN JAPANESE – TEXTE EN JAPONAIS]

経済上の連携に関する日本国とモンゴル国との間の協定

目次